SPIRIT
OF THE BLUES

CHRISTOPHER BEESLEY

SPIRIT
OF THE BLUES

Everton's Most Memorable Matches
& Goodison Park's Greatest Games

FOREWORD BY KEVIN RATCLIFFE

pitch

First published by Pitch Publishing, 2025

pitch

Pitch Publishing
9 Donnington Park,
85 Birdham Road,
Chichester, West Sussex,
PO20 7AJ
www.pitchpublishing.co.uk
info@pitchpublishing.co.uk

A CIP catalogue record is available for this book
from the British Library.

ISBN 978 1 83680 163 4

Typesetting and origination by Pitch Publishing

FSC MIX
Paper | Supporting
responsible forestry
FSC® C013604

Printed and bound in the UK on FSC® certified paper in line
with our continuing commitment to ethical business practices,
sustainability and the environment.

Printed and bound by CPI Group (UK) Ltd, Croydon, CR0 4YY

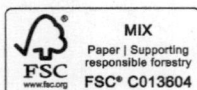

Contents

This book is dedicated to all the Evertonians who did not live to see Goodison Park's final Premier League fixture and the move to the new stadium.

My thoughts turn especially to 'Super' Kevin Campbell (he scored in a scramble), who was Everton's hero when they most needed one, and Michael Jones, who died while building a brighter future for fellow Blues. Both were cruelly taken from us far too soon.

Foreword by Kevin Ratcliffe

LIKE MANY of you reading this book, Goodison Park has been a very important place in my life, and I've been able to experience it as both an Everton fan and then a player.

Some of you will remember me from when I was fortunate enough to be the captain of the most successful team in Everton's history, but my personal Goodison Park story starts long before that.

For the younger generations, the 'Grand Old Lady' might seem to appear the same as she's always done but I can remember when she looked quite different, especially the bit I knew as I would watch the games in the old Main Stand.

Back when I first went to Goodison Park, my matchday routine started with getting into a squashed car with my father and his three brothers – two of whom were disabled so we had a wheelchair in there too – and being driven to Liverpool from our home in North Wales.

They'd sit on the end of the row for accessibility and my dad, who had a season ticket, fashioned a small homemade stool for me to sit on.

I can't remember the exact date of my first match but it was after the 1966 FA Cup Final and as well as watching the likes of the 'Holy Trinity' of Colin Harvey, Howard Kendall and Alan Ball – the first two of course would both go on to have huge influences on my own playing career – I saw other greats like Brian Labone and England World Cup winner Ray Wilson while in opposition there were stars such as Manchester United's George Best.

That was my dream as a footballer. If I was going to be a footballer then I wanted to play for Everton, I wanted to play at Goodison Park and I wanted to play for Wales. I never actually had the ambition to be a captain but that just seemed to follow suit. I was lucky enough to play with some good players, some class players.

There was no game too big for us at that moment in time – the bigger the game, the more we rose to the occasion. It was mainly down to the team we had that meant we bonded together. The team spirit that we had, I've never experienced it before or since.

I think when we go out now, people look at us and see why we won things. Just being in our company for five minutes, the way we speak to each other, very rarely do we pat each other on the back.

Playing at that time was special and our 3-1 comeback victory over Bayern Munich to reach the 1985 European Cup Winners' Cup Final is still widely regarded as being Goodison Park's greatest night.

Bayern were a hugely talented side themselves, but they couldn't live with us.

They couldn't live with our fitness even though we weren't run into the ground by Howard.

I think they thought we must have been on something but believe me, we weren't on anything other than a cup of tea at half-time.

I can always remember that I never ever felt tired at a night game at Goodison Park, I felt that I could run forever.

It's been our ground, our home, our fortress for so long, we'll miss it.

It's going to be a hard job to get that atmosphere we've had at Goodison Park at the new stadium.

I really hope we take that with us, especially in the night games when you feel unbeatable.

Acknowledgements

EVERTONIANS KNOW all about the importance of family and that has been a crucial element for me when putting together this book, whether the 'family' in question are Blues or not or actual kin or not.

First and foremost, I must thank my wife Chloe who has been the yin to my yang for the past 20 years and a pillar of support who – unlike all those that have obstructed my views at Goodison Park over many seasons – ensures my existence is a happy one.

Her backing of me both during this project and with my work in what have been some of the most difficult and challenging seasons in Everton's history throughout recent years has been unwavering, just as it always is in our lives together, which is why I hope she realises just how loved and appreciated she is.

The same goes for my mother, both with her help diligently reading the manuscript drafts and all her support throughout the years.

Despite Mum having no real football interest herself, she has still always dutifully played her part, including taking me to Goodison for Everton v Borussia Mönchengladbach in 1992 and the Brazil v Japan Umbro Cup game in 1995 because my father was working.

Which brings me to my dad.

It's over 35 years now since he took me to my first ever football game at Goodison Park with his work colleague 'Billy from

Maghull' for Everton's 2-1 comeback win over Charlton Athletic on 10 February 1990, and for that and all the many subsequent times that we've been to the match together, and for every other aspect in life that he and my mum have been there for me, I am eternally grateful.

Thanks must also go to the 'Dynamite' Paul Trevillion for his incredible illustrations – he really is the 'Master of Movement' – plus another dear friend of mine, Dr David France, for his comments and advice; David Prentice, Gavin Buckland and Steve Johnson, a 'Holy Trinity' of Everton authors in their own right, who helped me out with some of the selections of matches at the start of this project; all my colleagues at the *Liverpool Echo*; and finally Pitch Publishing of course for giving me the platform to produce my first book.

Christopher Beesley

Prologue

THE CLUB that would become Everton FC was founded in 1878 as St Domingo's FC so members of the congregation at St Domingo Methodist New Connexion Chapel in Breckfield Road North (in Everton) could play sport all year round in addition to their cricket in the summer.

Defeating Everton Church Club 1-0 in their inaugural fixture, the club changed their name to Everton the following year as men outside the congregation wished to participate in the team, and they overcame St Peter's 6-0 in the first game after the change.

Despite their name, the club have never technically played home matches in Everton as they originally turned out on an open pitch in Anfield in the south-east corner of Stanley Park, which had opened in 1870, before briefly moving to a site with turnstiles on Priory Road where they beat Hartford St John's 3-1 in their first match, on 3 November 1883.

Landowner William Cruit quickly lost his patience with the noise and unruly behaviour of the team's increasingly large crowds though, and in the following March he gave them notice to quit.

In September 1884, the *Liverpool Courier* reported that Everton were moving to a patch of land owned by Joseph Orrell on Anfield Road and on 18 May the next year, their president, a certain John Houlding, bought it outright to become landlord of his own club.

Playing at Anfield, Everton started to attract some of the biggest attendances in the country and it was this kind of pulling power that helped them get the nod over their local rivals Bootle FC – who arguably had a better on-field record at the time – when it came to being admitted to the pioneering Football League in 1888.

Everton attracted the only five-figure crowd of the Football League's opening day on 8 September as they defeated Accrington 2-1, and they would boast the highest average gates throughout the first decade of the competition, meaning Evertonians can lay claim to being the English game's first major fanbase.

While still at Anfield, they became the first club to lift the league championship trophy at the end of the 1890/91 campaign – Preston North End, the title winners for the first two seasons, had to make do with a flag – but after their maiden success, the Everton committee and Houlding became embroiled in a deep and bitter conflict over their rent.

The result was that Houlding was left with his ground empty and decided to fill the void with a new team he had created from scratch.

It might not sit well with many modern-day Kopites but whereas Everton, the senior club in the city, were formed because a group of young Scousers wanted to play football, Liverpool FC only exists because a Tory businessman wanted to make more money.

'King John', as Houlding was known, wanted to call his new side Everton but the Football League would not recognise such claims so he picked the name Liverpool FC instead and his hired guns, dubbed the 'Team of Macs' because he raided Scotland to manufacture a ready-made squad, had to start in the Lancashire League while Everton crossed Stanley Park to a new site called Mere Green field in Walton where they constructed Goodison Park, England's first purpose-built football ground.

Genesis

BOTH CLUBS have their own differing versions of events that resulted in Everton's move and the creation of Liverpool FC, but with John Houlding's proposal again defeated, James Corbett's *Everton: The School of Science* records that during a special general meeting at the former Liverpool College building on Shaw Street on 25 January 1892, Everton board member George Mahon suggested that the existing team relocate to another site and when a heckler shouted, 'You can't find one,' he replied, 'I've got one in my pocket.'

Mere Green field, next to Goodison Road – less than a mile from the Anfield Road ground at their nearest points – was owned by Christopher Leyland with Everton renting until they were in a position to buy outright.

Mr Barton was contracted to excavate the site (levelling the field, installing a drainage system and laying the turf) at a cost of £552.

Walton-based builders Kelly Brothers erected two uncovered stands, both holding 4,000 spectators, plus a covered stand for an additional 3,000 at a cost of £1,640, while exterior hoardings were added for £150 and a dozen turnstiles at £7 each with Everton committee man and future chairman Dr James Baxter donating a £1,000 interest-free loan to help towards the funding.

The president of the Football Association, Lord Kinnaird, came up from London for Goodison Park's official opening on

24 August 1892, attending an inaugural lunch at the Adelphi Hotel in Liverpool city centre before a procession of open carriages made their way up to the ground through streets of flag-waving crowds.

The *Liverpool Mercury* reported that during his speech at the dinner table, Kinnaird said it was his desire that Everton should follow in his footsteps, [in] his endeavours to hold for association football a position of respect for sportsmen as a national game.

He believed association football to be as good a game as any other, and his object, and the object of the Everton club, was to maintain the game as a national sport, and not to allow it to play second fiddle to cricket.

In common with the Everton club, it was his endeavour to save the game from the taint of rowdyism and betting, and he looked to the club to support him and his colleagues on the council of the association in the decisions they might come to when such points were raised.

Any committee putting its foot down at any piece of rowdyism would, he was sure, receive the support of players and spectators.

It was because Everton had always upheld these principles that gave him great pleasure to propose such a toast.

* * *

1 September 1892: Everton 4 Bolton Wanderers 2 (First ever game at Goodison Park)

Goodison Park's first ever football match – played a week after the official opening by Lord Kinnaird, which came complete with an athletics display and fireworks – was a high-profile curtain raiser to Everton's upcoming First Division campaign.

The *Liverpool Mercury* reported, 'The weather was threatening, but in spite of that unfavourable condition there was a capital attendance, numbering 10,000.'

In contrast, across Stanley Park, at the Anfield ground that Everton had vacated in acrimonious fashion, Liverpool were watched by what the same publication described as a 'moderate attendance' (estimated at around 1,000) as they thrashed Rotherham Town 7-1 in their first ever game.

While Everton's neighbours would soon catch them up in terms of both stature and support, the longer-established outfit were still very much in the ascendancy for the short term at least.

The choice of Bolton as friendly opponents to christen Everton's new home ahead of competitive action seemed an obvious one.

The Trotters had finished the previous season in third position in the Football League – two places above Everton – and the roles would ultimately be reversed in 1892/93.

Also, just 48 hours before the respective sides' opening First Division fixtures (the game was played on 1 September, not 2 September as widely reported in later chronicles), Bolton were geographically Everton's closest top-flight rivals with their Pike's Lane ground situated just 27 miles up the East Lancs Road.

The *Mercury* recorded that 'a most cordial reception' was accorded to each 11 with Everton chairman George Mahon eliciting cheers with the ceremonial kick-off, an act Houlding would replicate that same night at Anfield.

The report added, 'The play at once became of an earnest character, the ball being impelled quickly from end to end. Excitement was thus aroused at the outset.'

Bolton's Kilmarnock-born centre-forward Jim Cassidy – who in 1890 had netted five times in a 13-0 FA Cup mauling of Sheffield United in which Davie Weir, namesake of a future Everton defender, also bagged four – had the honour of scoring Goodison Park's first-ever goal early in the contest.

Joe Dickenson doubled the visitors' advantage as neither side held back and the *Mercury* observed, 'The play was most interesting, and quite as keen as it would have been in a league match.'

Fred Geary – who later returned to the club as groundsman despite a subsequent playing spell at Liverpool – became the inaugural Everton goalscorer at Goodison as his low shot beat Bolton keeper John Willie Sutcliffe (the last man to represent England at both football and rugby union).

Alex Latta then netted to draw Everton level and it's at this point the report states that they 'soon caused the Wanderers to beat a retreat and literally stormed the goal' with the siege culminating in Edgar Chadwick scoring to give the hosts a 3-2 lead at the interval.

Everton started the second half in a similar fashion and bagged what proved to be the final goal of the night as Dickie Boyle netted from the rebound from an Alf Milward shot.

In an era long before floodlights, the absence of any further scoring after the earlier frenzy might be attributed to the setting sun with the report concluding, 'The light grew faint, though play continued to be followed with zest.'

When Everton returned to action two days later for their first competitive fixture at Goodison Park, an even bigger crowd of some 14,000 turned up to watch them play Nottingham Forest, who were making their own debut in the competition.

The East Midlanders, who joined neighbours Notts County in the top flight and would finish above their relegated local rivals in 1892/93, had won what proved the be the final edition of the Football Alliance (an alternative to the Football League that Bootle had entered when Everton had controversially been chosen ahead of them) the previous season.

Forest, who the *Mercury* noted were 'in the charmed circle for the first time', proved to be worthy adversaries and held Everton to a 2-2 draw in what was described as 'a capital game'.

2

Glory days

WHILE – as already mentioned – Everton's first league championship came when they were still playing at Anfield, all their subsequent honours have been achieved at Goodison Park.

The Blues have lifted a further eight titles, five FA Cups and a European trophy during this time – and there might have been more had it not been for the post-Heysel ban on English clubs or the two world wars (Everton were reigning champions on both occasions that competitive football was paused due to global conflicts).

Despite their 30-year drought as of the time of writing being the longest period in the club's history that they have failed to secure major silverware, Everton's enduring longevity and consistency still ensures that only Manchester United and neighbours Liverpool can top their record of winning trophies across nine separate decades.

Following her final Premier League fixture, the 'Grand Old Lady' as Goodison Park was affectionately known, had staged more top-flight matches in English football than any other ground, some 2,327 in total.

* * *

24 April 1985: Everton 3 Bayern Munich 1 (Goodison's greatest night)

Four decades after it was played, this match has taken on almost mythical status, but you'd struggle to find an Evertonian who would deny that the famous victory over Bayern Munich was the greatest night in Goodison Park's 133-year history.

Offering his reflections of the evening on the BBC series *Match of the Eighties* in 1997, shortly before he returned to Everton for a third stint as manager, Howard Kendall said, 'The night was absolutely deafening. When I talk to Everton supporters now, when I talk to players who were involved that night, they still regard that as their greatest night at Goodison, and I most certainly do as well.'

Kendall's half-time rallying cry to his players when they trailed 1-0 that the Gwladys Street 'would suck the ball into the Bayern net' and the complaints over Everton's physical approach from visiting boss Udo Lattek of 'Mr Kendall, this is not football', which were met with an X-rated response from the home dugout, have become ingrained in the fabric of the club's heritage.

Speaking on the 30th anniversary of the European Cup Winners' Cup semi-final in 2015, the *Liverpool Echo*'s David Prentice, who was there as a fan rather than as a reporter, said, 'Just over 49,000 fans were at Goodison Park that night and I think looking back, probably a quarter of a million claim they were there. It was an incredible night as far as atmosphere goes, it was just absolutely electric.'

The first leg in Munich's Olympiastadion had finished goalless so the Blues knew they'd need to score twice to go through after Dieter Hoeneß had put Bayern ahead at Goodison with an away goal on 37 minutes.

It was the one moment on the night that for a couple of seconds, the raucous crowd fell silent.

Prentice said, 'I remember when Ludwig Kögl was through on goal, bearing down on Neville Southall, having an absolute assurance that Nev was going to save it because he was just so unbeatable that year. He did but the ball span loose and fell really kindly for Hoeneß. There was just this absolute flatness, followed by a defiant roar.'

Kendall's instructions at the interval to go route one paid off as Everton turned the tie on its head with a couple of goals from long throw-ins by Gary Stevens.

The headed equaliser on 48 minutes by Graeme Sharp came via a flick-on from fellow Scot Andy Gray who tapped in the second from point-blank range on 75 minutes after keeper Jean-Marie Pfaff had let the ball slip through his fingers, flapping at the delivery under pressure from Sharp.

But the beauty of that Everton team was the way they outthought as well as outfought opponents and the passage of play for the decisive third goal four minutes from the end was pure 'School of Science' stuff.

Prentice said, 'That wonderful move. Kevin Sheedy played it into Gray, and he touched it on to Trevor Steven. If you ever wanted a man going clean through on goal, your money would be going on Steven, there was never any shadow of a doubt that he was going to clip the ball past Pfaff.'

Speaking in 2020 on the fifth anniversary of his father's death, Howard Kendall's son Simon revealed to the *Liverpool Echo* that he missed that great Goodison moment in front of the famous end of the ground that would later bear his dad's name.

He said, 'It was by far the best atmosphere I've ever experienced in any football stadium. The crowd were our 12th man that night; no more so than the Gwladys Street. As a ten-year-old boy, when Trevor Steven was put through for the third and the whole crowd rose in expectation, I knew I had no chance of seeing what was about to happen, so I remember sitting down with my head in my hands waiting for the roar!'

Andy Gray, who epitomised Everton's fighting spirit on the night, summed things up by proclaiming, 'I played 600 to 700 football matches at the professional level. If I could take one with me when I go, that will be the one. We were the fittest side and the strongest side I'd seen for many a year and we physically battered them.'

After defeating Bayern, Everton were confident they'd go on to lift their first European trophy and Austrians Rapid Vienna were duly dispatched, also 3-1, in the final with Blues fans savouring the moment and behaving impeccably in Rotterdam.

Their club's best-ever side were primed for greatness and a crack at the greatest prize but would be robbed of their destiny by tragic events ahead of another European final in the Low Countries involving their neighbours just a fortnight later.

* * *

30 August 1969: Everton 3 Leeds United 2 (Power shift)

Leeds United arrived at Goodison Park as reigning league champions and on a club record 34-match unbeaten run in the First Division but despite a late fightback, they were blown away by Everton's sensational start which would signal a power shift over the coming months culminating in the Blues taking their crown.

The 1960s had been a golden era for English football. Not only had the national team – containing Everton left-back Ray Wilson and soon-to-be Goodison idol Alan Ball – won the World Cup for the only time to date but there were several great club sides, guided by a generation of legendary managers.

The decade started with former Everton inside-forward Harry Potts steering Burnley to the title, while a couple of years later, Alf Ramsey's success with another unfashionable outfit, Ipswich Town, would lead to him being appointed England boss.

Otherwise, the period was dominated by big-name managers at big teams with Harry Catterick's Everton vying for honours with Bill Shankly's Liverpool, Matt Busby's Manchester United, Bill Nicholson's Tottenham Hotspur, Joe Mercer's Manchester City and of course Don Revie's Leeds.

As much as any of those sides, Leeds, who had not won any major honours before Revie's arrival, could claim to be the creation of one man's work.

Something of a tactical pioneer as a player, he'd operated as a deep-lying centre-forward for Manchester City in a system dubbed the 'Revie Plan', which was a variation on the Hungarian formation that had inflicted an emphatic first Wembley defeat, 6-3 to the Magyars, for England to continental opposition, in 1953, and the man from Middlesbrough set about transforming Leeds both on and off the pitch following his appointment in 1961.

Arriving at a club in debt with little pedigree in what had been a predominantly rugby league area, Revie instigated sweeping changes.

He adopted an all-white kit like Europe's most successful club, Real Madrid, ditching the old blue and yellow colours, while the club crest lost its owl and the team its 'Peacocks' nickname due to Revie's superstitious belief that birds were bad luck.

Revie was also diligent when it came to preparation for matches and would prepare extensive dossiers on opposing teams to ensure his players knew every possible detail about their adversaries and were able to exploit weaknesses and nullify threats.

This work saw them rise from being Second Division strugglers to winners of the Inter-Cities Fairs Cup in 1968 – a competition they'd triumph in again in 1971 – and league champions for the first time in 1968/69, ten points clear of third-placed Everton, who had nevertheless that season produced some of their own best football.

When they met at Goodison, however – one of the rare occasions from the era captured on film at the ground – the Yorkshire side's great run in the First Division, which had stretched back to a 5-1 thrashing at Burnley on 19 October the previous year, came to an abrupt halt.

The truncated domestic season ahead of the 1970 World Cup in Mexico ensured a busy start and this was Everton's seventh game in August.

Victories in all those matches bar a 1-1 draw at Manchester City had already ensured they'd climbed to the top of the fledgling table, a position they would also finish in.

Jimmy Husband fired the Blues ahead on four minutes with his stinging effort going through keeper Gary Sprake's hands before Joe Royle bagged a brace on 21 and 49 minutes, first with a double header after his initial effort rebounded off the crossbar and then with a hooked shot from the edge of the area, ensuring goals from close range by Billy Bremner (52) and Allan Clarke (75) proved too little, too late.

In the *Liverpool Echo*, Michael Charters wrote, 'Everton thrilled a capacity Goodison Park crowd with their best display for seasons to go three up on champions Leeds United within 49 minutes. With outstanding performances from Johnny Morrissey and Joe Royle, who scored two brilliant goals, Everton played superbly, their defence also doing their part in containing the Leeds attack.'

He added, 'Royle was having the game of his life. He was making space for himself that I have never seen him achieve before. We'll be lucky to see a better match than this all season. Leeds were putting everything into the game to try and get back into the chase. The game never let up for a minute in pace and interest with the play non-stop in action and excitement.'

The two sides would finish the season in first and second with champions Everton on 66 points, nine clear of runners-up Leeds.

* * *

26 April 1915: Everton 2 Chelsea 2 (Blues celebrate a wartime title handed to them by Liverpool 48 hours earlier)

Of all Everton's title triumphs, the championship of 1914/15 must be the most surreal as it was played out against the backdrop of the first world war and handed to the Blues by neighbours Liverpool whose manager Tom Watson was dying of pneumonia.

Unfortunately, death had been on the minds of everyone since the outbreak of the Great War the previous summer, and the decision of the Football League to continue playing despite the conflict –

they would ultimately halt at the end of the 1914/15 season and not resume until 1919/20 – was a source of deep controversy.

With rugby union and cricket both suspended, football's initial insistence to play on was deemed unpatriotic by many, and writing in his *History of the Everton Football Club 1878–1928*, Thomas Keates recalled the dilemma that he and his fellow Goodison Park board members faced in regards of continuing to play.

He said, 'To the impulsive, panic-stricken section of the community, the idea of any entertainments, or sporting games being tolerated, was unthinkable.

'The experienced governing bodies of the country were soon convinced that the wise and sound policy was to carry on, as far as it was possible, as usual.

'Every suspension would create additional unemployment, undermine the courage of the population, deepen their inevitable depression, and be commercially and economically disastrous.

'Diversion and cheering entertainment was found to be the most essential tonic and sustainer for the men at the front as well as those by the home fires.'

The wartime season also produced one of the closest-fought title battles in First Division history, with champions Everton pipping runners-up Oldham Athletic by a single point, while from third to sixth place, Blackburn Rovers, Burnley, Manchester City and Sheffield Wednesday were all just a further two points back.

Everton didn't play their final fixture until 48 hours after the majority of the other teams, so Liverpool's 2-0 victory over Oldham at Boundary Park on Saturday, 24 April is credited with handing the Blues their first title since their own days at Anfield in 1890/91.

Although highly unlikely, in truth, Everton still needed to avoid what would have been a record-breaking 15-0 defeat to Chelsea in their own last game.

Despite being beaten 3-0 by Sheffield United in the 'Khaki' FA Cup Final at Old Trafford just two days earlier, the west

London outfit – who had defeated Everton 2-0 in the semi-final but were fighting to avoid relegation – showed they were no pushovers at Goodison Park as they held the champions-elect to a 2-2 draw.

Writing in 'Bee's Sports Notes' in the *Liverpool Echo*, Ernest Edwards observed, 'Had you or I faked this football season we could not have made a more startling finish than the ordinary course of events is producing.

'Last night the value of Liverpool's win at Oldham was made evident. Liverpool have reason to be proud of their share in making Everton's position secure.

'Chelsea showed that they can play real football when allowed – they were utterly opposite to their Saturday selves.'

Edwards added, 'Somehow there was not the enthusiasm one expected would be seen. First the league champions received a reception that was not too hearty. Chelsea in truth having a heartier reception from the crowd. Not until Everton became fiery did the crowd warm to Everton's cause.'

Chelsea took the lead through Harold Brittan just nine minutes in and despite Tom Fleetwood equalising on 70 minutes, Tommy Logan's 78th-minute penalty briefly put the visitors back in front and it looked like Everton's title could be secured by the narrowest of margins on mere goal average.

However, just a minute later, the First Division's leading scorer Bobby Parker netted his 36th goal of the campaign to ensure honours finished even.

Describing the strike, Edwards said, 'It was a wonderful hook, as will be recognised when I tell those not present at the game that Parker had to press his leg so far that he fell full length as soon as he had touched the ball.'

Glaswegian Parker was one of 13 players on the club's books who would go on to serve in the first world war while there were a further 22 former Everton men who also went to fight with ten of them – including Leigh Richmond Roose, recipient of the Military Medal – killed in action.

Although Parker survived to continue his playing career after the war, he suffered from having a bullet lodged in his back and the injury made him a shadow of his former self, leading to him being sold by Everton to Nottingham Forest in 1921.

When recalling Everton's 1915 success over a dozen years later in the club's 50th anniversary jubilee history, Keates remarked on the muted celebrations by noting, 'Our gratification was chilled by the catastrophe of the Great War.'

* * *

6 May 1985: Everton 2 Queens Park Rangers 0 (Title clincher)
The class of 1984/85 were such a magnificent side that they've had a film – *Everton: Howard's Way* – made about them and their achievements fully deserve to be captured on the silver screen.

Their excellence is the benchmark for all other Blues teams before or since to be measured against as they delivered both the league championship plus the club's only European trophy to date while also coming agonisingly close to securing a domestic double only to run out of legs in extra time against ten-man Manchester United in the FA Cup Final.

Everton: Howard's Way captures the agony and ecstasy of being an Evertonian in what was, off the pitch at least, a troubled period for Merseyside with high unemployment, political militancy and at times, rioting on the streets.

From a football point of view, until former midfielder Howard Kendall returned to restore the glory days, Blues fans had also been forced to endure a painful decline in their own club's fortunes while watching neighbours Liverpool's conquests both at home and abroad.

When Everton had last lifted the championship in 1970, they and the Reds had seven titles each to their name but before

Kendall's side won the FA Cup with a 2-0 victory over Watford some 14 years later, a further eight championships, one FA Cup, four League Cups, three European Cups (a fourth was about to follow) and two UEFA Cups had made their way into the bulging Anfield trophy cabinet across Stanley Park without reply.

Finally, long-suffering fans at Goodison had something to shout about with their own set of heroes who were, for a couple of seasons at least, able to turn the Mersey tide.

The belief brought by ending Everton's silverware drought on the day that Elton John cried at Wembley provided the springboard required for the following season.

Those hopes were further boosted by a 1-0 win over Liverpool on 20 October 1984 – a first success at Anfield since the 1970 title season – courtesy of Graeme Sharp's spectacular strike which was arguably the greatest goal, and certainly one of the most important, in Merseyside derby history.

BBC commentator John Motson famously enthused, 'The Evertonians have gone berserk,' before adding after the full-time whistle, 'The balance of power may be shifting on Merseyside and Everton needed this result to prove it.'

The Blues had climbed to the summit by November but lost diminutive attacker Adrian 'Inchy' Heath to injury.

Andy Gray, who had been largely out of the side until that point but came in to prove a talismanic strike partner to fellow Scottish target man Sharp, recalled on *Match of the Eighties*, 'A lot of people thought Everton's chances died that day with Adrian's injury because they looked at Sharpy and I and thought "nah, they can't play together".'

That proved not to be the case as from Boxing Day onwards, the Blues went on a club record 28-match unbeaten run in all competitions and won ten consecutive league games from March.

Following a 4-0 drubbing at Goodison in January, Newcastle United manager Jack Charlton was asked if he was disappointed only to reply, 'No, I'm delighted. Really, that could have been 8-0. They are the best-balanced team in the division.'

The ninth fixture in the ten-match winning run, against Queens Park Rangers, clinched the title as 50,514 crammed into Goodison on a bank holiday Monday.

Centre-back Derek Mountfield, who finished the season with 14 goals, smashed in the opener via the crossbar on 24 minutes before Sharp sealed proceedings with a lovely header from the edge of the area eight minutes from the end.

Ken Rogers of the *Liverpool Echo* reckoned it was a goal that the great Everton centre-forwards of yesteryear would have been proud of, declaring that the player rose majestically, 'Like some latter-day Dixie Dean, Tommy Lawton or Joe Royle.'

On the general proceedings, Rogers said, 'The royal blue dream machine powered on to glory as the league championship trophy returned to Goodison Park for the first time in 15 years.

'The FA Cup Final and European Cup Winners' Cup Final are yet to come but this was the prize that Howard Kendall and his outstanding young side wanted most of all. It was a day for Evertonians to savour from start to finish and 50,000 of them packed into the ground to get the celebrations off to an early start.'

After the full-time whistle blew it was a well-earned party time for players and supporters alike and Rogers added, 'The old battle hymn "We Shall Not be Moved" echoed around the terraces. Everton were home, dry and deserved champions.'

* * *

17 September 1938: Everton 5 Portsmouth 1 (Sixth straight win at the start of title season)

A sixth consecutive win represented a record-breaking start to a season for Everton and would prove the springboard to their fifth league championship success as they looked forward to the year of 1939 with optimism; what could go wrong?

Dixie Dean, the club's – and indeed English football's – greatest goalscorer had been ushered out to Notts County in the previous campaign but in Tommy Lawton, Everton had an exciting teenage protégé in his place who was assisted by a talented supporting cast of team-mates.

Snapped up from Burnley for £6,500 in January 1937, Farnworth-born Lawton had been tutored by Dean during his early days at Goodison Park but the old master was well aware the precocious youngster had been signed to replace him.

Lawton already topped the First Division scoring charts with 28 goals in 1937/38 but his total of 34 in 1938/39 would inspire the first success of the post-Dixie era.

Everton were far from being a one-man band though and oozed quality throughout the side.

Gordon Watson was a Goodison stalwart on and off the pitch for over six decades and although he was never shy of calling out those in royal blue he didn't rate, he waxed lyrical in *Gwladys Street's Blue Book* when it came to describing some of his team-mates from the 1938/39 title-winning team.

TG Jones, 'The most polished British defender of all time.'

Joe Mercer, 'A world-class wing-half … he made the game look deceptively easy.'

Torry Gillick, 'An outrageous crowd-pleaser … he was always surrounded by breathless admirers – his team-mates.'

Jock Thomson, 'On my debut he made the hardest tackle I've ever seen or heard.'

Alex Stevenson, 'Pound for pound, one of the best ball players of his era.'

Ted Sagar, 'A cross between Neville Southall and Peter Schmeichel.'

Although Everton have never won back-to-back titles, the championship trophy remained at Goodison Park between 1915 and 1920 then 1939 to 1947 because the Blues were reigning champions on both occasions that the Football League was suspended for the two world wars.

It's a curious coincidence that has often had Evertonians pondering whether those teams might have achieved more if it wasn't for the disruption caused by huge global conflicts.

While the class of 1914/15 didn't seem an overly special vintage primed for a period of prolonged success, the boys of 1938/39 did appear to possess the potential to forge a dynasty.

As Watson said of Lawton, 'I'm convinced we never saw him at his peak. Tommy was just 19 when he led our title charge and then lost six years to Mr Hitler.'

After wins over Blackpool (2-0 away); Grimsby Town (3-0 at home); Brentford (2-1 at home); Aston Villa (3-0 away) and Arsenal (2-1 away), Everton's six of the best against Portsmouth saw them fall behind for the first time that season when William Bagley netted for the visitors after just seven minutes.

However, 'Stork' recorded for the *Liverpool Echo* that the early setback proved to be the 'spur' needed to play their normal game that was 'assertive, more conclusive and scintillating'.

Stan Bentham restored parity on 17 minutes. Lawton, who had netted in all five previous wins, fired in his eighth goal of the season to put Everton ahead on 31 minutes, Gillick added a third on 62, Lew Morgan's own goal made it four on 72 and Wally Boyes completed the rout four minutes from full-time.

Also in the *Echo*, 'Ranger's Notes' said, 'Had they won by seven or eight goals it would be no more than they deserved. Everton are an eye-opener this season. Who maintains now that class football does not pay? What have the biff-and-bang exponents to say?

'Everton's wonderful run of success has come at an appropriate time, for this season marks the club's diamond jubilee. It is 60 years, almost to the day, that a body of youths connected with the Methodist Chapel at the top of St Domingo Vale formed in their modest way the club that was later to become one of the most famous in the country.

'So far Everton have taken no steps towards celebrating their 60th birthday officially. Probably the directors consider the players have taken the matter into their own hands sufficiently satisfactorily!

'Maybe the board will have to do something in the celebration line – by the way of signifying another championship – by the time next May comes round?'

If only the nation's politicians could have possessed such foresight when it came to what 1939 would actually bring.

* * *

20 April 1963: Everton 1 Tottenham Hotspur 0 (Blues defeat rivals to close in on title)

This was the game that signalled the start of a bright new era for Everton in the swinging 60s – albeit under the stewardship of their strait-laced manager Harry Catterick and owner John Moores.

Two years earlier, in the 1960/61 season, Tottenham Hotspur became the first club in the 20th century to do the league championship and FA Cup double and most of that great side were still around in 1963 when they pushed the Blues for the title, netting 111 goals in 42 matches.

During the north Londoners' historic campaign, lifelong Spurs fan Paul Trevillion – who watched Dixie Dean play at White Hart Lane in the first game he attended in 1937 – travelled up to Merseyside to collaborate with the legendary Everton centre-forward on his illustrated life story in the *Liverpool Echo*.

A previously confident Trevillion was having jitters about his team's chances, but his nerves were soothed following a pep talk that included some tough love from the prolific marksman, who also encouraged him to stretch the series out to a marathon 21 weeks to take it up to the cup final.

The world-renowned sports artist, who produced the cover illustrations for this book, said, 'Nobody believed so positively as Dixie Dean … we went through to the end of the season and we "did the double" together.'

Although he didn't play at Goodison Park on this occasion, captain Danny Blanchflower, by now 37, was still turning out and would lift the European Cup Winners' Cup the following month as Tottenham became the first British side to win a UEFA competition.

Those who did face Everton included Scottish trio Bill Brown, John White and Dave Mackay, a hard man who could also play and was the 'heartbeat' of their side, long-serving full-backs Peter Baker and Ron Henry, Welsh winger Cliff Jones, fellow wide man Terry Dyson and up front Bobby Smith had been joined by Jimmy Greaves, signed for £99,999 in December 1961, who would go on to net more top flight goals than Dean.

Everton – who would finish 1962/63 unbeaten at home for the first time – started the campaign strongly and were at the summit by the time of the 'big freeze', a brutal winter (the coldest in the UK for over 200 years) that ensured they wouldn't play a league game between 22 December and 12 February.

The enforced break delayed the debut of the club's new record signing, wing-half Tony Kay, a £55,000 purchase from Catterick's previous club Sheffield Wednesday, while the Blues boss also used the fallow period to snap up Rangers winger Alex Scott for £40,000.

Everton went into the game in third place, below Spurs and leaders Leicester City in the table, but Alex Young's goal ensured they leapfrogged both to return to top spot where they would stay for the remainder of the campaign.

The 1962/63 season was also the first and only time to date that Everton's average home crowd topped 50,000 (51,603) – a figure they can now better at their new 52,888-capacity stadium by the banks of the Mersey – and 67,650 crammed into Goodison Park to watch this title showdown.

The headline in the *Liverpool Echo* proclaimed 'The game that lived up to its label' with Leslie Edwards enthusing, 'Tottenham not-so-hotspur! That was the way of it at Goodison Park where Everton, now fractional leaders of the First Division, won by a goal to nil.

'Sixty-seven thousand people, many of whom must have feared the tension of this vital league match might spoil it, went away delighted with the football in difficult conditions; satisfied that Everton's championship claims are legitimate and sorry only that the margin of a goal gave no hint of the hammering Tottenham had to take.'

He added, 'Tottenham, usually directors of the football scene, were forced to leave that role to Everton.

'I don't say that Spurs were not more polished artistically, the occasional bursts of applause from "enemy" supporters proved that they were, but they were firmly run off their feet on a heavy, grassless pitch which the strong wind (initially with Everton) made even more formidable as a test of stamina.

'The game was a sustained, non-stop serial of fine football: hair's-breadth Everton misses and general excitement.

'When the goal came, after 16 minutes (Tottenham's best 16 of the match), the applause literally shook the place. I'll swear the press box moved inches up and down from the reverberations of the din.'

Catterick's paranoia over allowing cameras into Everton matches – he feared it could give opponents insights into how his side played – ensured that many highlights from this era are lost to posterity, but Edwards's words paint a picture of the match-winner from fans' favourite the 'Golden Vision'.

He said, 'Jumping half his own height, Young soared over one opponent, John Smith, edged the ball, almost gently, high over the line. If he never scores again, he will always be remembered for this historic goal.'

Everton superfan Dr David France later insisted Young had an eye-catching grace like no other and proclaimed, 'He didn't run, he glided; he didn't turn, he pirouetted; he didn't jump, he floated; his first touch was like a mother's tender kiss; he possessed radar vision and his boots launched missiles.'

A 1-1 home draw with Arsenal followed four days later but then four successive victories saw Everton crowned champions, six points clear of Tottenham, although they had to wait until their 4-1 win over Fulham in their final game to clinch the title.

* * *

11 April 1987: Everton 4 West Ham 0 (Blues go three points clear at the summit with a game in hand as Liverpool lose at Norwich)

Everton's most recent league championship was a real triumph against adversity and although the title wasn't secured until they won at Norwich City some three weeks later, this was the day the odds finally tipped in their favour as Liverpool lost on their own trip to Carrow Road.

The Reds' capitulation against the Canaries, having gone ahead through Ian Rush on 36 minutes only to be sunk by late strikes from Trevor Putney (71) and Kevin Drinkell (88) combined with the Blues' emphatic victory, ensured Howard Kendall's side moved three points clear at the summit with a game in hand.

Going into the 1986/87 campaign, Everton had lost the previous season's 40-goal top scorer Gary Lineker with the prolific marksman – acquired from Leicester City just a year earlier – sold to Barcelona for £2.2m on the back of winning the Golden Boot at the 1986 World Cup in Mexico.

Although Lineker's departure arguably enabled the Blues to share the goals around more – five players finished on double figures in all competitions with a three-way tie for leading scorer between Kevin Sheedy, Adrian Heath and Trevor Steven, all on 16, while Graeme Sharp netted 13 and Paul Wilkinson 12 – the team were beset by the prolonged absences of their stars that remained.

Goalkeeper Neville Southall, usually so durable, had been out since March 1986 with an ankle ligament injury picked up on a pothole in the turf on the Lansdowne Road pitch, playing for Wales against the Republic of Ireland, and would not return until late October.

Paul Bracewell missed the entire season through injury, but he had plenty of company on Bellefield's overworked treatment table as Gary Stevens didn't play until December, Peter Reid until January and Pat Van Den Hauwe until February.

Kevin Sheedy was out between January and April while Graeme Sharp was absent between February and May, although Everton's success epitomised not just the character of their squad but their strength in depth.

New left-back Paul Power – almost 33 at the time of his arrival following over a decade at Manchester City – enjoyed an Indian summer by becoming a mainstay, starting 40 league matches.

Other recruits such as future captain Dave Watson, Ian Snodin and Wayne Clarke – who netted a vital long-range winner against Arsenal at Highbury a fortnight before West Ham's visit – represented a changing of the guard.

The hammering of the Hammers was dubbed the 'Day the championship took a dramatic twist in Everton's favour' in the *Liverpool Echo*.

All four of the goals came within a dramatic spell of fewer than 20 first half minutes as Clarke broke the deadlock with his first Goodison Park goal, a smart two-touch manoeuvre – one to control and one to pick his spot – from the edge of the area.

For the second, just three minutes later, Peter Reid cut inside from the right to fire in what television commentator Clive Tyldesley described as 'a left-footed volley that Kevin Sheedy would have been proud of!' from outside the area.

Right-back Stevens then got in on the act with a long-range arrow of his own ten minutes later before Watson completed the rout on 38 minutes by poking home from much closer when the east London outfit failed to clear their lines from a corner kick.

Under the headline 'By the left, it's a step in the right direction', both the *Echo*'s Ric George and Reid himself took a humorous approach to the 'collector's item' strike.

The midfielder, once lauded by Kendall as being Everton's most important signing since the war, quipped in the tunnel, 'With Kevin Sheedy and Liam Brady out there, you've got to show them what to do with the left peg.'

George declared in his match report, 'In this life there are some aspects generally accepted as impossibilities – such as [Liverpool City Council deputy leader] Derek Hatton voting Tory, me shedding a few pounds and Peter Reid drilling in a goal with his left peg.

'But even I might actually consider changing my diet, believing it could produce results, having witnessed Reid's magnificent strike with the foot he normally only uses for standing.

'Not exactly renowned as a prolific marksman, the tigerish midfielder, back to his England best, earned rich applause for a goal that will live forever in the memories of the Goodison faithful.'

Everton were closing in on their ninth championship but just weeks later Kendall would depart for Athletic Club Bilbao.

He'd ultimately come back twice as manager but was unable to restore the glory days and now, for the longest period in the club's history, the Blues are yet to return to the top of the English game and add a tenth crown.

* * *

13 August 1966: Everton 0 Liverpool 1 (World Cup, league championship and FA Cup all on display for the Charity Shield)

The city of Liverpool has accumulated 29 league championships and 13 FA Cups between its two professional clubs but never had such a glittering array of trophies been present at a single game than on this proud day.

As well as the Charity Shield that was being contested, hosts Everton paraded the FA Cup that they had won in May by coming from 2-0 down to defeat Sheffield Wednesday 3-2 while Liverpool showed off the league championship they had won for the second time in three seasons under Bill Shankly.

In addition to all that silverware, there was also a small but extremely valuable prize made of gold-plated sterling silver and lapis lazuli – an intense deep blue semi-precious stone – the Jules Rimet Trophy.

This came courtesy of Everton left-back Ray Wilson and Liverpool forward Roger Hunt who had both played for England in the 4-2 extra-time win over West Germany in the World Cup Final just a fortnight earlier, while Hunt's Anfield team-mates Gerry Byrne and Ian Callaghan were also members of Alf Ramsey's squad.

It was the second occasion that Liverpool had been crowned champions and Everton FA Cup winners in the same year, but the previous time in 1906 had preceded the first Charity Shield game by some two years.

The fixture did not become an annual challenge between the league champions and FA Cup winners until 1921, with that becoming the regular format from 1930 onwards but again with some exceptions.

This loss was one of just two defeats the Blues have suffered in 11 Charity Shield matches. The other was also at Goodison Park, 3-0, to Herbert Chapman's Arsenal in 1933, while they shared the trophy after a 1-1 draw with Liverpool at Wembley in 1986.

Everton's Charity Shield wins came in 1928: 2-1 at Old Trafford v FA Cup winners Blackburn Rovers, goalscorer Dean (2), attendance 4,000; 1932: 5-3 at St James' Park v FA Cup winners Newcastle United, Dean (4), Johnson, 10,000; 1963: 4-0 at Goodison Park v FA Cup winners Manchester United, Gabriel, Vernon (penalty), Stevens, Temple, 54,844; 1970: 2-1 at Stamford Bridge v FA Cup winners Chelsea, Whittle, Kendall, 43,547; 1984: 1-0 at Wembley v league champions Liverpool, Grobbelaar (own goal), 100,000; 1985: 2-0 at Wembley v FA Cup winners Manchester United, Steven, Heath, 82,000; 1987: 1-0 at Wembley v FA Cup winners Coventry City, Clarke, 88,000; 1995: 1-0 at Wembley v league champions Blackburn Rovers, Samways, 40,149.

On this occasion, the pre-match parade proved a greater spectacle than the action itself.

Leslie Edwards of the *Liverpool Echo* wrote, 'For me the game did not even come alive. It never produced the sparkling, sustained moves one anticipated from teams which had won the league championship and the FA Cup. Maybe the World Cup had sated one's appetite?

'It was for many of the 63,000 present, more an occasion to remember for the appearance in the lap of honour, of the three trophies in the collection of which this city has had such a hand.

'The sight of Roger Hunt and Ray Wilson, sharing a grip of the World Cup with Brian Labone and Ron Yeats, a few paces behind, carrying their trophies, was as unforgettable as any great moment, including Dixie's 60th, at Goodison Park.

'The crowd rose to the players spontaneously. One felt that inter-club rivalry and jealousy was, for two minutes at least, buried in the genuine affection of the lover of football for two city teams who had proved themselves worthy of their patronage.'

Although Hunt had watched on while fellow England frontman Geoff Hurst had helped himself to a hat-trick at Wembley to beat West Germany, he netted the only goal of this game on nine minutes.

Edwards remarked, 'Hunt's goal was beautifully taken after Peter Thompson had feinted to shoot and had opened up the way for his partner to crack a shot to the far goal angle.'

Given the occasion, it was a worryingly flat display from Everton.

Edwards observed that they 'started lethargically; took more than an hour to get going and even then, never looked like giving the others a game, narrow though the margin was.'

Galvanised into action, Harry Catterick would add another World Cup winner to his ranks just a couple of days later in the shape of Wembley man of the match Alan Ball for an English record fee of £110,000 from Blackpool.

* * *

1 April 1970: Everton 2 West Bromwich Albion 0 (Blues clinch the title)

An early finish to the English domestic season ahead of the 1970 World Cup in Mexico ensured Everton were able to wrap up their seventh league championship by 1 April with Alan Ball, the most-gifted player in one of their greatest sides, declaring, 'I can see five great years ahead. All the players work hard for each other and with this behind us, how can we fail?'

Had Evertonians been told that before the next year was out, Ball – still just 26 – would have been sold to Arsenal and the Blues would spend the next 14 years trophyless while their neighbours would go on to dominate proceedings both at home and abroad then they'd have thought you were playing a cruel April Fools' Day joke on them.

But that's exactly what happened as the title-winning side was broken up too soon and the health of both Everton and their successful manager Harry Catterick went into sharp decline.

If the title of 1963 marked the start of a golden era in the club's history, then the triumph of 1970, though nobody knew at the time, signalled the beginning of the end.

The truncated First Division season over eight months rather than the usual nine had seen Everton fly out of the traps and they'd remain in top spot for five months between 17 September and 17 February.

However, a bleak late- rather than mid-winter included a sequence of results that brought just two wins from nine matches, including an FA Cup exit at the hands of Second Division Sheffield United.

There would be a further blow in March as captain Brian Labone was ruled out for the rest of the season with a back injury.

The centre-half would recover in time to take his place alongside Goodison team-mates Ball, Tommy Wright and Keith Newton in Alf Ramsey's squad for England's World Cup defence in Mexico but Catterick used the setback to make the inspirational decision of appointing Ball as skipper.

The fiery midfielder, with the red hair to match, led the Blues to eight wins and a draw in their last nine games of the campaign as they clinched the title with a couple of games to go, ultimately finishing nine points ahead of the previous year's champions, Leeds United.

Goals from Alan Whittle (his eighth in ten games) on 20 minutes and Colin Harvey on 65 sealed the success in a Wednesday night game against a West Bromwich Albion side that had stunned them in the FA Cup Final two years earlier.

In the *Liverpool Echo*, Michael Charters wrote, 'Champions … and they played like it. Everton's performance against West Bromwich at Goodison was full of the brilliance which has established them as a superb footballing side, a side which plays the game with a skill and speed as fine as anything we have seen for many years.

'I consider them a better team than the one which won the title seven years ago. The championship is harder to win these days, but

Everton thrilled and entertained crowds up and down the country with football of the highest quality.

'It was fitting that they should delight their own deliriously happy fans in their last home game of the season with a title-clinching display which contained all the joys and delights of their skills in one effective package.'

This was the side which of course bossed matches from the centre of the park through the revered engine room combination later dubbed the 'Holy Trinity' and Charters declared, 'Everton's complete domination stemmed rightly from the department which has been their greatest asset all season – the midfield trio.

'Ball, Harvey and Kendall were tremendous, and they will be the backbone of a side which I expect to improve over the next few years.'

The Evertonians who formed the majority of the 58,523 crowd were determined to enjoy the evening, and Charters added, 'The game itself was played to the background of a continuous roar of applause and acclamation from the fans.'

That great Blue Colin Harvey, who netted the clincher midway through the second half, later recalled he was able to pick out a familiar face among the throngs of ecstatic supporters though.

He said, 'When we went up into the stands to receive the trophy, I walked through the directors' box and could see my dad in the stands.

'It was one of the greatest moments of my career and there was my father – who like me had been an Evertonian all his life – watching us lift the trophy. Winning the league with Everton was something I'd dreamed about when I was a kid and looking back on that memory now later on in life is something special for me.'

* * *

27 October 1984: Everton 5 Manchester United 0 (Old Blue Joe Mercer blown away by current crop's title credentials)

Grand old man and revered lifelong Blue Joe Mercer was three score years and ten when he watched this game, but having reached the age of 70 he insisted, 'It was the best performance by any Everton side I remember.'

The former Everton player, who as a manager went on to win all of English football's domestic honours plus the European Cup Winners' Cup with Manchester City before a stint as caretaker boss of the national team, added, 'I've seen Brazil play in blue today.'

In terms of the evolution of Howard Kendall's side who would become the Blues' best ever, this was a watershed moment.

If the 1-0 victory over Liverpool at Anfield – their first success across Stanley Park since the 1969/70 title-winning season – had given them belief, then this follow-up display was the confirmation that they had the ability to conquer all before them.

The players themselves could feel it. Writing in his autobiography, *Cheer Up Peter Reid*, Everton's tenacious midfield dynamo declared, 'This is in no way an exaggeration, our performance was the best that I was involved in as a professional footballer.'

Meanwhile Kevin Sheedy, who had opened the scoring on five minutes with a far from typical goal for him – a looping header from the edge of the area that resulted in an aerial collision with Kevin Moran – remarked in his own book, *So Good I Did It Twice*, that it was 'the day I fully realised that I was part of an Everton team that was heading for the stars.'

This was a very able United side who went into the fixture above their hosts on goal difference.

They'd finish the season fourth like they'd done the previous campaign and of course give the Blues a bloody nose after extra time in the FA Cup Final the following spring to deny them the double despite being reduced to ten men after Moran was sent off.

But such was the one-sided nature of this encounter, their Old Swan-born manager Ron Atkinson kept them locked in the dressing room for an hour after the full-time whistle.

Sheedy's second goal, on 24 minutes, was a more orthodox effort as, slipped through by Adrian Heath, he guided a low left-footed shot past Gary Bailey.

Heath then went from provider to finisher on 35 minutes as he was first to the ball in a crowded penalty area to hook in a shot from Trevor Steven's right wing cross.

In the second half, Arthur Albiston cleared a goal-bound Andy Gray header off the line, but Everton's relentless pressure paid off on 81 minutes as a powerful low drive from Gary Stevens made it 4-0 and Graeme Sharp completed the rout four minutes from the end as he headed in a Heath free kick from the left flank.

Under the headline 'Blues title rivals in a spin' in the *Liverpool Echo*, Ian Hargraves concurred Mercer was not exaggerating with his bold verdict.

He wrote, 'Even allowing for the natural enthusiasm of the moment, he was not far wrong. You have to go back to the playing days of Kendall and Harvey, whose coaching skills were behind this latest triumph, to recall anything comparable, and it certainly overshadowed the whole of the last decade.

'Manchester United arrived at Goodison as championship favourites, fairly stuffed with internationals, and having lost only one match previously.

'They were totally outclassed by opponents whose all-round speed and inventiveness made a mockery of United's title pretensions.'

Gary Stevens acknowledged that it was as good as weeks go for Everton, but their results had convinced them they could go on to achieve even more going forward.

That started with an instant rematch against United in the League Cup just three days later as the Blues would triumph 2-1, recovering from an Alan Brazil strike to equalise through Sharp before progressing thanks to a John Gidman own goal.

The right-back said, 'We had threatened to put on a performance like this a couple of times this season – and now we have done it. Peter Reid was unbelievable in midfield. Bryan Robson is a great player and captain of England, but Reidy outshone him.

'We had a good win at Anfield the previous Saturday and in Europe midweek [1-0 at Inter Bratislava], but we were really looking forward to doing something in this game in front of our home crowd.

'Hopefully we will keep it up. If we can get a good result at Old Trafford, the world is our oyster.'

3

Landmark occasions

IN THIS section, some of the matches were great games in their own right while others were less so, but they all had considerable historical significance and that is why they are housed here.

**

4 November 1970: Everton 1 Borussia Mönchengladbach 1 AET, 4-3 pens (First European penalty shoot-out)

With just six wins from 19 penalty shoot-outs over the years, Everton's record in football's nail-biting tie-break format is not great but the Blues do hold the distinction of being victorious in the first one in European competition with their understudy goalkeeper the hero – and it came against German opposition too!

After losing the final of the 1976 European Championship on penalties when Czechoslovakia's Antonín Panenka clipped home the winner with a cheeky, lightly-hit shot down the middle of the goal that would become so iconic that the technique later took his name, West Germany (and more recently Germany) have subsequently won their last six shoot-outs in major international tournaments.

Such a fearsome reputation for German players did not exist back in 1970 with the new format having been brought in to replace the infamous coin toss that had been used twice in the previous season's European Cup, with Celtic progressing against Benfica and Galatasaray against Spartak Trnava through such an unsatisfactorily arbitrary method.

Having exited Europe at the first time of asking in 1962/63 and 1963/64 against Dunfermline Athletic and Internazionale respectively, Everton had at least embarked on a hat-trick of runs before they returned to the premier tournament at the start of the new decade.

A couple of Inter-Cities Fairs Cup forays began in 1964/65 when they got past Norwegians Vålerenga and Scotland's Kilmarnock before succumbing to Manchester United in an all-English tie.

The following year they defeated West Germany's 1. FC Nürnberg but then fell to Hungarians Újpest Dozsa while in 1966/67 they were in the European Cup Winners' Cup for the first time, defeating Denmark's Aalborg but then losing out to Real Zaragoza of Spain.

There could have been two more seasons in the Fairs Cup but twice Everton missed out to another capricious ruling in European football at the time, limiting the competition to one club per city.

Thus in 1967, the fifth-placed Blues and seventh-placed Tottenham Hotspur were each omitted with Liverpool (third) and Chelsea (sixth) both having qualified.

This enabled tenth-placed Newcastle United to sneak in and they promptly went and won it.

Then in 1968 Everton finished third but again had to miss out because runners-up Liverpool had taken a spot.

The penalty shoot-out with Borussia Mönchengladbach came about due to a couple of 1-1 draws between the sides.

The first leg at the Bökelbergstadion saw Howard Kendall's 47th-minute effort cancel out Berti Vogts's 35th-minute opener. Back at Goodison Park, Johnny Morrissey fired the Blues ahead after just 23 seconds before Herbert Laumen restored parity on 34 minutes.

The *Liverpool Echo* described the action as a match of guts, glory and heart-stopping drama as Michael Charters wrote, 'The Goodison legend persists that the 6-4 FA Cup replay between Everton and Sunderland 34 years ago [see Chapter Seven] was the greatest game ever seen on the ground.

'Well, if it was more exciting, more dramatic, more tense or more compelling than the epic at Goodison in the European Cup against Mönchengladbach, then it must have been the greatest match of all time.'

Charters acknowledged that the new format was better than the old system, but it was tough on the players involved.

He said, 'I suppose the idea of deciding a European tie by taking penalties is as good a compromise as anyone can think up, at the moment. It is certainly better than tossing a coin. But the strain it imposes on the penalty takers and the goalkeepers – as well as the spectators – is unbelievable in its intensity.'

Charters then recounts the shoot-out, blow by blow.

'The tension reached heights I have not experienced before at Goodison as Joe Royle's penalty was saved by [Wolfgang] Kleff. Then [Klaus-Dieter] Sieloff put his side ahead, only for Alan Ball to make it 1-1. Laumen, scorer of Gladbach's goal, pushed his shot well wide … still 1-1. Morrissey put Everton in front 2-1, [Jupp] Heynckes made it 2-2. Kendall, [Horst] Köppel and [Sandy] Brown made the score 4-3 with one penalty to come.

'Ludwig Müller, a great figure in the Germans' superb defence, hit the ball hard enough, Andy Rankin [only playing because regular number one Gordon West was injured] dived to his right, pushed the ball away and was promptly engulfed by the ecstatic congratulations of his team-mates.'

The dramatic win should have propelled Everton on to a European conquest that season but the following spring they went out in the next round to Greek side Panathinaikos, via another vagary of UEFA competitions, the now abandoned away goals rule.

* * *

13 October 1894: Everton 3 Liverpool 0 (First league Merseyside derby)

The Merseyside derby is the fixture that can bring the greatest joy and despair to the fans in England's most passionate football city, and this is where it all started.

Although there have been strong showings from Manchester and London in recent decades, Liverpool remains the unofficial footballing capital in the game's homeland, holding the unique distinction of being the only city to have hosted top-flight football in every single season since the Football League began.

Whatever the Blues and Reds think about their neighbours, they have spurred each other on for over 130 years now in a way that other dual-club regions have failed to do.

Without Everton FC, there would be no Liverpool FC and if it wasn't for Liverpool FC, there would have been no Goodison Park.

Despite their 14-year head start over the club who would quickly supersede Bootle as their major local rivals, Everton soon found Liverpool competing on equal terms with them.

Consecutive titles in the Lancashire League and then the Second Division saw Liverpool reach the top flight within just two years of formation and they'd already beaten Everton 1-0 in their first meeting of any sort, the Liverpool Senior Cup Final at Bootle's Hawthorne Road ground on 22 April 1893.

The first league meeting came some 18 months later but the visitors weren't yet 'The Reds.'

They wouldn't adopt that colour scheme until 1896 and instead wore sky-blue-and-white-halved shirts.

Everton, who had worn salmon shirts and navy shorts in their final season at Anfield, switched to blue shirts and white shorts at Goodison but until 1901 they too were sporting a sky hue rather than the deep royal blue they'd later become synonymous with.

Up until this point, Goodison's record attendance had been 30,000, but 44,000, including the Lord Mayor, packed in for this historic fixture, bringing gate receipts of £1,026.

However, there was only one Scouser on the pitch, Liverpool's Harry Bradshaw, in a team otherwise composed entirely of Scots.

Everton themselves had seven players from north of the border plus a Welshman and three Englishmen: centre-forward Jack Southworth from Blackburn; 5ft 4in centre-half Johnny Holt from Church near Accrington and goalkeeper Tom Cain who hailed from Sunderland.

The *Liverpool Mercury* reported, 'The long-looked-for meeting of these local rivals excited all the interest anticipated.

'A great game from a scientific point of view was not expected, but the public appetite was whetted by the fact that Everton and Liverpool were to oppose each other seriously and in full strength for the first time in their history.

'The event recalled recollections of those keen games in which Everton and Bootle some six or seven years ago used to take part; but the parallel ends with keen local rivalry.

'The entertainment on Saturday surpassed in attractiveness every great event that had occurred before.'

League leaders Everton would comfortably triumph 3-0 in the end.

Glaswegian forward Tom McInnes, a recent recruit from Third Lanark, was the man who scored the first ever goal in a league derby with an 11th-minute header.

The otherwise very detailed match report sadly gives no more additional description of the landmark effort.

As the half-time whistle sounded, the hosts were 'in command' but there was still 'very even play'.

Everton doubled their advantage on 59 minutes, 'As on John Bell centring, Alex Latta [both Scots from Dumbarton] sent in, and the ball from a cluster of players was put into the net.'

Conditions changed as 'rain now began to fall quickly, rendering the grass slippery' but Bell added a third two minutes from the end.

'Everton attacked with the desired effect, as on the right-wing making ground, Bell breasted into the net. The home side were now in a safe position.'

Everton were top of the table at this point and would ultimately finish the season as runners-up, but Liverpool ended up bottom of the table.

The return match at Anfield on 17 November finished 2-2 while the clubs also squeezed in friendlies at Goodison Park (26 December, 2-1 to Everton) and Anfield (15 April, 1-1) that season plus a Lancashire Senior Cup semi-final at Goodison (9 March, 1-0 to Everton).

The Merseyside derby was up and running.

*　*　*

16 March 2002: Everton 2 Fulham 1 (David Moyes's explosive first game in charge)

Whether his words were calculated or merely off the cuff, David Moyes struck exactly the right note with Evertonians by dubbing the Blues the 'People's Club' when unveiled as their new manager.

While one Scot had replaced another in the Goodison Park dugout, they were contrasting characters and the 38-year-old Moyes, little older than some of his senior players, especially those who would soon be ushered out of the exit door (Paul Gascoigne left for Burnley days after Walter Smith's sacking and David Ginola was let go at the end of the season), brought a youthful energy and outlook to a team who had run out of ideas under his predecessor, and, without a league win since 12 January, had appeared to be sleepwalking into relegation trouble.

Everton had been dismantled 3-0 at Middlesbrough in an FA Cup quarter-final broadcast to the nation on BBC One the previous weekend with all the goals coming in the space of seven manic minutes late in the first half.

It was the cue for the 54-year-old Smith, a serial winner north of the border with Rangers who had acted with great dignity throughout his often troubled spell at Goodison, to go but the Blues moved swiftly that week to replace him.

Although Moyes did not possess any top-flight experience, his work at Preston North End had earned him the reputation as one of the game's brightest up and coming managerial talents and he looked primed for a crack at the big time.

When speaking to the media for the first time as Everton manager, he said, 'The people made me come here. I am from a city not unlike Liverpool myself. I have been brought up with Glasgow Celtic and Glasgow Rangers and I am now in a city where football means as much as it does up there.

'I think I am joining a football club which is probably the people's football club in Liverpool. The people in the street support Everton and I hope to give them something over the next few years that they can be very proud of.'

Those words struck a chord with Evertonians at a time they needed a lift, and proved so popular that the 'People's Club' phrase came to be adopted as a quasi-official tag that still irks many Kopites to this day.

Having got 'the people' of Goodison Park onside, Moyes was given a tumultuous baptism of fire for his first game against Fulham.

David Prentice of the *Liverpool Echo* picked up upon the mood, writing, 'Optimism was the new buzzword at a bouncing Goodison Park, and it gripped everybody.

'From Golden Goal timers to tartan talismans, a wave of enthusiasm washed over a stadium which had witnessed frustrated resignation just a fortnight earlier.

'The man with the stopwatch got so carried away he slashed five seconds off the time of the opening goal. David Unsworth's sugar-sweet strike was undeniably quick, but it was more 32 seconds than the 27 officially given out.

'Then there was Duncan Ferguson, winning headers, taking throw-ins, heading off his goal line and even chasing down the goalkeeper's clearances.'

He added, 'When the roof almost came off Goodison Park at referee Graham Barber's final whistle, Moyes swiftly blocked Ferguson's traditional early dart for the tunnel and sent him back out to join his team-mates and pay tribute to the outstanding support they had received.

'That crowd noise, as much as anything else, had helped Everton to the victory which was absolutely imperative to their Premier League survival hopes.'

Ferguson had put Everton 2-0 up with just 12 minutes played after 'unselfishly chasing down a goalkeeper's clearance' but any hopes this might be a stroll for Moyes's boys were dashed when Thomas Gravesen was dismissed for his second bookable offence with over an hour still left to play.

Steed Malbranque stabbed in Fulham's lifeline on 55 minutes which ensured a nervous finale but while they did 'creak' at times, 'the Blues refused to buckle'.

Prentice concluded, 'This was all about new starts, fresh ideas and bold impetus. If that proves enough to keep Everton in the top flight to celebrate their 100th season in England's most elevated echelon, Bill Kenwright will have got it right.

'By five o'clock on Saturday, though, most of Goodison Park had already made their minds up.'

Not only would Moyes keep Everton up, he'd stick around for the next 11 years – a tenure second in length only to Harry Catterick – and steer the Blues to nine top-eight finishes over that spell after just one in the previous decade, before his dramatic return in Goodison's final season.

* * *

15 April 1961: Everton 5 Cardiff City 1 (Manager Johnny Carey bows out after being told he was getting the sack by John Moores in a taxi)

'Taxi for xxx' – insert a suitable name – has become the shorthand phrase for any football manager on their way out but back in 1961 an Everton boss really was told by the club's owner he was getting the sack while the pair of them rode together in a cab.

John Moores and manager Johnny Carey were travelling to London for a Football Association meeting.

James Corbett records in *The Everton Encyclopedia*, 'Although Everton had beaten Newcastle United 4-0 at St James' Park the previous Saturday, speculation was more intense than ever about Carey's future.

'Wanting clarification, he demanded a meeting with his chairman. Moores suggested that they reconvene, and the two men took a taxi to the Grosvenor Hotel.

'During that journey, Carey repeated his request for clarification on his future. Moores, always a man of principle, was straight and to the point. He told Carey that he was being replaced.'

Despite being a respected figure in the game, Carey seemed to lack the ruthlessness, and his Everton team the consistency, that Moores demanded.

There's a clip of Moores on the BBC's *The Official History of Everton FC* video in which he boldly declares, 'Everton expects success. We've a very good crowd and our crowd are very loyal. But, of course, they pay money, and they expect to see us do well.

'If we don't do well then something should be done about it, and something *will* be done about it.'

Despite being born in Eccles, self-made man Moores had amassed his fortune in Liverpool with his Littlewoods retail and football pools company and having joined Everton's board in 1960, he was determined to restore the Blues to their former glories.

The fitful 1950s had seen a three-year period in the Second Division, the club's longest spell outside the top flight, and for too long Everton's proud Latin motto of *Nil Satis Nisi Optimum* ('Nothing but the best is good enough') had been ignored, but Moores used his financial muscle to try to ensure that the new decade produced an upturn in fortunes.

This started with a £56,000 interest-free loan to the club to buy new players and the Blues were soon dubbed the 'Mersey Millionaires'.

Such spending had enabled Everton to improve on the back-to-back 16th-placed finishes they'd had under former Manchester United captain Carey in 1959 and 1960 to come fifth in 1961 but the manager was replaced by Sheffield Wednesday's Harry Catterick with just two fixtures remaining of the season.

Carey was allowed one last match in charge the day after he'd been told he was being relieved of his duties and his players rewarded him with a crushing 5-1 victory over Cardiff City at Goodison Park. Captain Bobby Collins netted a hat-trick with goals on four, 29 (a penalty) and 49 minutes, while Alex Young bagged a brace (44, 46).

After conceding the fifth, visiting goalkeeper Maurice Swan, a Dubliner like Carey, had retired injured on 54 minutes and been replaced between the sticks by forward Derek Tapscott by the time Dai Ward struck an 83rd-minute consolation for the Welsh side.

The *Liverpool Echo* went with the headline 'Jeers and cheers mingle in thrilling display', with Michael Charters reporting, 'The crowd at Everton were more interested in the occupants of the directors' box than they were in the appearance of the teams on the pitch.

'There was some jeering when chairman John Moores appeared and took his customary seat in the front row of the directors' box and the crowd, some of them slow hand-clapping, set up the cry "We want Carey".

'Mr Carey came in the box as the match kicked off and sat in the second row. His usual seat was next to Mr Moores.

'After this preliminary burst of excitement, the crowd settled down to see how Everton played with Mr Carey as manager for the last time.'

The Everton players, whose wild inconsistencies at times that season had contributed to Carey's dismissal – they'd won 3-1 at defending champions Burnley on Boxing Day only to be beaten 3-0 by the Clarets at Goodison Park just 24 hours later – set about producing a masterclass for their departing gaffer.

Charters said, 'Everton were indeed giving Mr Carey the finest of send-offs for their football had not been better all season.'

It was too late to save him though, and despite later remembered by Moores as being 'a nice man, an honourable man and a good practitioner', Carey made way for Catterick who was the winner that Everton's ambitious owner demanded.

* * *

18 September 1948: Everton 1 Liverpool 1 (Record Goodison attendance for what proved to be the last game before the club's first manager was replaced)

As an historical footnote, this game was Goodison Park's record attendance but the fact it also proved to be the last fixture before Everton chose to replace their first official manager, Theo Kelly, had the greater long-term significance.

Everton played 16 matches in front of crowds of over 70,000 at Goodison and all of them came between 1948 and 1962.

Despite this being an era in which the Blues collected no major honours, the popularity of the game boomed in postwar Britain with spectators searching for some much-needed escapism.

Everton were one of the last major clubs to appoint a manager.

Although William Barclay, one of the few members of the club to remain at Anfield at the time of the move to Goodison in 1892, has been listed by some as a 19th-century forerunner of Rafael Benítez in terms of being 'manager' of both clubs having subsequently worked alongside fellow Irishman John McKenna in running Liverpool's team between 1892 and 1896, his title with Everton was that of secretary.

Barclay had already relinquished his role of picking the team at Everton after the inaugural Football League season anyway and Prescot-born Dick Molyneux is the man credited with being in charge for their first title in 1890/91.

Molyneux's reign ended in 1901 having been suspended by the club for suspected drunkenness and director Will Cuff, who was later the chairman, oversaw selections until the first world war.

Upon the resumption of the Football League after the conflict, Tom McIntosh, who would pave the way for other later County Durham-born bosses Harry Catterick and Howard Kendall, took charge.

He was the man who brought Dixie Dean to the club, and he remained in the post until his death aged 56 on 29 October 1935.

Between 1935 and 1939, teams were picked by committees but following the 1938/39 championship season, Theo Kelly manoeuvred himself into the position of being Everton's first manager.

Born in Liverpool on 17 October 1896, Kelly was of Celtic stock with a Manx father and Cornish mother.

Kelly certainly seems to have been a highly driven individual. He's the man who devised the original version of the now iconic Everton crest using the emblem of the Everton lock-up/Prince Rupert's Tower complete with the *Nil Satis Nisi Optimum* motto.

However, his style was referred to as remote and autocratic and having seen the start of his reign delayed by the second world war, as well as sanctioning the sale of the Blues' biggest star Tommy Lawton, he also fell out with other leading lights such as Joe Mercer, who joined Arsenal, and T.G. Jones, who would have signed for Roma were it not for red tape.

With Everton still propping up the First Division table, having lost six of their previous seven matches, Kelly would revert to his old role of secretary with former Blues wing-half Cliff Britton replacing him as manager.

However, unlike Liverpool's Brendan Rodgers, who was also replaced after a 1-1 Merseyside derby draw at Goodison in 2015, being sacked that same evening, it took another three weeks for Britton's release from Burnley to be secured.

The new man was pictured arriving and shaking hands with predecessor Kelly under the watchful eye of trainer Harry Cooke on 11 October despite his imminent arrival being reported in the *Liverpool Echo* just 48 hours after the game with the Reds.

As for the match itself, 'Stork' speculated in the *Echo* that the attendance record might be broken, observing, 'Each section of the ground looked to be well and truly packed, and there were many thousands outside.'

Much was made of Everton selecting six of their 1939 title-winning side for the fixture and 'Stork' said, 'All good footballers admittedly but with a big streak of age,' adding, 'The big surprise was the staying power of the old guard. They were up and down going right to the end, playing as well as any of the younger members.'

Liverpool's Willie Fagan broke the deadlock ten minutes from full time with 'the ball going in off the upright'.

However, Jock Dodds earned a share of the spoils for Everton by equalising from the penalty spot four minutes later with 'a pile-driver that Cyril Sidlow got his hand to' after full-back Bill Shepherd 'had took over the goalkeeper's role and tipped Wally Boyes' shot over the bar' in an era when you could do that and still not get yourself sent off.

* * *

4 May 1991: Everton 1 Luton Town 0 (Gwladys Street's last stand)

For almost a century Everton's most vociferous supporters had congregated in various incarnations of the Gwladys Street terrace but this was to be their last stand.

Those same passionate fans who – as predicted by Howard Kendall – would 'suck the ball into the Bayern Munich net' on Goodison Park's greatest night would still be there but from now on they would have to 'officially' sit down during matches.

What goes on in theory compared to the reality of practice though are often two very different things and for over three decades more, eager Evertonians behind the goal would routinely still rise to their feet whenever their side crossed the halfway line but from this point onwards they would be placed in designated seats rather than against crush barriers.

Football was changing. The following year the English First Division would become the Premier League while the European Cup, ironically by letting in non-title-winning clubs, would be rebranded as the Champions League.

The biggest alteration for spectators though was the way in which they watched matches and nowhere was that felt as deeply as Merseyside.

One of the major recommendations of the Taylor Report, the inquiry into the Hillsborough disaster which resulted in 97 Liverpool fans eventually losing their lives due to events at an FA Cup semi-final against Nottingham Forest in 1989, was that terraces were unsafe and must be replaced by all-seater stadia.

Although lower-division clubs had a longer period of grace to complete the transition, teams in England's top two tiers had until August 1994 to convert and many, like Everton, abandoned their standing areas well ahead of time.

In terms of the action on the pitch, this end-of-season encounter between a mid-table Blues side and struggling Luton Town, who the following weekend would avoid relegation on the final day for the third year on the run, was hardly a fitting finale for the grand old terrace.

At least the only goal of the game was scored in front of the Gwladys Street as four minutes into the second half, Stuart McCall's bravery going into a 50-50 challenge saw the ball rebound into the path of Tony Cottee and the striker coolly rounded former Everton understudy keeper Alec Chamberlain and dispatched a left-footed finish into the open net.

The Gwladys Street terrace itself was typically packed but Goodison had just 19,809 in total in the ground, less than half the number who had watched Everton defeat Liverpool 1-0 in an FA Cup fifth round second replay just nine weeks earlier at the same venue.

One of those present on the Gwladys Street was Ken Rogers of the *Liverpool Echo* who ditched his usual place in the press box to be among the huddled masses.

He wrote, 'I joined the faithful to say goodbye to an old friend. The Gwladys Street terrace, as we know it, is now just part of Goodison folklore. Everton's answer to the Anfield Kop will be all-seater in time for the start of next season and so the game against Luton Town marked the end of an era.

'I report on Everton AND Liverpool these days, hopefully showing no bias, but I was a Street-Ender as a lad and proud of it, sneaking in at three-quarter time to cheer on wonderful characters like Dave Hickson – the original Cannonball Kid.'

Rogers added, 'Saturday's odyssey was therefore very special. It was the first time I had stood to watch in the Street End for years.

'I'm a watcher now rather than an active participant, working from the Main Stand press box.

'But it was fascinating to climb on to the shelf, that slightly elevated section of terracing halfway up the Gwladys Street, reclaim my old "spec" behind the goal and listen to the banter and views of the only sponsors who really matter in football – the grassroots fans who are the lifeblood of every club.'

Back among the people, Rogers was able to hear the many quips 'neatly parcelled and tied up with barbed wire' from those standing around him.

Remarks chronicled included, 'Peter Beagrie's made a tackle. Get the smelling salts out for Howard,' and the cry, 'If you all hate Souness clap your hands,' which was followed by a standing ovation.

Rogers was left disappointed by the low-key exit of most of the Everton players, 'One or two glanced towards the partisan hordes and clapped but the vast majority headed straight for the dressing room. Modern players have no sense of theatre.'

Man of the match Cottee, though, complete with bottle of bubbly in his hand, was the only one who 'broke ranks'.

Rogers mused, 'The champagne should have been sprayed on the Gwladys Street. It will never quite be the same again.'

* * *

31 December 1983: Everton 0 Coventry City 0 (Kendall faces protests as less than 14,000 turn up before new year revival in fortunes)

It's often said that the darkest hour is just before dawn and that proved to be the case with this dour New Year's Eve stalemate for Howard Kendall, who would go on to become the most successful manager in Everton's history.

By the time the 1983/84 season had finished, Kendall's side had ended the club's 14-year trophy drought by winning the FA Cup Final with a 2-0 victory over Watford.

It would be the start of a golden era as the Blues added two league championships and the European Cup Winners' Cup over the following three campaigns.

However, nobody could have envisaged that the good times were just around the corner as Everton saw out 1983 with a whimper.

Indeed, there weren't many inside Goodison Park to witness it either as just 13,659 turned up to watch.

Pre-coronavirus restrictions, there had only been three lower top-flight attendances at the ground in the post-second world war era, two of which came that same season while the other was in the previous campaign – also against Coventry City.

Among all the Goodison gloom, Ken Rogers, writing in his end-of-year review for the *Liverpool Echo*, highlighted one colourful tale that had captured the imagination in Everton's ongoing attempts to land Brazilian international striker Nunes, who had already endeared himself to Blues fans by netting twice for Flamengo in their 3-0 Intercontinental Cup win over Liverpool back in December 1981.

Rogers recorded, 'Another year has slipped by without a trophy to brighten up the Goodison cabinet, but the Blues get the prize for the most unusual soccer story of 1983.

'Nunes himself was on the line from Rio, emphasising that he is ready for a new challenge in England.

'The long-drawn-out process of obtaining a work permit is still going through. The Brazilian blend is still a distinct possibility as Everton step into 1984.'

That transfer never happened but while the Blues could have done with some slick Samba moves to help break the deadlock against Sam Allardyce and company on this occasion, they found the answers they needed from within the camp in the weeks ahead.

Various theories abound as to the moment that marked the watershed in their fortunes the following January.

First there was Kendall opening the window of the visiting dressing room at the Victoria Ground for Everton's players to be inspired by hearing their travelling fans ahead of an FA Cup third round tie with Stoke City with his galvanised side triumphing 2-0.

Then 11 days later, Everton were trailing 1-0 at Third Division Oxford United in the League Cup quarter-finals before Kevin

Brock's misplaced backpass was intercepted by Adrian Heath who equalised and forced a replay.

Although beaten by Liverpool in the final, following another replay after the rivals met in a first all-Merseyside Wembley showpiece, the run had proved the Blues were finally becoming a match for their all-conquering neighbours.

The faith shown in Kendall during these dark days by chairman Philip Carter and the way in which he was subsequently rewarded by a period of sustained success is a lesson to today's impatient Premier League owners who are often all too eager to press the panic button, including Farhad Moshiri who went through eight managers in as many years.

About to turn 35 when he returned to the club as manager in 1981, Kendall had presided over finishes of eighth and seventh in his first two seasons but with Everton hovering just above the relegation zone ahead of Coventry's visit and having netted just 11 goals all season – the lowest tally in all four divisions of English football – Carter was under increasing pressure to dispense with the young gaffer's services.

Kendall went on to coach in Spain where fans wave white handkerchiefs when they don't like what they see on the pitch, but Carter would have been alarmed when cushions were thrown from the Main Stand's more elevated seats around him on to the Goodison turf on this day.

There was precious little action to record from the match itself with Ann Cummings of the *Liverpool Echo* reporting, 'Everton's goal famine continued. Despite dominating much of the play against high-flying Coventry [who were seventh] they struggled to convert their chances.

'At times the crowd gave vent to their frustrations when the Blues' attacking moves fizzled out disappointingly.

'But prompted by the hard-working Peter Reid bolstered by Kevin Ratcliffe, they kept looking for that elusive opening.'

Safe in the knowledge that he'd later been part of Everton's greatest side, Reid declared on Twitter after another goalless bore draw at Goodison in December, this time against Arsenal in 2019, 'Nearly as bad as the Everton v Coventry game I played in many years ago. NEARLY.'

* * *

19 October 2002: Everton 2 Arsenal 1 (Remember the name – Wayne Rooney)

'Remember the name – Wayne Rooney!' roared Clive Tyldesley with five of the most succinct but appropriate words in a long and glittering career of commentating.

How could any of us forget?

It's deeply regrettable that Evertonians only got to enjoy the footballing genius of Rooney, one of their own, during two short spells that bookended his English top-flight career.

In between that, Rooney won every major honour in club football with Manchester United and was the all-time leading goalscorer for both the Red Devils and England by the time he returned to Goodison Park some 13 years after his exit, when aged just 18, he had broken Blues' hearts.

Everton would do well to remember their most-gifted homegrown talent at his precocious, youthful best though, when as a freakishly gifted man-child he was a force of nature that frightened the life out of senior pros twice his age.

After watching him play while still a schoolboy, Colin Harvey, never prone to bouts of hysteria, let it be known (on the quiet) that the prospect from Croxteth was like Kenny Dalglish – only quicker.

Walter Smith had hoped that the wonderkid – who was almost taking on opponents single-handedly in Everton's run to the 2001/02 FA Youth Cup final – might help save his job but he ran out of time, and it was his successor David Moyes who was tasked with nurturing and protecting the jewel in the academy's crown.

Rooney started the Blues' first match of the 2002/03 season, but his manager tried to ease the 16-year-old as gently as he could into senior football, deploying him off the bench for 20 of his 37 appearances in his first campaign.

It was on one of those occasions, as an impact substitute, that Rooney famously announced himself to the footballing world at large.

There had already been whispers about what he had the potential to go and do – a stadium announcer at Austrian part-timers Weiz where Rooney netted a hat-trick in a 10-2 mauling ahead of his first season hailed him as 'Der neue Alan Shearer' – but nobody was quite expecting the grand entrance he made against Arsenal.

The youngster had bagged the first two goals of his fledgling career in a 3-0 League Cup win at fourth-tier Wrexham at the start of the month, but here, introduced just ten minutes from the end, he was facing the defending Premier League champions and league leaders with a backline featuring England internationals Ashley Cole, Sol Campbell and goalkeeper David Seaman.

The Gunners had taken the lead just eight minutes in through Freddie Ljungberg but Tomasz Radzinski, who Rooney replaced, equalised midway through the first half.

David Prentice of the *Liverpool Echo* described the wonder strike in detail, writing, 'Such is the hype which has surrounded Wayne Rooney's blossoming talent, he was never going to break his Premier League duck with a scruffy fourth goal in a one-sided rout of West Brom.

'He was always going to choose the grand stage. He almost did it at the Theatre of Dreams a fortnight ago, against Manchester United.

'But this boy has been made at Everton, and Goodison Park was always going to be the most appropriate venue to deliver his first League goal.

'Not even the most wildly optimistic Evertonian, however, could have dreamed of an icebreaker like this one.

'It was his last chance to score in the Premier League as a 16-year-old, against the England goalkeeper, and an Arsenal team which hadn't lost a match for a record-breaking 30 Premier League games.

'Oh, and the 89th minute was almost up.'

He added, 'As if that wasn't enough, the strike was one of breathtaking brilliance. It deserves recording in freeze-frame detail.

'Thomas Gravesen hoisted a long ball forwards from the halfway line, which Rooney instantly plucked from the sky with one sure touch of his right instep.

'Such was the quality of that first touch he was able to turn immediately inside, glance upwards at the distant target then explode a wickedly curving shot – from 25 yards – over Seaman and off the underside of the Park End crossbar.

'It was a reverberating moment – one which Goodison has not witnessed for years.'

With over five minutes of stoppage time played, Rooney almost added another goal after 'lifting the ball with the deftest of chips with the outside of his boot on to the roof of the net'.

As Prentice quipped, 'If that had gone in, the fans [more than 30,000 stayed behind 15 minutes after the players left the pitch] might still be inside Goodison Park now.'

* * *

17 August 1996: Everton 2 Newcastle United 0 (The world's most-expensive player, Alan Shearer, is put in the shade on his debut)

In the summer of 1996, we were told 'football's coming home' as England hosted the European Championship but while David Baddiel and Frank Skinner epitomised the game's new image in the Premier League era, this match was a throwback to a previous age.

With their weekly television show *Fantasy Football League* based around the new phenomenon of fans picking their select XIs from across the division to score points for their imaginary teams and competing against friends and colleagues, comedians Baddiel and Skinner had become two of the most recognisable figures in the early years of the Premier League.

While they would always give a cheeky nod to football's past through their 'Phoenix from the Flames' sketches in which they'd recreate memorable moments – one included a glorious starring role for Evertonian folk hero Eddie Cavanagh who had to be rugby tackled to the ground after running on to the Wembley pitch in celebration during the 1966 FA Cup Final against Sheffield Wednesday – in essence, their programme celebrated the more light-hearted nature of the game in the 1990s.

After the previous decade had been marred by hooliganism and stadium tragedies, we had now progressed from violence to more family-friendly atmospheres, albeit with a large dollop of laddish banter from the 'Cool Britannia' generation.

Unlike Baddiel and Skinner's song 'Three Lions', England didn't quite make it to number one at the Euros – suffering predictable penalty heartbreak against Germany – ensuring the 'years of hurt' (which have subsequently doubled from 30 to 60) continued, but one of their team emerged from the tournament as the world's most expensive player.

Newcastle United paid £15m to take Alan Shearer – a Premier League title winner with Blackburn Rovers just a year earlier – back to his home city and he'd make his highly anticipated debut for his boyhood club at Goodison Park.

While the Magpies had to go back much further than Everton for their own glory days, having been promoted to the Premier League one year after its creation, under manager Kevin Keegan they were seen as one of the swashbuckling new forces now English football was different.

Many Blues resented the amount of attention the Geordies received in the national media while more recent powerhouses like themselves were already being dismissed as yesterday's men after a few lean years.

Indeed, the FA Cup had only just left the Goodison trophy cabinet having been won the previous year while at the time, the last major silverware for Newcastle, whose most recent league championship came in 1927, was the 1969 Inter-Cities Fairs Cup, a competition they'd gained entry to at Everton's expense through the one team per city rule despite the Blues finishing higher than them.

You had to look to 1955 for their last domestic success, the FA Cup, before – buoyed by the sovereign wealth fund of the House of Saud – the 70-year drought was finally ended with a 2-1 victory over Liverpool in the 2025 League Cup Final.

But back in the 1990s, with lavish purchases of the likes of local lad Shearer, the Toon were thinking big.

It's not as if Shearer didn't pose a threat on his debut but this just wasn't his day. David Prentice of the *Liverpool Echo* said, 'The £15m forward was one of the few Newcastle players to do himself justice. He was denied a customary debut goal only by one outstanding Neville Southall save and referee Mike Reed's decision to rule out a first-half header for pushing.'

Everton took the lead through a 29th-minute penalty after Duncan Ferguson was fouled by future Blue Steve Watson, and David Unsworth 'calmly stroked the ball to Shaka Hislop's right'.

The victory was sewn up five minutes before the break by an Everton debutant who would leave the club for Newcastle 18 months later in acrimonious circumstances – Gary Speed, 'Ferguson created the opening with a prodigious leap and the £3.5m summer signing just beat Hislop to the ball and rapped it firmly past him.'

Prentice proclaimed, 'Back when Everton were last really, really good, but no one had quite begun to realise it, a Newcastle manager described the Blues as "the best-balanced team in the division".

'Jack Charlton's words raised a few eyebrows back in 1984. His early analysis of Howard Kendall's fledgling side, however, ultimately proved spot on.

'The present-day Toon Army wouldn't want to hear Big Jack's assessment of the current Everton and Newcastle line-ups.

'While Kevin Keegan's side appears to possess all the balance of a drunk, Joe Royle's slick unit is well-oiled and potent.'

He added, 'Keegan's post-match press conference, while handing Everton the praise they deserved, also contained a liberal sprinkling of the F and B words – "fighting" and "battling".

'If it was an underhand attempt to undermine Everton's achievement, nobody was taken in. This was no Dogs of War-style victory.'

* * *

9 January 1946: Everton 2 Preston North End 2 (First competitive postwar fixture sees double-legged FA Cup tie settled after golden goal extra time)

What a return for Everton as they were sunk in their first postwar fixture at Goodison Park by a penalty from Bill Shankly in golden goal extra time before the phrase even existed.

The Blues had gone into the second world war as English champions but just as those who survived the biggest mass slaughter in human history had to rebuild their lives after the fighting was over, so Everton had to sift through the rubble with what was left of their once great team.

In 1939, they had a hugely talented side who were the best in the land and looked set to enjoy a potential period of dominance.

Tommy Lawton – a worthy heir to Dixie Dean – had been the First Division's leading goalscorer for the past two seasons and had still yet to turn 20. His all-star supporting cast included the likes of T.G. Jones (21) and Joe Mercer (24) with all three men young enough to have their best footballing years ahead of them.

Lawton would later claim, 'The next year we should have won the league again, the FA Cup and the bloody boat race if they'd put us in it.'

Leading aircraftman Thomas Robson, a former Blues wing-half, was in the RAF when his death aged 34 from a heart condition was announced in 1942 while four players on Everton's books who hadn't turned out competitively also died during the conflict (leading aircraftman Brian Atkins; sergeant Alfred Penlington; lance corporal William Reid and pilot officer William Sumner).

While all the Blues' first-teamers came home safely, the war had robbed them of a significant chunk of what even at the best of times is a notoriously short career.

Everton accepted a £15,000 offer from Roma for Jones, dubbed 'the prince of centre-halves', but the transfer was ultimately blocked by foreign exchange regulations.

Lawton and Mercer both had plenty of football left in them but sadly it was away from Everton.

With his marriage having deteriorated, Lawton wanted to leave the Liverpool area, and he'd already joined Chelsea in November 1945 before the Blues had even returned to the field competitively.

It was a decision he would live to regret, remarking, 'On reflection I should have stayed and transferred the wife!'

Mercer – a lifelong Evertonian from Ellesmere Port – stayed on for a further year but joined Arsenal after falling out with secretary turned manager Theo Kelly.

Football had continued to be played throughout the second world war, but it was an ad hoc affair with many players away and others making guest appearances for different clubs.

With Liverpool suffering the largest tonnage of bombing of any British city outside of London during the Blitz, Goodison Park itself did not escape the destruction.

A bomb landed directly in Gwladys Street and the £5,000 splinter damage repairs to the structure of the stand

– only completed in 1938 – was paid for by the War Damage Commission.

Football League action did not resume until the 1946/47 season, but FA Cup matches were played in 1945/46 with a two-legged format for the only time in the history of football's oldest competition.

Everton were drawn against Preston North End in the third round, losing 2-1 at Deepdale in the first leg, despite Harry Catterick having put them ahead.

The return match at Goodison saw Everton 1-0 up after 90 minutes to level the aggregate score, courtesy of Mercer's 17th-minute penalty, but with no away goals rule, the tie went into extra time (ten minutes each way rather than the 15 that later became standard).

Thomas Elliott looked to be putting the Blues through when he netted a second for the hosts four minutes into the additional period, but Billy McIntosh scored for Preston a minute later to ensure the game went into what later became known as 'golden goal' extra time and it was eventually settled by a penalty converted by Bill Shankly.

The match is covered in the *Liverpool Echo* under the headline 'Extra-extra time – sternest test of stamina' but seemingly hampered by print deadlines due to the extended play, what had otherwise been a detailed report fizzled out when it came to the dramatic conclusion with Shankly's name not even mentioned in regards to his goal.

With the match starting at 2pm on a Wednesday in midwinter in an era before floodlights, 'Ranger' simply remarked, 'There was an exciting finish when, after the nine minutes of extra time, Preston were awarded a penalty for an offence, which in the failing light, I could not see.'

And there it ends. Welcome back Everton.

* * *

12 May 2013: Everton 2 West Ham United 0 (Moyes's Goodison farewell after over 11 years in charge)

Over 11 years on from his tumultuous Goodison Park arrival, dubbing Everton the 'People's Club' and presiding over a barnstorming 2-1 victory over Fulham, there were mixed emotions for Blues as long-serving manager David Moyes signed off.

Back when he was appointed in 2002, Evertonians sang, 'He's got red hair, but we don't care.'

By 2013, those ginger locks on the head of Moyes, now 50, had faded and the worry lines on his face had deepened but what did he and the club have to show for his lengthy tenure?

Despite turning down the position of Manchester United assistant manager before coming to Goodison, he was now leaving for the top job at Old Trafford – although there'd be no bumper compensation package for Everton after Moyes had let his contract run down – having been hand-picked by the retiring Sir Alex Ferguson to be his successor.

Yet for all the multitude of undoubted good work that he'd done with the Blues, delivering nine top-eight finishes, including fourth position in 2005 – which remains their highest Premier League placing to date – with a club that had achieved just one in the previous decade, the Glaswegian had failed to secure silverware, something he would only finally rectify with West Ham United by lifting the UEFA Europa Conference League aged 60 in 2023.

There were personal gongs for Moyes – his work saw him named League Managers' Association Manager of the Year in 2002/03, 2004/05 and 2008/09 – but not the trophies that long-suffering Evertonians craved so much.

When it came to the big games, the opportunities to make a statement and smash through that glass ceiling to challenge the established elite, he could never take that last step.

Everton defeated Liverpool and Manchester United en route to Wembley in 2009 but despite going ahead through Louis Saha scoring the quickest goal in FA Cup history at the time, they lost 2-1 to Chelsea.

It was a similar story when they surrendered a lead at the national stadium against an out-of-form Liverpool in the 2012 FA Cup semi-final while just two months before he left, there was the painful 3-0 FA Cup quarter-final exit at Goodison Park to Roberto Martínez's Wigan Athletic.

Not lifting the UEFA Cup in 2008 was also viewed as a huge opportunity wasted while throughout Moyes's reign he never won a Premier League fixture away to Liverpool, Manchester United, Arsenal or Chelsea.

It felt frustrating to many at the time, but with the benefit of hindsight, Moyes could be considered extremely unfortunate considering that the spine of his team – Phil Jagielka, Mikel Arteta and Ayegbeni Yakubu – were all out injured for the FA Cup Final loss.

Also, having to compete against Chelsea's new money early in his reign, he then came up against Manchester City's petrodollar-fuelled riches, which he compared to 'taking a knife to a gun fight'.

Given the subsequent records of his successors and what has happened to the club before he returned, you could also argue that nobody else has managed Everton as well in the Premier League era.

As Greg O'Keeffe of the *Liverpool Echo* mused after Sam Allardyce's Hammers were put to the sword, 'It could have been the champagne which flowed at Goodison yesterday – instead it was tears.

'As David Moyes emphasised after regaining his composure following that emotional farewell on the pitch, Everton might have been celebrating the prospect of Champions League football but for the unfortunately relentless form of the three London clubs above them.

'That would have been an even more fitting way for the Scot to sign off his 11-year reign as he departs for Manchester United.

'His side's tally of 63 points with one game remaining means they still have the opportunity to record their highest ever Premier League points total.

'A convincing win over West Ham also ensured they can claim supremacy as the ascendant club on Merseyside for the second consecutive season.

'But neither were much consolation to the supporters, who watched a poignant lap of the pitch by their outgoing manager after the final whistle with a mixture of melancholy and concern for the future.

'This was a triumph which neatly summed-up the evolution of Everton under Moyes.'

Everton, who were heading for sixth place, triumphed in comfortable fashion thanks to a brace from Kevin Mirallas.

The first, on six minutes, with the hosts 'capitalising on a scintillating start' saw the Belgian coolly side-foot home.

His second, on the hour, came via a deflection off James Collins after a nicely weighted pass from Darron Gibson.

Former midfielder Tim Cahill, who had departed for New York Red Bulls the previous summer having been so instrumental for much of Moyes's reign, flew in from the USA to join in the farewell guard of honour alongside retiring captain Phil Neville who hadn't been picked since the Wigan debacle.

O'Keeffe observed, 'But it was Moyes who predictably brought the house down. Standing alone near the centre circle, blowing out his cheeks and wearing a smile of pure pride and affection, he signalled his goodbyes.'

* * *

9 October 1957: Everton 2 Liverpool 0 (First use of floodlights)
Goodison Park under the lights often produced a special atmosphere for players and fans alike but for the first half of the ground's existence there was no such thing.

Midweek matches had to be finished before dusk – particularly tricky in winter – which hampered attendances too.

However, the development of lighting technology – and gradual acceptance of the English football authorities to embrace it – would pave the way for the nighttime fixtures that many prefer and of course the scope for continental competition between Europe's leading clubs.

Former *Liverpool Echo* sports editor Ken Rogers described Everton's original floodlights in his book, *Goodison Glory*, 'Four giant pylons, each 185ft high and operating initially with 36 lamps each, towered over the pitch, one in each corner of the ground.

'The towers, the tallest in the country, could accommodate a further 18 lamps on each pylon if it was felt that the illumination generated was insufficient.

'The company installing the system claimed that each lamp would last for at least 500 hours, or 330 matches, and the makers suggested the club install new lamps every three to four years. It was claimed that the light output was the equivalent of 400 good-sized houses.'

As Rob Sawyer explained in his illuminating article, 'The Story of Goodison Park Under Floodlights' on the Everton fan website Toffeeweb, Anfield had played host to trial matches using gas-fuelled Wells Lights when Everton still played there in 1890 but while the interesting novelty drew in crowds, the light was deemed insufficient for sporting contests.

Sawyer added that with the bill coming to £38,000 – just shy of £1m in today's prices – the Blues had considered inviting an overseas opponent but with Anfield also installing floodlights (their ones only cost £12,000), a two-legged Floodlit Challenge Cup competition against Liverpool was devised.

With no league derbies since 1951 due to first Everton's and then Liverpool's spells in the Second Division, there was an appetite for the two local rivals to meet and a silver-gilt cup valued at £300 was commissioned to be contested.

'Ranger's Notes on Sport' recorded the game in the *Liverpool Echo*, 'If anybody had lingering doubts regarding the drawing power of floodlit football on Merseyside, they were set at rest at Goodison Park when 58,771 watched the "Liverton" game.

'True, it was an extra-special occasion, but as time goes on, I think the crowds in this almost fantastically enthusiastic soccer area will continue to roll up even when there is no derby label to the match.

'Conditions of course were all in favour of a good crowd apart from a slight mist which reduced visibility a little, for it was a mild and gentle night.

'The light did not strike me as quite as good as those at Old Trafford but as I saw the latter on a very clear night the comparison may not be a fair one.

'The haze hanging over the ground was a handicap. In any case, if Everton consider it necessary to step up the power it can be done at little cost and without loss of time. They wisely made provision for that in the original plans.'

Both goals for Everton came from Eddie Thomas, who was a modern player in this modern match given that he was a substitute.

The Football League wouldn't permit replacement players until 1965 but Thomas had come on for Wally Fielding at the start of the second half after the Blues' London-born veteran had suffered a twisted ankle.

Thomas broke the deadlock on 52 minutes, but his second goal 13 minutes later prompted 'Ranger' to go into chapter and verse about Kopite complaints about it supposedly being offside, 'Certainly the Anfielders thought so, for they surrounded the referee and begged him to consult the linesman, holding up the restart for a minute or so as they argued the point.

'Dave Hickson was certainly yards offside when the movement began but he was played on when the pass to him struck a defender [Gerry Byrne] en route.

'Hickson metaphorically rubbing his hands with glee at this stroke of luck, took the ball on 20 yards and then squared it to the on-coming Thomas to slot it home with the greatest of ease.'

The return match took place at Anfield some three weeks later on 30 October and although Liverpool won 3-2 having raced into a 3-0 lead with goals from Billy Liddell (16 penalty, 18) and future Blue Johnny Morrissey (25), Hickson (38) and Jimmy Harris (82) reduced arrears to give Everton a 5-3 aggregate success.

* * *

15 August 1992: Everton 1 Sheffield Wednesday 1 (First ever Premier League game at Goodison Park)

'It's a whole new ball game' claimed broadcaster Sky in its advert for English football's rebranded top flight but nothing much seemed to have changed at Goodison Park for Everton's first fixture in the new Premier League.

Although Sky would revolutionise television coverage, not just by taking it away from the terrestrial channels but with the ways it marketed and packaged the product, for those inside grounds up and down the country, little other than the name of the competition appeared to have altered, overnight at least.

In the 1970s and 80s, going to watch football was hardly a family-friendly day out. Not only was the sport blighted by hooliganism at times, but it was also played in often dilapidated venues with the May 1985 Heysel disaster the prime example of what a deadly combination those two factors could be.

Earlier that same month, after the Bradford City stadium fire had killed 56 people at Valley Parade, a *Sunday Times* leader column proclaimed that football was, 'a slum sport played in slum stadiums increasingly watched by slum people, who deter decent folk from turning up'.

Looking to build on the new type of fans that the game was now attracting – including the middle classes and women – on the back of the 1990 World Cup in Italy and an increasingly sanitised environment in stadia, Sky tried to project a more wholesome image.

A player from each of the 22 Premier League founder member clubs was invited to appear on the 'Whole new ball game' promotion (for Everton it was Peter Beardsley) set against the musical backdrop of the song 'Alive and Kicking' by Simple Minds.

The rival footballers were shown laughing together as they made their way by coach to a studio for filming and the smiles continued in a mock dressing room/gym environment as they donned their kits.

Everton legend Peter Reid – by now manager of Manchester City – was shown delivering a team talk, calmly instructing his players, 'It's important that we get that ball back as soon as we can … let's go and win it.'

The measured, squeaky-clean approach was in stark contrast to the reality of the expletive-filled verbal volleys delivered by Reid and his staff shown in the *Premier Passions* documentary later in the decade.

But while Sky brought gimmicks such as fireworks, cheerleaders and giant inflatable sumo wrestlers to the early live games, in truth other than green shirts for referees and Premier League badges on the players' sleeves, there had been no radical overhaul.

Football's greatest alteration that summer, the introduction of the backpass rule, had nothing to do with the Premier League but in time the game would evolve into something very different.

Crowds increased, but it took time. Everton's final game of the first Premier League season against Sheffield Wednesday's neighbours United attracted just 15,197, much less than half the number they'd average in the early decades of the 21st century.

Squads also became cosmopolitan with players from across the globe – substitute Robert Warzycha from Poland was the Blues' only non-Brit in their line-up against the Owls – but back on day one, the words 'Premier League' were not even mentioned in Ken Rogers's match report in the *Liverpool Echo*.

Instead, he took the tone that this game had been much like the start of any other campaign, declaring, 'The opening day of the football season is always fraught with danger. Expensive new signings are paraded on bowling green pitches in front of fans with hopes raised high. But that's the beauty of it all. It's a day for reaching for the stars, with every chance that 90 minutes later, you might be crashing down to earth with an ignominious bump.'

There were a couple of oddities to note from the action though concerning a brace of Welshmen in the Everton side, one an already experienced star at the club and the other making his debut.

Nigel Pearson was gifted a 15th-minute opener, 'the simplest of volleyed chances', by something as rare as hen's teeth – a Neville Southall mistake. Rogers described how 'the greasy ball slipped through his gloves like a lump of lard'.

Lifelong Evertonian Barry Horne, making his Blues bow aged 30, then lulled his new fans into believing their new signing might be a regular goal threat, equalising a minute before half-time as he 'rifled home a superb volley that found the net off the underside of the bar'.

He'd only ever do that once more, on what proved to be a much more significant day when it came to Everton playing in the Premier League.

* * *

29 April 1978: Everton 6 Chelsea 0 (Bob Latchford breaks the 30-goal barrier)

Some Everton supporters have speculated about the prospect of getting water taxis to arrive at the club's new stadium at Bramley-

Moore Dock but if their claims about Bob Latchford were true then the 1970s Blues icon could just stride across the Mersey.

Writing in *The Everton Encyclopedia*, James Corbett said, 'A player who followed in Everton's famous tradition of number nines, only Dixie Dean and Graeme Sharp have ever bettered Bob Latchford's phenomenal goalscoring for Everton.

'Latchford may have lacked the charisma of Dave Hickson, the grace of Alex Young or the scintillating pace of Roy Vernon, but in an Everton career that spanned more than seven years he was a Goodison icon, a player who the fans used to chant "walks on water".

'A modest, articulate man, he helped restore pride to Evertonians during a time when living in Liverpool's shadow had become a way of life.'

The middle sibling among three brothers who were professional footballers, Bob had always scored goals while David and Peter stopped them and carved out careers as keepers.

Latchford's impressive scoring ratio of almost a goal every other game for his local club Birmingham City prompted Everton to shell out a British record fee equivalent to £350,000 for his services in February 1974 but with Howard Kendall and Archie Styles heading in the opposite direction to St Andrew's, only £80,000 was actually handed over.

With Joe Royle being sold to Manchester City at the start of the following season, Latchford quickly became the spearhead of the Blues' attack but his prolific scoring couldn't bring back the glory days to Goodison Park.

Despite going into the final month of the 1974/75 season on top of the table, Everton blew their title chances with Derby County ending up as champions while in 1976/77 the club reached their first League Cup Final with Latchford scoring in the replay and second replay (the only time the competition's showpiece has required three games) against old foes Aston Villa only to succumb to a 3-2 defeat after five and a half hours of gruelling combat.

With trophies continuing to elude their team, Blues fans enthusiastically got behind Latchford's bid to claim a £10,000 prize from the *Daily Express* newspaper for any player who could score 30 league goals in the 1977/78 season.

Nobody had achieved the feat since Manchester City's Francis Lee hit 33 in 1971/72 but by the turn of the calendar year, Latchford was almost two-thirds of his ways towards the total.

A new year drought was followed up by a purple patch over Easter but after drawing a blank at Middlesbrough and West Bromwich Albion, he required two more goals on the final day of the season at home to Chelsea to claim the bounty.

Everton, who would finish the season in third place but nine points adrift of champions Nottingham Forest, were always in command against their visitors from west London who had just survived a relegation battle.

Martin Dobson fired the Blues ahead on seven minutes, Billy Wright doubled their advantage on 14 minutes and Neil Robinson, who had become a vegetarian in 1970 and a decade later claimed to be the first vegan in professional football, made it 3-0 on 54.

However, with 20 minutes to go, the 39,504 crowd were still waiting on Latchford to bring home the bacon.

On 72 minutes Latchford finally got his first goal of the day with a header but when Mick Lyons added a fifth just three minutes later, he recalled celebrating alone, lamenting, 'Everybody just stood and looked at me. It's the only time I've scored at Goodison and felt sick about it.'

A further three minutes on, Lyons did help Latchford reach his target as he went down in the area under a challenge from Mickey Droy, with the Chelsea man insisting, 'I never touched him. He just fell over.'

There was never any doubt over who would take the penalty and the *Sunday Mirror* reported that when Latchford 'stepped up to bang the ball past Peter Bonetti it heralded an ecstatic invasion of the pitch by Everton fans.'

While the moment was one of the biggest highlights of Latchford's career, the aftermath proved to be seriously problematic for the kind-hearted striker.

He donated half of his £10,000 prize to the Professional Footballers' Association Benevolent Fund before sharing the rest with his team-mates, leaving him with just £192 and a three-year wrangle with the Inland Revenue as he had to convince the taxman he hadn't pocketed a £5,000 bonus.

* * *

18 September 1963: Everton 0 Internazionale 0 (First European Cup game at Goodison)

No Evertonian needs reminding that the Blues have not enjoyed the same kind of love affair with the European Cup as their neighbours but their first foray into UEFA's premier club tournament started here.

Of course, Everton's greatest side were denied their place at European football's top table in 1985 because of the post-Heysel ban in an era when English clubs had won seven out of the previous nine finals, including six in a row from 1977 to 1982, while Howard Kendall's men themselves had proven their pedigree in continental competition just a fortnight before that tragic night in Brussels by lifting the European Cup Winners' Cup.

They would also miss out in 1987/88 after their last league championship with English clubs not being invited back until 1990/91 when, like Everton the previous time out, Manchester United won the Cup Winners' Cup in Rotterdam.

But back in the 1960s all this was to come, and the Blues became the first club from Merseyside to compete in the European Cup in 1963/64 having made their European debut the previous season in somewhat underwhelming circumstances.

They didn't even make it to the continent on that occasion having been drawn against Scottish side Dunfermline Athletic. Although the hosts triumphed 1-0 in the first leg at Goodison Park, Harry Catterick was undone by the great Jock Stein – the manager who would deliver Britain's first European Cup with Celtic in 1967 – suffering a shock 2-0 defeat in the return match in Fife.

While the Blues only had themselves to blame on that occasion, they could count themselves extremely unfortunate to have been paired with Internazionale in an unseeded preliminary round of the European Cup the following year when there were minnows from the likes of Cyprus, Malta, Northern Ireland, the Republic of Ireland and Albania, and even the champions of Finland and Luxembourg playing against each other at the same stage.

Inter – often incorrectly dubbed 'Inter Milan' by British football followers (nobody refers to them as such in Italy) – would go on to lift the trophy for the first time that season, defeating the already five-times winners Real Madrid 3-1 in the final in Vienna, and would retain their crown on their home San Siro turf in 1965 by beating Benfica 1-0.

Writing in the *Liverpool Echo*, Michael Charters admitted that a goalless draw for Everton did not bode well ahead of the return match in Lombardy, stating, 'The Milan maestros duly took back with them the goalless draw they had hoped for from the first leg of the European Cup preliminary round at Goodison Park.

'And, on the evidence of this game, Everton's chances of anything at Milan next Wednesday are very slim indeed.

'The Inter coach, Helenio Herrera, pulled off one of the confidence tricks of the age when he said, pre-match, that his intention would be to play a defensive game.

'Instead, the 62,000 crowd saw some superb attacking play from the Italians, particularly in the first half. They packed their defence when they had to, but their whole play was so fluid, so slick in turning defence into attack, they were much the better team.'

Legendary Inter boss Herrera, an Argentinian of Spanish parents who became a naturalised Frenchman (his family left South America for the French colonial city of Casablanca in modern day Morocco when he was just ten), was one of the first managers credited with orchestrating his team's success through a detailed tactical approach.

His style was dubbed *catenaccio* (meaning door bolt) and was based around a 5-3-2 formation which included four defensive markers with a sweeper behind them.

Such a disciplined nature was evident in frustrating Everton at Goodison Park with Charters observing, 'The essence of the difference in the two sides was the well-drilled execution of the Italians in everything they did.

'Their defensive covering was superb, they obviously worked to a set plan, and when they moved into attack, they went like lightning. Everton were never allowed to take command for a moment, and although they went all out all the game, they could not make any impression.'

The second leg was settled by a solitary strike from Brazilian right-winger Jair on 48 minutes but with Jimmy Gabriel ruled out there was one bright spot for Blues with the start of a legendary Everton career as 18-year-old homegrown hero Colin Harvey, who had been told he was only travelling to carry the skips containing the kit, made his debut.

* * *

4 December 1993: Everton 1 Southampton 0 (Kendall resigns again)

In more recent years Dion Dublin has become something of a national treasure, delighting television viewers with his 'stairs up to the bedrooms' catchphrase on *Homes Under the Hammer*, but back at the end of 1993 he was the reason behind Everton's most successful manager's fairytale return coming to an end.

After the full-time whistle of this low-key encounter, settled by a close-range header from Tony Cottee in the 35th minute and watched by just 13,667 fans (a mere eight more than had witnessed the infamous stalemate against Coventry City on New Year's Eve 1983 in Howard Kendall's first spell in charge), neither the boss nor the assembled press pack seemed to display the merest suggestion that anything out of the ordinary was about to happen.

It was a first win in five games for his side and they'd been knocked out of the League Cup with a 2-0 loss to Manchester United midweek, but they were in no immediate danger, sitting 11th in the Premier League table.

Kendall, who had spectacularly been appointed at Goodison Park for a second time just over three years earlier, immediately reinstalling his sacked predecessor (and successor from his first spell) Colin Harvey as his assistant and explained his decision to quit Maine Road by insisting that while Manchester City for him was 'a love affair', Everton was like 'a marriage'.

On Saturday evening, the *Liverpool Echo*'s *Football Pink* just went with the headline 'Cottee the goal hero' and actually tagged a line on the end of its report to seemingly play down any potential drama at the game, stating, 'A rumour circulating around the ground that Virgin empire boss Richard Branson was linking up with club director Bill Kenwright for a possible takeover was denied by the club.'

Instead, there would be rather more shocking news related to the existing hierarchy that would have to wait in print on Merseyside until the Monday.

After speaking to his chairman Dr David Marsh, a former amateur golfer from Southport, Kendall had made his decision to resign and went back up the staircase of the Main Stand to tell reporters, but it was too late for the deadlines of local publications.

Some 48 hours later, though, things were much clearer as Evertonians also digested the news that their 1963 title-winning captain Roy Vernon had died aged just 56.

Writing in his 2024 book *The End*, Gavin Buckland covered the matter in more detail and suggested there was more to Kendall's departure than the failure to prise Dublin from Manchester United alone, but Alex Ferguson confirmed the Blues' interest.

The Scot had beaten Everton to the signature of the target man in August of the previous year but just one month later Dublin had broken his leg.

During his period on the sidelines, Ferguson had signed the talismanic Eric Cantona and although Dublin had subsequently returned to full fitness, he nevertheless found himself down the pecking order behind the Frenchman and Mark Hughes, who were by now the regular front two.

Ferguson had told Kendall that he was determined to keep Dublin, who he still rated highly as a prospect, but the pair discussed the matter further when their sides had met in the League Cup at Goodison the previous Tuesday.

Ken Rogers of the *Liverpool Echo* wrote, 'Kendall asked again, and Ferguson told him, "Look, I would need an exceptional offer to even consider parting with the player." Kendall asked what Ferguson thought was "exceptional" and asked, "Would £1.5m do the trick?"

'"That's not exceptional enough," said Ferguson, who demanded £1.8m. Kendall put this figure to his board and the rest is now history. When the money was not forthcoming, Kendall clearly felt his position was untenable.'

Rogers added, 'Chairman Dr Marsh admits that Kendall possibly gave him an inkling of what was to come when they walked across the pitch prior to the game but is adamant that the final decision came as a complete surprise.'

However, Kendall revealed that in his heart of hearts he had already decided before the match he was going to quit but wanted to act like it was business as usual to protect his players.

He told Rogers, 'In a strange kind of way, I take as much satisfaction from that victory as I do from winning the championship.

'If we had lost against the Saints in front of 13,000 people and I had walked out, people might have got the wrong impression.

'In my mind it was done before that. I was feeling for the players. I didn't want to upset them before an important match.

'I have dealt with it in the way I thought was right and proper. That is the way Everton Football Club have always done things and this is why I have been privileged to manage the club twice.'

* * *

4 August 2010: Everton 2 Everton Viña del Mar 0 (The Blues defeat their Chilean namesakes in historic friendly)

It was the day that Everton couldn't lose, or perhaps they were bound to (depending which Everton that was), but then again it could also have been a draw.

Confused? Well, this was the occasion that Goodison Park hosted a friendly, although a trophy called the Brotherhood Cup was contested, between Everton and their namesakes from the Chilean city of Viña del Mar.

Over the years, there have been several 'Evertons' across the sporting world. There has been a clutch of Brazilian footballers called Everton, including the international Everton Soares who was linked with a potential move to the Blues before departing Gremio for Benfica in 2020.

Birmingham-born winger Mark Everton Walters could have also joined his namesake club from Rangers but opted for Liverpool instead.

Sir Everton Weekes was a West Indian Test cricketer while there was also Clive Everton, the snooker commentator.

Derived from the Saxon word *eofor*, meaning wild boar that lives in the forest, Everton is not a name merely confined to one particular corner of Liverpool.

There are villages called Everton in Bedfordshire, Hampshire and Nottinghamshire; there are at least three places in the

USA bearing the name in Arkansas, Indiana and Missouri; two in Australia in Victoria and Queensland; one in Ontario, Canada; plus an Everton that is part of Kloof in KwaZulu-Natal, South Africa.

In terms of football teams though, the club from Chile's Pacific coast gambling resort, nicknamed *Ruleteros* (Roulette players) are the most famous after the Merseyside originals although there was an Everton FC from Port of Spain who won the Trinidad and Tobago Cup four seasons in a row from 1929 to 1932.

Despite Everton's crest depicting the Everton Lock-Up or Prince Rupert's Tower, a Grade II-listed building built in 1787 that still stands on Everton Brow, Everton FC have never actually played their home games in the district.

St Domingo Methodist Chapel, from which the club took their original name in 1878 before switching to Everton the following year, was in Everton but their early grounds were in Anfield while Goodison Park is in neighbouring Walton and their new home at Bramley-Moore Dock is in Vauxhall.

Curiously, if John Houlding had his way, there could have been two Everton FCs in Liverpool alone.

After Everton decamped to their newly built ground on Goodison Road from Anfield where he was landlord in 1892, Houlding tried to have his new team's company registered as The Everton Football Club and Athletic Grounds Limited, but the Football League would not recognise them under that name.

Therefore, despite there already being a rugby union outfit of the same name, the oldest open rugby club in the world, formed in 1857 (now Liverpool St Helens since a merger in 1986), he changed to Liverpool FC.

So, in 2010, some 101 years after they had been formed by a group of Anglo-Chilean teenagers in deference to the Blues' pioneering tour of South America, the other Everton made their 7,000-mile pilgrimage to Goodison Park.

Greg O'Keeffe of the *Liverpool Echo* wrote, 'It must have been an exciting Everton side which embarked on that all-conquering tour of South America back in 1909. So exciting in fact, that those early 20th-century Toffees inspired a whole new team named in their honour. That club, from the picturesque coast of Viña del Mar in Chile, made their first ever visit to the land of their forebears for a long-planned friendly. They were comfortably beaten by another Everton side with the potential to excite a generation and maybe even make history.

'Whether David Moyes's peaking team are able to inspire a namesake somewhere else across the globe is a tall order, but they certainly seem able to achieve something special when the Premier League kicks off in a few weeks' time.

'Because as the inaugural Brotherhood Cup was lifted aloft by Phil Neville and Mikel Arteta on the pitch after last night's game, Evertonians of a Merseyside persuasion were dreaming of more meaningful silverware finally arriving at Goodison next season.'

Although for David Moyes's side it was just a pre-season fitness exercise, there must have been relief that the original Everton triumphed 2-0 thanks to goals from new signing Jermaine Beckford with 'an emphatic header his reward for a non-stop performance' and Diniyar Bilyaletdinov via 'a sweetly struck volley'.

While O'Keeffe concurred it was 'a game which, in every sense, Everton couldn't lose', he also saluted the 171 Chilean fans – 'more than Fulham brought to Goodison last season' – who had crossed the Andes, Amazon and Atlantic to be there.

* * *

3 May 1989: Everton 0 Liverpool 0 (Merseyside unites for Liverpool's first competitive post-Hillsborough fixture)

After the greatest ever loss of life at a European football ground, it seemed fitting that Liverpool made their return to competitive action against Everton.

On 15 April 1989, 94 fans died in a human crush at the FA Cup semi-final between Liverpool and Nottingham Forest in the Leppings Lane End of Sheffield Wednesday's Hillsborough stadium. This figure had increased to 95 by the time the Reds took to the Goodison Park turf and for many years was 96 before going up to 97 when Andrew Devine died in 2021.

Ever since Everton departed Anfield for Goodison in 1892 and John Houlding formed his new club, the neighbours either side of Stanley Park have been fiercely competitive. The respective quests for glory helped spur each other on to greatness but for all the two clubs' differences, which have become increasingly marked over recent decades, this passionate partisanship remains a sibling rivalry.

There are no clear geographical or – despite what some might say – religious divides when it comes to the city's footballing allegiances with many families and indeed individual households split along those lines within the region.

Everton chairman Bill Kenwright's choice of the Hollies' song 'He Ain't Heavy, He's My Brother' was poignant and inspired ahead of the Blues' home fixture with Newcastle United on 17 September 2012, five days after the Hillsborough Independent Panel concluded that fans were not responsible for the disaster.

A child in an Everton shirt with the number 9 stood holding hands with a child in a Liverpool shirt with the number 6 in the centre circle while warm applause rang out as the names of the victims were displayed on Goodison's big screens (the memorial plaque outside the Park End has since been amended to display 9 and 7 on their jerseys).

Just as they had done since 1989, the Blues stood united with their Scouse brethren, a fact that younger followers of both clubs who weren't around back then would do well to remember.

Some of the first scarves and floral tributes that would come to fill Anfield's Kop in the days after the tragedy came from

Evertonians and with their own team also playing in the other FA Cup semi-final that day – defeating Norwich City 1-0 at Villa Park in another 3pm kick-off, unaware of the horrors unfolding 90 miles away in South Yorkshire – there was also a sense of 'There but for the grace of God go I'.

Everton had played two more fixtures before Liverpool returned to action, both in London, losing 2-1 to Tottenham Hotspur in the First Division and 4-3 after extra time to Nottingham Forest in the Full Members' Cup Final at Wembley.

For their part, the grieving Reds had defeated manager Kenny Dalglish's former club Celtic 4-0 in a fundraising friendly watched by 60,437 in Glasgow the previous Sunday.

Ahead of the derby, a line of linked Everton and Liverpool scarves tied together surrounded the pitch and Ken Rogers of the *Liverpool Echo* vividly depicted the events before kick-off.

He wrote, 'A giant banner from the Stanley Park stand carried a simple but moving message from Kenny Dalglish's army, "The Kop Thanks You All. We Never Walked Alone".

'And then chairmen John Smith and Philip Carter, followed by managers Dalglish and Colin Harvey, led their teams out on to the pitch. Goodison erupted. Within seconds, a hush fell across the stadium when Everton announced, "Your loss is ours too. We will observe a minute's silence."'

Of the match itself, Rogers continued, 'Liverpool and Everton paid their respects with pride, passion and total commitment. It was the ultimate tribute to the 95 fans who died so tragically at Hillsborough.

'The 140th league derby finished goalless, but it was a riveting, fiercely competitive affair that confirmed what we have known for years … that Merseyside is the undisputed soccer capital of Great Britain – always has been, always will be. Liverpool failed to claim the maximum points that would have sent a championship shockwave reverberating all the way from Goodison Park to Highbury.

'But in the light of everything that has happened in the last two and a half weeks, their performance was little short of magnificent.

'In the final reckoning, they ran out of steam – mentally and physically exhausted by the events of the last 17 days.

'Everton were never going to make life easy for their neighbours. Football doesn't work like that in this city, no matter what the circumstances.'

He added, 'It was still end-to-end stuff. Both goalkeepers [Neville Southall and Bruce Grobbelaar] were in dominant mood and a draw was not only honourable, but a fair reflection on proceedings.'

The two sides would meet again at Wembley on 20 May in an emotionally charged FA Cup Final – the last to date between them – with Everton losing 3-2 after extra time.

* * *

1 February 2025: Everton 4 Leicester City 0 (The fastest goal in Everton history comes in their final year at Goodison Park)

The fastest recorded goal from an Everton player in the club's 147-year history came in their final year at Goodison Park, just eight league games from the end before they departed.

It also came on the first day of the month that the historic first game at the new stadium took place as the Blues' under-18s played a friendly against their Wigan Athletic counterparts in an inaugural test event for 10,000 spectators at the 52,888-capacity venue.

Given what loyal but long-suffering Evertonians had been through during a tumultuous few years before the move, the lightning-fast strike felt like another piece of long-overdue good news to signal an upturn in fortunes ahead of a bright new dawn.

Before the global coronavirus pandemic, Everton had Europe's most decorated coach, Carlo Ancelotti, at the helm but in the summer of 2021, just weeks before the herculean construction task of transforming Bramley-Moore Dock into the 21st-century arena to replace Goodison Park began, the Italian was lured back to Real Madrid after a season played mostly behind closed doors.

Fans duly returned to matches en masse, but the Blues had former Kop idol Rafael Benítez at the helm.

The Spaniard only lasted for half a season, and under Frank Lampard Everton finished by staying up with a 3-2 comeback win over Crystal Palace in their final home game despite posting the joint-lowest equivalent points total in their history.

That figure dropped even lower in 2022/23 with the Chelsea legend also dismissed in the January as the Blues sat joint bottom of the table, and under replacement Sean Dyche they avoided a first relegation in 72 years by a single goal on the last day, scored by Abdoulaye Doucoure.

In 2023/24 there was an unprecedented brace of sporting sanctions for historic Profit and Sustainability Rules breaches, which saw Everton deducted a total of eight points, set against the backdrop of Farhad Moshiri attempting to sell to 777 Partners, whose global portfolio of football clubs subsequently collapsed.

Therefore, beleaguered Blues just wanted to be able to enjoy their final season at Goodison Park without any further dramas.

The campaign started with four straight defeats, though, including back-to-back 3-2 losses in which Everton surrendered 2-0 leads and despite the takeover by the Friedkin Group being completed in the week before Christmas, by the halfway point the team had accrued just 17 points – less than 50 per cent of their lowest-ever equivalent total of 36 in 2022/23 – with Dyche appearing to have ran out of ideas and being dismissed after showdown talks with the new owners in the wake of a 1-0 loss at Bournemouth in which his side failed to register a shot on target.

Almost a dozen years after he left and just shy of 23 since he was first appointed, cue a sensational return to the dugout for David

Moyes, who had gone from being the Premier League's youngest manager at 38 when plucked from Preston in 2002 to the division's elder statesman at 61.

Despite losing 1-0 at home to Aston Villa in his first game back, the 4-0 demolition of Leicester City completed a hat-trick of consecutive wins for the Scot with a side that previously hadn't produced back-to-back successes all season.

Dyche so often struggled to harness the power of Goodison, but Moyes gave supporters 'their' Everton back.

A team that had looked so toothless just weeks before, was now making goalscoring history.

James Garner's kick-off was hit straight back to goalkeeper Jordan Pickford who, after taking a touch, punted the ball back upfield. As it bounced, Doucoure – who had struck 11 times in the first year under Dyche but hadn't found the net in the Premier League all season – controlled the ball on his chest before smashing a controlled right-footed finish beyond Mads Hermansen with officially just 10.18 seconds on the clock.

The Mali international's historic effort knocked Howard Kendall off top spot after he had struck the opener in a 5-2 home win over Chelsea after 14 seconds in the 1969/70 title-winning season.

A brace from Beto, with a first-time finish from James Tarkowski's curled ball upfield on six minutes, and then confidently rolling in from Garner's 'eye-of-a-needle' through ball two minutes into first-half stoppage time, put the hosts in command before Iliman Ndiaye completed the rout on the 90-minute mark, coolly capitalising on hesitancy in the Foxes' defence.

Joe Thomas remarked in the *Liverpool Echo*, 'The most obvious change since Moyes replaced Sean Dyche has been the intent shown by Everton.

'A fortnight ago, the first win of the second Moyes reign was secured in first-half stoppage time when, rather than protect a two-goal lead into the break, Everton pushed for a third and scored it. The goal was the difference when Spurs fought back late on.

'The same approach was repeated with the same impact against Leicester, Beto's second sealing this win before Goodison could take stock of a win of enormous magnitude.'

4

1966 World Cup and other major non-Everton games

THIS BOOK is about Everton's long-time home so is therefore mostly about the Blues, but some significant matches have taken place over the years at the ground that did not feature them.

Some are mentioned in later chapters, but this section focuses on the 1966 World Cup, when Goodison Park became the only English club ground to host a World Cup semi-final, plus an FA Cup Final (hosting in 1894 and the replay in 1910) and a landmark fixture for women's football.

***

12 July 1966: Brazil 2 Bulgaria 0 (Goodison sways to a Samba rhythm)

As winners of the previous two tournaments, there was great excitement on Merseyside at the prospect of welcoming Pelé and friends as Brazil were based at Goodison Park for all their Group 3 matches at the 1966 finals, but ultimately the Samba carnival on the pitch failed to hit the right notes for the defending champions.

Claudia Street, in the shadow of Goodison, just off Walton Lane, was lovingly decorated by residents with colourful flags and flowers, while the *Liverpool Echo* interviewed a Wirral missionary who had returned home after living in the Brazilian interior state of Mato Grosso, a region comprising Amazon rainforest, tropical wetlands and savannah.

Robert Watson, of Heswall, who had spent five years in South America before coming back for the sake of his wife's health, said, 'The Mato Grosso is a large tract of unexplored and underdeveloped country. But this is one of the rapidly growing areas of Brazil and the people there are just football-mad like the rest.'

Recalling the previous World Cup in 1962, which Brazil won in Chile, he added, 'The moment a goal was scored they [the locals] rushed out of their homes and set off giant firecrackers.'

Meanwhile, with Spellow Lane Church preparing to offer refreshments to Brazilian fans, their former vicar the Rev Mervyn Bufton, who had moved to São Paulo, had written to them to warn over what drinks should and should not be provided to the South American guests.

He implored, 'Don't offer them coffee because you can't possibly make it the way they like it! Merely to try would, in their eyes, be like insulting their coffee. Offer them weak tea instead. They love it.'

On the pitch, Brazil's World Cup campaign at Goodison ultimately flattered to deceive as they were knocked out in the group stage but there had been no early signs of their malaise in their opening game as they defeated Bulgaria 2-0 with goals from Pelé and Garrincha.

In the *Liverpool Echo*, Michael Charters reported, 'Brazil moved smoothly through the opening defence of their world title at Goodison Park last night and showed in their 2-0 victory over Bulgaria that it will take a highly talented team indeed to prevent them from going on to a hat-trick of World Cup successes.

'Brazil showed the sort of football which makes all the effort of staging the World Cup here worthwhile and must make spectators feel they have seen something for their money – and big money at that.'

Bulgarian centre-forward Georgi Asparuhov caught the eye, with Charters observing that 'he can get up for a ball like Tommy Lawton' but adding that he was 'poorly supported, and could not do it all himself'. Both of Brazil's goals came from free kicks with Pelé having the honour of being Goodison's first World Cup scorer some 15 minutes into the contest before Garrincha sealed the holders' victory on 63 minutes.

Charters wrote, 'Brought down by [Dobromir] Zhechev, just outside the penalty area, Pelé swerved a low ball past the defensive wall and goalkeeper [Georgi] Naydenov, who played very well, looked unsighted as he went down for the ball, which hit him on the arm and was deflected high into the net.

'The other free kick goal was right out of the top drawer. Again, the man who had been fouled took the kick and scored. This time it was Garrincha, who hit an incredible shot from 20 yards past the Bulgars' line-up and Naydenov was airborne when the ball was in the top corner.'

On the goalscorers, he noted, 'Pelé's artistry was there for all to see. For long periods he was out of the game, but he moves like lightning when the crucial moment arrives. His chipped passes with either foot, his deft and deadly passing through a wall of defenders opened the way for Alcindo and others.

'Garrincha, the Little Bird of great fame, quickly delighted the crowd with his intricate dribbling, not all of which succeeded but still showed the sort of high individual skill which makes spectating a pleasure.'

Indeed, while suitably impressed by the holders, Charters was taken aback by the cultural differences with his South American counterparts in the Goodison Park press box, adding, 'If this is World Cup football, let's sit back and enjoy it. The staging of the game on the superb Goodison pitch was excellent although it was rather strange to be surrounded by Brazilian press men who cheered every move of their own side!'

* * *

15 July 1966: Hungary 3 Brazil 1 (World champions are stunned)

Brazil's World Cup debut at Goodison Park had finished with Michael Charters of the *Liverpool Echo* proclaiming that they could secure a hat-trick of titles after their 1958 and 1962 successes, but the South Americans were brought back down to earth by Hungary in their second group game.

After a 2-0 win over Bulgaria in their opener, Charters wrote, 'These Brazilians not only play the game for keeps, they can also entertain with their great technique and artistry. They can lift the game when they want to, and this attribute could make them once again the outstanding side of the tournament.'

It wasn't just Brazil's players who were receiving plaudits though and the *Echo* revealed that a report in Sweden had praised the population of Liverpool for the way they had embraced the tournament.

Stockholm-based publication *Dagens Nyheter* was quoted as saying, 'This is the football city of England, not stiff and serious London where you can hardly tell that there is a World Cup competition going on.

'The people here are really the supporters and friends of football. They have decorated the streets near the stadium and windows and doors bear paper garlands and flowers. They have put up notices on walls welcoming friends of football from all over the world.'

But while nobody was left in any doubt about Scousers' hospitality credentials, the Brazilian blossom quickly wilted after the bouquets they had received from their first fixture.

Of their loss to the Magyars, Charters said, 'Another great game at Goodison Park last night – in fact one of the finest ever seen on this famous ground.

'Hungary turned the north-west group inside out with their 3-1 victory over the favourites and holders, Brazil, and their magnificent display gave the soaked crowd something to talk about for years.

'Hungary turned on a type of attack, urged on by the locals in the crowd who swept them to victory with their support, which had the Brazil defence fully exposed as suspect against such flowing, thrilling play.'

Pelé was ruled out of the game with a knee injury and without their star man, Brazil 'never found their rhythm' and struggled with the conditions, as Charters observed, 'The wet turf seemed to disturb them and upset the flow of their passing.'

The Hungarians took the lead just two minutes into the contest with what Charters described as 'a brilliant individual goal' by Ferenc Bene as the forward 'beat three men, sent Gilmar the wrong way in the Brazil goal, and then turned the ball into the other corner'.

Indeed, when Brazil equalised a dozen minutes later through Tostão, Charters remarked that it was 'fortunate', 'Lima took the free kick from 25 yards, the ball struck a Hungarian defender and was deflected to Tostão who cracked it high into the net.'

However, as the rain started to get heavier, the European side began to take control and they went close several times with Brazil 'defending desperately' before finally restoring their lead on 64 minutes as János Farkas 'smashed the ball home from a low centre by Bene'.

The Hungarians sealed their famous victory with a penalty on 73 minutes after Bene was fouled by Altair. Charters wrote, 'Kálmán Mészöly made no mistake from the spot, although two of his colleagues in front of the main stand turned their heads away in anguish while he was taking the kick.'

While Brazil are often one of the neutrals' favourites at all World Cups and had earned plenty of cheers from the Merseyside public in their previous fixture, Hungary's biggest star, Flórián Albert, a one-club man with Ferencváros who would be voted

European Footballer of the Year in 1967, hailed the tremendous encouragement his side – who were based in Birkdale for the competition – received from the Goodison crowd.

He said, 'I was very pleased, and sometimes felt that we were playing at home. I want to thank, on the behalf of the Hungarian team, the crowd for the wonderful support they gave us today.'

Another 3-1 victory over Bulgaria at Old Trafford five days later would see the Magyars progressing to the knockout stages before a 2-1 quarter-final defeat to the Soviet Union at Roker Park, but for Brazil, the defence of their crown was about to come to a premature end at Goodison.

* * *

19 July 1966: Portugal 3 Brazil 1 (Painful exit for Pelé and company)

Needing to beat Portugal 3-0 to progress to the knockout stages of the competition, Brazil's eight-year grip on the World Cup was already dangling by a thread as they went into their final group game at Goodison Park, but in the end their opponents added injury to insult through a series of vicious challenges that resulted in Pelé hobbling off the field.

In a desperate attempt to try and secure the emphatic result needed to progress, Brazil made nine changes to their starting line-up, including bringing back Pelé who had missed the 3-1 defeat to Hungary last time out, but it was to no avail as they were not just beaten but beaten up.

Michael Charters of the *Liverpool Echo* was unimpressed by the cynical tactics of the victors who had gone into this fixture with a brace of wins at Old Trafford against Hungary (3-1) and Bulgaria (3-0).

He said, 'When Pelé was carried off after half an hour with a crippling knee injury, any chance Brazil had of staying in the World Cup went with him. Pelé was chopped mercilessly out of the game. Within ten minutes he had been scythed down twice with double tackles and was marked so closely by his shadows that Brazil stuttered and came to a full stop.'

The irony was that Portugal, who had a Brazilian coach in Otto Glória, didn't have to play dirty as they were dominating proceedings through their football anyway, going 2-0 up in less than half an hour to extinguish any fading hopes for the holders.

Charters wrote, 'With Pelé they might have had a chance of pulling it back but when he went off for attention shortly after the second goal and thereafter was only a passenger, Brazil slipped rather ingloriously off their perch as world champions.

'Brazil showed against Hungary that without Pelé they were only half the team they can be. Portugal learned that lesson and went out of their way to make sure. But give credit in every other way to a superb Portuguese display.

'They were the better team from the start and far from settling on defence, their attacking ideas always carried more directness and fire than Brazil, who looked a team in need of considerable rebuilding.'

The deadlock was broken 15 minutes into the contest with a move that Charters suggested represented a changing of the guard among the global game's dominant powers.

He said, 'Eusébio, who on this performance must take over Pelé's crown as the number one player in the world, made Portugal's first goal as he slipped cleverly down the left before crossing the ball to the goalmouth where Manga tamely punched it out to the head of António Simões who nodded it straight back past him.'

When Portugal added a second a dozen minutes later, Charters felt the match was over as a contest, especially due to Pelé's lack of mobility after being hacked out of proceedings, '[Mário] Coluna floated over a free kick which the tall [José]

Torres headed back past the indecisive Manga and there was Eusébio to head it in.

'The game lost a good deal of its entertainment value with Portugal cruising comfortably along and although Brazil had the crowd cheering them on at times, they could not raise their game with Pelé, who could not use his right leg at all, limping, almost hopping on one leg, down the left wing.'

Brazil finally reduced arrears on 73 minutes as 'Rildo came up from deep in defence to hit a good shot from 20 yards past José Pereira in the Portugal goal.'

Charters observed, 'There was a fleeting sight of a comeback but Portugal were too strong, too confident, too good to permit Brazil to offer more than a token rally,' and they sealed victory with a third goal some five minutes before the end when following a corner, the ball came out to Eusébio 'who smashed it back into the net like lightning, the perfect example of a master player taking advantage of half a chance'.

There was more of that to come from the Benfica star in Goodison's next World Cup game but Pelé – who would ultimately bow out from the World Cup in a blaze of glory at Mexico City's Azteca Stadium four years later – departed Merseyside threatening to quit international football, angrily proclaiming, 'I don't want to finish my life as an invalid.'

* * *

23 July 1966: Portugal 5 North Korea 3 (Eusébio inspires great comeback)

While Pelé could be forgiven for having painful memories of his time at Goodison Park at the 1966 World Cup, fellow legend Eusébio loved his time playing at Everton's home.

The Portuguese centre-forward finished as the tournament's top scorer with nine goals, six of which came at Goodison, and on returning to the ground in November 2009 when his old club defeated the Blues 2-0 in a Europa League group game, he said, 'Sorry, I don't speak good English. But today for me, for my family, it's a good day, for Benfica to play here. This stadium for me is the best stadium in my playing life.'

Mozambique-born Eusébio could lay claim to being the first footballer from sub-Saharan Africa to excel on the global stage, after the continent had produced a previous World Cup Golden Boot winner in the shape of Just Fontaine – born in Morocco to a French father and Spanish mother – whose 13 goals for France in the 1958 finals remains a tournament record.

Eusébio struck three times in the group stage, opening his account in a 3-0 win over Bulgaria at Old Trafford before bagging a brace at Goodison in the 3-1 victory that knocked out Brazil.

It was his incredible four-goal display in Portugal's 5-3 quarter-final comeback success against North Korea that he'll best be remembered for though, as Goodison witnessed one of its most remarkable encounters.

Back in 1966, the North Koreans were even more of an unknown quantity than they are today with their continued political isolation, but they had already shocked the world with their exploits at Middlesbrough's Ayresome Park in the group stage.

Recovering from a 3-0 defeat to the Soviet Union, an 88th-minute equaliser from Pak Seung-zin earned them a 1-1 draw with Chile before their momentous 1-0 victory over the already two-time World Cup winners Italy courtesy of Pak Doo-ik's 42nd-minute strike had propelled them into the knockout section. English football spectators in general and Scousers in particular love an underdog and in reporting on the quarter-final against Portugal at Goodison, Michael Charters of the *Liverpool Echo* wrote, 'The crowd quickly indicated they were on the side of the men from Korea.'

Seemingly buoyed by the encouragement of the Goodison roar, North Korea, who were 'delighting the fans with the cleverness of their passing', raced into a 3-0 lead after 25 minutes.

Just a minute into the contest, Pak Seung-zin fired them ahead 'with a great shot from 18 yards into the top corner of the net' before two goals in the space of three minutes from Li Dong-woon, who turned the ball over the line from close range, and Yang Song-guk, who 'cracked' into the net, put them temporarily in command.

However, the side from Pyongyang peaked too early and Charters's report explained how they struggled to match the physicality of their opponents, stating, 'The Koreans had plenty of quality football but at rather a slow pace and there was no comparison with the power the Portuguese could develop when they attacked.'

Despite the sluggish start, Eusébio then set about almost single-handedly pulling the Koreans apart.

He'd grabbed two goals – the first after getting on to a through-ball 'like a flash' and the second a penalty – by the interval, and the increasingly inevitable equaliser came with his hat-trick strike 11 minutes into the second half, when he got on to the ball 'like lightning' before he 'smashed' it into the net from an angle.

Charters added, 'Eusébio's finishing was really fantastic, and the Koreans could make nothing of this master footballer whenever he got within sight of the goal.'

A second penalty on 59 minutes saw Eusébio grab his fourth of the afternoon for Portugal to finally take the lead while their passage to the last four was secured through José Augusto ten minutes from the end with a close-range header.

After the final whistle, the Goodison crowd saluted both sides who had produced an enthralling contest.

The Koreans were given 'a wonderful reception having done far better than anyone could have expected' while the Portuguese players, who surrounded Eusébio and 'not only hugged him but kissed him', stood in the centre of the pitch and waved.

Eusébio was handed the match ball by the referee following 'as great a one-man performance as has been seen on this ground for many years.'

* * *

25 July 1966: West Germany 2 Soviet Union 1 (Fury after semi-final switch)

In terms of what was at stake, the 1966 World Cup semi-final between West Germany and the Soviet Union was the biggest game ever staged at Goodison Park, but many angry supporters stayed away, leaving Everton's home with its lowest crowd of the tournament.

Goodison was supposed to be the venue for hosts England's semi-final against Portugal, but the ties were the subject of a late switch, prompting understandable fan fury.

The normally reserved *Liverpool Daily Post* blasted that Merseysiders were calling the FIFA decision to play that tie at Wembley as 'the greatest betrayal in sporting history'.

So, what happened?

The *Liverpool Echo* reported that when the draw for the finals was originally made, it was indicated that the winners of quarter-final one, which turned out to be England, would face the winners of quarter-final three, ultimately Portugal, at Goodison Park.

All four quarter-finals were played on Saturday, 23 July and with what now seems incredibly short notice – the Goodison semi-final was played just two days later on the Monday night – the decision to change the games around and deny Scouse fans the chance to cheer on Alf Ramsey's side in the flesh was taken a mere 48 hours beforehand.

In Monday's edition, the *Liverpool Echo* warned that demonstrations were likely with Merseyside fans 'incensed' at what they claimed was a snub to the city of Liverpool with many having bought tickets to see England at Goodison, only for a 'draw' for the semi-finals to be made after the weekend's results were known.

Michael Charters, who had been covering all of Goodison's World Cup games for the *Echo*, stuck the boot into FIFA, insisting that the decision by their organising committee was 'contrary to everything that has been understood at Everton since the first planning for the World Cup was made' and that he was 'told last week, on the best possible authority, that whatever else happened, England would be at Goodison Park for the semi-final if they beat Argentina'.

Charters blasted that the actions of FIFA – whose president at the time was Englishman Sir Stanley Rous – left them open to three major criticisms, 'That the tournament was a "money-making racket" with a principal aim of getting as much cash as possible from a capacity gate at Wembley; that they were being unfair to other countries by allowing England to treat Wembley as their home pitch and play every game on it; and they were failing to keep faith with the fans in the north-west, particularly Everton, who had planned and prepared for seeing England at Goodison.'

Everton chairman Edward Holland Hughes was more diplomatic, stating, 'At Goodison Park we are naturally disappointed that we have been denied the privilege of receiving England in the semi-final.

'We had been led to believe, and indeed so had the public, that if England got this far the privilege was to be ours.'

Stay-away fans let their feet do their talking over the decision through their absence and just 38,273 were at Goodison for the semi-final, more than 20,000 fewer than the 58,479 who had watched Portugal beat Brazil in the group stage.

Those who did turn up let their anger be known through homemade banners containing slogans such as 'Down With FIFA'; 'England Fix Insults Liverpool' and 'England Snubs Liverpool'.

Despite the quality on the pitch as a Uwe Seeler-led West Germany side that would push England all the way in the final locked horns with Lev Yashin and his comrades, the mood of

Charters and the crowd did not seem to have been lifted by the action in the *Liverpool Echo* match report.

Helmut Haller fired the Germans ahead on 42 minutes before Beckenbauer doubled their advantage midway through the second half. Valeriy Porkujan reduced the deficit for the Soviets two minutes from the end, but it was too little, too late.

Charters complained, 'I suppose it was too much to expect to see a fifth great World Cup game at Goodison Park. What we did endure – and the locals in the crowd made their feelings very clear – was rubbish between West Germany and Russia which ended with both teams being jeered off the pitch.'

He added, 'The sum total of proceedings were two fine goals from the Germans, some brilliant goalkeeping by Yashin, too many fouls, and too little good football. At times the game dropped to Fourth Division standard, and perhaps that is too harsh on our Fourth Division.

'The crowd gave the game its rightful verdict by setting up chants of "England" followed by "Liverpool" and "Everton" with the crowning touch being the heartfelt singing of "Go home, you bums".'

* * *

31 March 1894: Notts County 4 Bolton Wanderers 1 (First FA Cup Final at a Football League ground)

Goodison Park has played host to two FA Cup finals – the second being a replay – but when it was chosen for the 1894 showpiece game, it was the first time the fixture had taken place at any club ground.

The decision reflected the fact that Everton's home, which had opened less than two years previously, was the first purpose-built football ground in England.

Up until that point, the Oval in Kennington, south London, home of Surrey County Cricket Club, had been the regular venue, hosting all but one of the finals up until 1892.

The sole deviation had been the use of the Lillie Bridge Grounds in Fulham for the 1873 final while the 1886 final replay took place at the Racecourse Ground in Derby, home of Derbyshire County Cricket Club.

In their first FA Cup Final in 1893, Everton themselves lost 1-0 to Wolverhampton Wanderers at the Fallowfield athletics stadium in Manchester, but then they had the honour of staging the game the following year as Notts County defeated Bolton Wanderers 4-1 in front of a 37,000 crowd.

The heavy defeat for Bolton, who had been Everton's first opponents at Goodison in 1892, must have been particularly humbling as Notts County were a Second Division club and became the first FA Cup winners from outside the top flight after the Football League had been founded.

Notts had finished third in tier two that term, behind unbeaten Football League new boys Liverpool who had romped to the title undefeated, and Small Heath, who were later renamed Birmingham City.

This earned them a place in one of the three end-of-season 'Test matches' a month after the cup final – an early precursor of the play-off system – only to be thrashed 4-0 at Sheffield Wednesday's Olive Grove ground by Preston North End, who had been champions in the first two Football League seasons but had finished 14th in 1893/94.

When it came to the final itself, the *Liverpool Mercury* reported that the locals at Goodison Park seemed somewhat apathetic towards the big fixture compared to the respective supporters of the two clubs involved, stating, 'The fact that the Everton ground was the scene of the final stage of the English cup competition caused unusual stir, but this was manifested more by the invasion of the town by excursionists from the Midlands, east Lancashire and other places, rather than the enthusiasm of the Liverpool people generally.

'A match of an ordinary kind, between Everton and Sunderland for instance, would have raised more enthusiasm among the latter.'

Indeed, the visit of Sunderland had produced Everton's largest gate that season, 30,000, but the *Mercury* continued with the downbeat tone as its correspondent's observations seemed at odds with the official crowd for the final being recorded at 37,000 which was Goodison's largest at this point until it was eclipsed for the first Merseyside derby in the league the following October.

The report continued, 'Increased stands were provided, barricades were erected, and a large posse of police was in attendance to keep order and help the management to make the gathering a success.

'The gates were thrown open about noon, but the populace arrived so slowly that it soon became evident that the company would not be of mammoth proportions, even if it exceeded that which one is accustomed to at Goodison Park.

'The popular side alone had become well tenanted, but even there, gaps were visible. The end stands were not half filled, nor were some portions of the reserved stand, and when all totalled up, they would not exceed much beyond 20,000 – a disappointing attendance.'

Notts County strolled to victory with Arthur Watson putting them ahead on 18 minutes before a Jimmy Logan hat-trick (29, 67, 70) made fellow Scot Jim Cassidy's 87th-minute goal for Bolton a mere consolation.

Of the action, the *Mercury* reported, 'Now and again the partisans would raise a cheer for their team, which was responded by the shouts of the followers of the opposition clan, and the time passed harmoniously.

'These two last successes [Logan's pair of second half goals came in the space of three minutes] had given Notts so big a lead that nearly all interest disappeared from the struggle.'

Although Logan was the hero of the day, he would tragically pass away two years later in bizarre circumstances related to wet weather in Manchester.

His side Loughborough turned up for a fixture at Newton Heath only to discover they had lost their kit. Unable to borrow any shirts, they took to the field in their ordinary clothes, losing 2-0 with rain falling heavily throughout the 90 minutes.

Returning home without getting changed out of their sodden attire, Logan caught a cold, developed pneumonia and died aged just 25.

* * *

26 December 1920: Dick, Kerr Ladies 4 St Helens 0 (Record crowd for a women's game)

How fitting that Goodison Park, the ground which attracted a bumper crowd that remained a world record for a women's club game for over 98 years when some 53,000 fans crammed in to watch Dick, Kerr Ladies face St Helens, should be given a new lease of life after Everton's men's first team moved out by the club's women's team moving in.

Everton's women's team moved into their own purpose-built 2,000-capacity stadium at Walton Hall Park in 2020 and had also occasionally used Goodison Park for matches in recent years, but just five days before the final Premier League fixture the club's new owners the Friedkin Group made the bold move of handing over the ground – albeit with plans to reduce the capacity and bring in stadium upgrades to enhance facilities – to Everton Women from the 2025/26 season, with a previous 'Goodison Legacy Project' on the site now shelved.

Who would have thought it over a century earlier when fans flocked for this female football fiesta? The Boxing Day 1920 gate, with an estimated 10,000 to 14,000 more locked outside, was finally eclipsed by the 60,739 who watched Atlético Madrid's women lose 2-0 at home to their Barcelona counterparts at the Metropolitano stadium on 18 March 2019, but what was also remarkable about the attendance – in a season in which Everton's average was 37,215 – was that it was the biggest on Merseyside over that year's festive period.

Just 35,000 watched the third-placed Blues lose 4-2 at home to Arsenal in their Christmas Day First Division fixture, while it also topped the 50,000 gate at Anfield for Liverpool's 2-1 win over Chelsea in the same competition on 27 December.

Dick, Kerr Ladies were like the Harlem Globetrotters of the women's game.

Originally formed as a factory team from the Preston branch of the Dick, Kerr and Company locomotive and tramcar manufacturer, they were the first women's team to play an organised match wearing shorts, and between 1917 and 1965 they turned out in 833 games, winning 759, drawing 46 and losing just 28.

In the same year that they came to Goodison Park, they defeated a French side from Paris in front of a 25,000 crowd in what was considered the first international fixture in women's football.

Although females had initially been discouraged from playing the game, women's football enjoyed a sudden boom period during the first world war.

With many young men away in the killing fields of Europe, it was believed that such organised sporting activity would be good for morale in wartime factories and would aid production, so competitive fixtures were encouraged.

The *Liverpool Echo* reported the Boxing Day game in 'Bee's Sports Notes' under the headline 'Ladies' skill with ball', and although there was a distinct chauvinistic tone by today's standards, it was ultimately a positive article, highlighting the charity fundraising nature of the match.

'Bee' wrote, 'Yesterday Mr Frankland of Dick, Kerr's and Mr Gordon of St Helens ladies' football sides, having asked me to accept their thanks for, they said, "being mainly responsible for the excellent attendance at the ladies' game", to thank also the Everton club's officers and staff – and all the ladies.

'They agreed and asked me to say to you all, "A big, big thanks for breaking the record."

'It appears that Dick, Kerr's best previously was £1,050 in France. Now they can claim to have helped produce in one game a sum of £3,100.

'The ladies at Goodison Park gave us all much pleasure. We appreciated their skill, their stamina, their determination and their manner of taking hard knocks without "turning a hair". Sometimes the cap didn't fit, and there was a hair turned, still one must say that they all played well and hard throughout.

'One lady on the right wing of St Helens loved to dribble, she lived for it. But she did not succeed in the manner that little Jennie Harris did – what a splendid little player.

'And what full-backs Dick, Kerr's have: they study their kicks and are the backbone of the side. What I am puzzled to know is will kind Ella Retford kiss the rival captains if she kicks off in a gents' match? If so, I'll fix one up!

'Another puzzle is this. How could referee Peers send anyone off the field for ungentlemanly conduct when all were ladies?

'Of course, it is the privilege of the ladies to be late (cough and say in 99 out of a hundred engagements!) and therefore none of the spectators grumbled.

'The ladies played to the whistle with a promptitude that did them proud. May gentlemen copy their example.'

Unfortunately, the first golden period of women's football proved to be short-lived. Despite the game at Goodison Park raising approximately £150,000 in today's money for charity, there would be no chance of a repeat the following festive period as less than a year after the record-breaking match, on 5 December 1921 the FA banned women's football from taking place at its member grounds.

Although the FA claimed that the reason for the ban was to 'protect' women, who they saw as not physically able to play football, it was widely purported that they felt the popularity of the team threatened the men's game.

The ban would remain in place for 50 years until finally being lifted in 1971, some six years after Dick, Kerr Ladies (who had become Preston Ladies back in 1926) folded.

Women's football in England wouldn't become absorbed into FA administration and funding until 1993.

* * *

28 April 1910: Newcastle United 2 Barnsley 0 (Pitch invasion ahead of FA Cup Final replay)

Goodison Park was packed to the rafters when it staged the 1910 FA Cup Final replay between Newcastle United and Barnsley, but club officials and the local police had to deal with the drama of a large pre-match pitch invasion which had threatened to put the game in jeopardy.

Newcastle triumphed 2-0 but the *Manchester Guardian* had complained that the choice of venue was unfair to Barnsley given that the local supporters would hardly be neutral after the Tykes had knocked out Everton in the semi-finals, also after a replay.

Unlike 16 years earlier when reports had mentioned the gaps in the stands for Goodison's first FA Cup Final, a crowd of 69,000 is recorded as cramming into the ground for the 1910 replay, which seems like a monster attendance given that Everton's record at the time was 52,455 for an FA Cup third round tie with Bolton Wanderers in 1907.

The *London Daily News* stated, 'Rain had fallen in Liverpool throughout the morning, and it was still pelting down when the crowd began to collect around the enclosure at one o'clock.

'Excursionists had packed into the city from all parts of the country, including trainloads from London, and a full hour before the time for the kick-off the ground was so densely packed that thousands of people broke the bounds of the cordon of police and stewards and swarmed over the playing pitch.

'The disorder had become so alarming before three o'clock that it appeared impossible for the game to be played, but a dozen mounted police were hastily summoned and they rendered such invaluable service that in half an hour the thousands of people who had scaled the low palings had been forced back into the enclosures.'

The *Liverpool Courier and Commercial Advertiser* proclaimed that despite the issues with the assembled hordes, the city had proven to be a worthy host.

It pointed out that the crowd was a record for any game outside of London or Glasgow and reported, 'At Goodison Park every person who entered the gates could follow the progress of play without much difficulty. The remarkable figures suggest the enormous holding capacity of the magnificent enclosure of the Everton club.'

Regarding the pre-match pitch invasion, it noted, 'Matters looked ugly, and there were visions of interference with the game.

'The timely appearance of a detachment of mounted police worked wonders. Assisted by their comrades on foot and by officials of the club, the too-impulsive spectators were quietly, but none the less firmly compelled to retire behind the barriers, so much so that when the players appeared on the field there was not the slightest sign of encroachment on the part of the crowd.'

The original game at Crystal Palace had ended in a 1-1 draw on St George's Day with underdogs Barnsley – who finished ninth in the Second Division that season – taking the lead through Harry Tufnell on 37 minutes.

However, Newcastle, the reigning league champions, who would finish fourth in the First Division in 1910, earned the

Goodison replay through a Jock Rutherford equaliser seven minutes from the end.

Despite winning three league titles in the previous decade, up until this point the Magpies had always been the bridesmaids in the FA Cup, having lost a hat-trick of finals (2-0 to Aston Villa in 1905, 1-0 to Everton in 1906 for the Blues' first triumph in the competition, and 3-1 to Wolverhampton Wanderers in 1908).

Their class finally told on Merseyside though as they secured a 2-0 success courtesy of a second half brace from Albert Shepherd (52, 62 penalty).

The *Liverpool Courier and Commercial Advertiser* reported, 'At last Newcastle United have attained the height of their ambition. Their victory was absolutely merited on the play.

'Newcastle United were an infinitely cleverer side, and though Barnsley battled bravely right to the last minute of play, they had to retire beaten, though by no means discredited.'

Yorkshiremen are typically known for plain-speaking but for its part, the *Barnsley Chronicle* said of the game at Goodison, 'Just as Byron awoke one day to find himself famous, so Barnsley has suddenly secured renown by the prowess of its exploits on the football field.

'The struggle in connection with the cup final will go down in local history as an epoch in the annals of Yorkshire sport.

'Rarely has local feeling been so stirred as it was over this Homeric encounter for the honour of winning the blue ribbon of the football world.'

It makes you wonder what the paper would have said if Barnsley had actually won the FA Cup. Thankfully for the locals, they only had to wait two more years to find out.

Hollow victories

NOT ALL memorable wins produce happy outcomes, and that has sometimes been the case for Everton over the years as certain Goodison Park victories failed to get them to where they wanted to be.

* * *

12 March 2008: Everton 2 Fiorentina 0 AET, 2-4 pens (Stirring display to cancel out first-leg deficit but penalty heartache for the Blues in competition they could have won)
This was Goodison's greatest European night since Bayern Munich and arguably Everton's best chance to win major silverware under David Moyes, but a failure to capitalise on their dominance and net a crucial third goal left the Blues paying the penalty.

Everton were left to rue their missed chances in the one-sided contest, after a 2-0 defeat in a sorry display in the first leg in Tuscany had left them chasing.

Moyes lamented, 'We battered them, the players played really well, but they have not been rewarded for it and I have to admit that is hard to take. The fans were fantastic, and they really made for a great atmosphere.'

A 16th-minute close-range effort off Andrew Johnson's chest had set Everton on their way and it felt like the roof was about to come off the 'Grand Old Lady' when Mikel Arteta's laser-guided missile of a strike made its way into the bottom corner of the net in front of the Gwladys Street midway through the second half.

Goodison hadn't experienced anything like this since Everton reached the Cup Winners' Cup Final some 23 years earlier but there was to be no fairytale ending on this occasion.

Fiorentina's goal continued to lead a charmed life as a shot was cleared off the line while Yakubu – who would hit the post in the resultant shoot-out – was denied by a stunning double stop from the visitors' French keeper Sébastien Frey, who would also go on to save from Phil Jagielka from 12 yards after extra time had finished.

David Prentice of the *Liverpool Echo* wrote, 'The European adventure is over ... for now. But Everton have whetted their appetite for the kind of nights which had Goodison Park rocking to its very foundations last night.

'Everton were utterly magnificent. They dominated Italy's fourth best team for 120 minutes. They outplayed Fiorentina, they outpassed them, outfought them and outran them. Only goalkeeper Sébastien Frey stood between his team and a rout. But football, like life, can be unfair.'

Captain Phil Neville declared that he was 'proud' of his team-mates, insisting, 'We should have won the game by four or five goals,' but Everton's frustrations weren't just down to the fine margins on the night.

Given the talent in the team that Moyes had assembled over the previous six years, this edition of the UEFA Cup was a competition they could have and perhaps really should have, gone all the way in.

After coming through a tricky qualification round tie with Metalist Kharkiv – missing two penalties in a 1-1 draw at Goodison before coming from behind to triumph 3-2 in Ukraine – they grew into the competition and became a real force.

A short-lived format of five-team groups with two home games and two away saw the Blues quickly get into their stride.

Greek outfit Larissa, whose striker Ibrahima Bakayoko made an emotional Goodison return over eight years after departing, were brushed aside 3-1; a 2-0 win in Nuremberg provided travelling Evertonians with one of their great European away days while eventual winners Zenit St Petersburg, with future Premier League stars Martin Škrtel and Andrey Arshavin in their side, were dispatched 1-0 at Goodison.

With qualification to the knockout stages already secured, Everton endured freezing temperatures to triumph 3-2 against AZ in Alkmaar to end the Dutch side's 32-game unbeaten home run which was the longest in European competition.

The Blues' next port of call in February would be Bergen but it was the Norwegian champions Brann who were caught cold, beaten 2-0 on their own turf before a 6-1 thumping at Goodison; perhaps Moyes's men peaked too early?

After dispatching Everton in the round of 16, Fiorentina made their way past PSV Eindhoven before suffering a shock semi-final exit to a Rangers side, managed by Moyes's Goodison Park predecessor Walter Smith.

To make matters worse for the Blues, the final was played just 35 miles from Goodison Park at the City of Manchester Stadium with Zenit beating Rangers 2-0.

It's far from being a fanciful claim that Everton could have contended for the trophy given that the likes of Middlesbrough, who have only ever won a solitary League Cup, had reached the final two years earlier, while Fulham, who have never lifted a major trophy, made it two years later.

Like in 1985 when the Blues were denied a crack at the European Cup, this was a great wasted opportunity for them, yet on this occasion they had nobody to blame but themselves.

* * *

3 May 1986: Everton 6 Southampton 1 (Saints smashed but to no avail as Liverpool clinch the title)

Such were the fine margins, Everton not Liverpool might have been the first club from the city to record a league championship and FA Cup double had Gary Lineker not been without his lucky boots for one crucial game in the run-in.

Instead, the Blues ended up empty-handed while their neighbours swept up both major domestic honours for the only time in their history to date as after the Reds won 11 out of their last 12 First Division matches to clinch the title, they also recovered from a 1-0 half-time deficit at Wembley through Lineker's 40th goal of the season to triumph 3-1 in the FA Cup Final.

Afterwards, Everton's nearly men had to endure the ritual public humiliation of joining Liverpool on a pre-arranged joint open-top bus parade around the city which was perhaps the true driving force behind the Blues clinching the championship for the last time to date the following year.

A 1-0 home win over Tottenham Hotspur on 1 February had returned reigning champions Everton back to the summit for the first time; they were eight points clear of the then third place Reds after a 2-0 victory at Anfield on 22 February and they remained there until a 0-0 draw at Manchester United on 31 March.

Once they had overcome Sheffield Wednesday 2-1 after extra time in their FA Cup semi-final at Villa Park, a couple of huge away wins in the space of three days at Arsenal (1-0) and Watford (2-0) returned the Blues to top spot and although they were overhauled again by Liverpool in a race that was nip and tuck, with just three games to go their destiny remained in their own hands.

Everton knew a hat-trick of victories would be enough for them to retain the title for the first time in their history, but their hopes were severely dashed on that strange night at the Manor Ground just three days before Southampton's visit.

Over 32 years later, Lineker recalled what happened on his *Behind Closed Doors* podcast with Danny Baker, stating, 'I had a pair of lucky boots. I used to go through several pairs a season, but I couldn't stop scoring, I was knocking them in for fun.

'We played at Oxford, we arrived, and the skip came full of the boots and my lucky boots weren't in it. I had to borrow someone's boots, they were a size too big, and I can't remember whose they were, and I missed two or three really good chances, and we lost 1-0 and it cost us the league title.'

Indeed, with Lineker and his big boots spurning a hatful of opportunities, Les Phillips landed the sucker punch for Oxford with only two games to go.

It ensured that although Everton had a subsequent fixture at home to West Ham 48 hours after the Saints' trip to Goodison on the Saturday, Liverpool could clinch the title when playing at the same time away to Chelsea.

To keep their title hopes alive, the Blues just had to fulfil their part of the bargain and pray for a helping hand at Stamford Bridge.

Ken Rogers wrote in the *Liverpool Echo*, 'Everton ran riot at Goodison Park with a Gary Lineker hat-trick helping to inflict a crushing defeat on Southampton.'

The Saints were without England goalkeeper Peter Shilton while his understudy Phil Kite was on loan at Middlesbrough, so the visitors fielded 17-year-old Keith Granger, who hadn't even played for their reserves, between the sticks and the Blues exploited the situation to the full.

They were 4-0 up at the break, Derek Mountfield opening the scoring with a close-range diving header just ten minutes in, while another header from Trevor Steven from a Lineker cross doubled their advantage on 29 minutes.

The roles were reversed two minutes later with Steven dinking the ball into the predatory Lineker's path and the First Division's leading marksman added another three minutes after that with a low shot from the edge of the area after being fed by Paul Bracewell.

A Graeme Sharp header from a lofted Kevin Sheedy cross made it 5-0 ten minutes into the second half, David Puckett slipping in Southampton's consolation four minutes after that before Lineker completed his hat-trick and the rout on 63 minutes, heading in substitute Adrian Heath's left-wing cross.

However, with Liverpool having led since player-manager Kenny Dalglish's goal midway in the first half, Lineker and Everton had long since resigned themselves to their fate.

* * *

3 May 1930: Everton 4 Sunderland 1 (Blues win but find out it's not enough to avoid first relegation)

While they were overtaken at the top of the all-time table a few years back, it remains a proud boast for Everton that they retain the record for the most seasons spent in English football's top flight.

As the Blues move to their new stadium at Bramley-Moore Dock, this figure now stands at 123 for the 2025/26 campaign.

Everton haven't had it all their own way either though. Although they've spent longer than anyone else in the elite, they have had to endure four years in the second tier (the 1930/31 season and 1951 to 1954) and the first time they were relegated, coming a mere two years after their Dixie Dean 60-goal inspired 1928 league championship, was a major shock to the system.

It seems remarkable the Blues could suffer such a fate at a time when their greatest goalscorer – whose image adorned the special badge on their players' sleeves during their 100th top-flight season in 2002/03 – was in the side.

However, much of their troubles that year could be attributed to Dean's injury-plagued campaign. Not only did he require operations on damaged ankles, he also suffered from leg muscle problems.

The centre-forward still averaged almost a goal a game when he was fit, scoring 23 times in 25 outings, but the fact that he was absent for 17 games proved crucial in what was a closely fought battle against the drop.

Everton's fate was virtually sealed by a wretched six-game losing run between 5 March and 12 April as they were beaten by Aston Villa (4-3 at home); Newcastle United (1-0 away); West Ham United (2-1 at home); Birmingham City (4-2 at home); Leicester City (5-4 away) and Grimsby Town (4-2 at home).

By the time of that penultimate loss, they were at the foot of the table and although the Blues would subsequently rally to finish the season unbeaten in five games and win their last three, it was too little, too late to save them.

A mere point behind third-bottom Sheffield United in an era when just two clubs were relegated, Everton went into their final fixture with the chance to still save themselves.

Playing in front of a crowd of 51,132 at Goodison Park, they went out all guns blazing by thrashing ninth-placed Sunderland 4-1.

'Stork' recorded the drama for the *Liverpool Echo*, reporting, 'Today saw Goodison's biggest gate of the season. It was difficult even to get into the press box, such was the jam at the top of the stairs.'

He added, 'As I looked around, I saw many anxious faces. The Everton mascot was busy shooting the ball into the net. I only hope that the Everton forwards will put it in there half as many times. Then a win, and we must have that, will be practically assured.'

Despite the Blues receiving 'a tremendous ovation' as they took to the field, with the stakes so high, the players and fans were both predictably jittery.

'Stork' continued, 'There was a groan when Warney Cresswell dallied with his clearance ... when he made another miskick there was a cry of derision from the crowd, they had not expected "nerves" from such a seasoned warrior.'

Tommy Johnson broke the deadlock on 23 minutes 'and was practically mobbed by his colleagues'. Although Willie Clunas equalised for Sunderland six minutes later, a hat-trick from Tommy White – who usually played centre-half but had switched to centre-forward in Dean's absence with the great man out for Everton's final five fixtures – ensured they romped home.

On the full-time whistle 'the mighty crowd waited on anxiously to hear the news from other quarters', but the other teams in danger had also won convincingly.

Sheffield United escaped by recording a 5-1 victory at Manchester United while Burnley went down with the Blues despite hammering Derby County 6-2 at Turf Moor.

The *Echo* pointed out that now only Aston Villa and Blackburn Rovers remained with an unblemished record from the Football League's 12 founder member clubs (they would both go down in 1936), lamenting, 'Everton relegated! There is a sad ring to those words. Everton stood for the real football.'

By the time of Monday's edition, 'Bee' was in a more reflective mood. He stated, 'They have played a style of game that is not suited to the new offside rule. Football had become more even in the last four years than ever before … never mind bothering your head *why* they have gone, let the slogan be "Make it a year – and a year only".'

* * *

6 April 2014: Everton 3 Arsenal 0 (Martínez wins the battle but not the war with Wenger for fourth place as Blues record their sixth of seven consecutive victories)

Roberto Martínez's Everton emphatically won the battle on this day, but it was Arsène Wenger's Arsenal who would win the war.

Although David Moyes's class of 2004/05 needed just 61 points to finish fourth, a Premier League era club record points haul of 72 for the Blues in 2013/14 still saw them ending up seven points adrift of the Gunners who secured Champions League qualification for the 16th straight season (they would eventually reach 19 before their sequence was broken).

Despite having acquired Everton's most prolific striker since Gary Lineker in Romelu Lukaku on a permanent deal following an initial season-long loan, things would unravel quite spectacularly for Martínez over his next two campaigns.

However, the Catalan's first season in charge represented the perfect blend of his fresh ideas and attacking impetus with the discipline and resoluteness left over from having Moyes at the helm for over a decade.

That hugely promising first 12 months would prompt Bill Kenwright to reward Martínez with a bumper new five-year deal at the end of his debut campaign – a decision that would cost the club £10m in compensation when he was sacked a couple of years later – but it was champagne football displays like this one that had convinced the chairman he was Goodison's man for the long-haul.

As the Gwladys Street chorus proclaimed at the time, 'The school of science – it's on its way back!'

Unlike predecessor Moyes who would often try and temper expectations, on Martínez's appointment, Kenwright declared that the new man's first words to him were, 'I'll get you in the Champions League.'

After this win, Greg O'Keeffe of the *Liverpool Echo* enthused, 'The prize on offer was not fourth place, even if this felt to all intents and purposes like a decider. Everton remain in fifth, a point behind the Gunners. But what they did seize – with two firm hands – was momentum, one of the most powerful forces in football.

'They did it *sin miedo*, without fear, as Roberto Martínez likes to say. They did it with swagger; witness Séamus Coleman nutmegging Santi Cazorla, or the Blues keeping the ball to a chorus of olés.

'And they did it with the hunger and vigour which suggests this Everton side is capable of special things.'

He added, 'It takes a long memory to recall the last time Arsène Wenger didn't steer Arsenal into the Champions League, but this season – on this evidence at least – his men are facing a team who appear quite simply to want it more.

'Everton did to Arsenal what the Londoners did to them at the Emirates in the FA Cup quarter-final last month [when the Gunners won 4-1]. They came out hell-bent on imposing themselves on the game and through sheer force of will and clever tactics they built an advantage which proved unassailable.'

The unexpected tweak that Martínez made to outfox the visitors was putting his usual centre-forward on the flank and the manoeuvre worked a treat.

O'Keeffe proclaimed, 'Martínez smelled blood with the unconvincing Nacho Monreal at left-back and deployed Lukaku over on the right to exploit their opponents' weakness. It worked, like almost everything else the Blues did in a blistering opening half.

'Lukaku is approaching the rampaging form just at the right time which made his loan acquisition seem such a coup earlier in the season. It was his shot which forced Wojciech Szczęsny to parry and allowed Steven Naismith to tuck away the crucial opening goal on 14 minutes.

'Lukaku needed no help with Everton's decisive second [on 34 minutes] and he delivered with style, then celebrated with Martínez like someone who feels nurtured and enriched by his time under such an intelligent coach.'

The coup de grâce was delivered on 61 minutes when former Everton fans' favourite Mikel Arteta, who had upset many Blues by kissing the Arsenal badge after scoring against them in the FA Cup the previous month while also rolling around trying to get their players booked, netted an own goal when sliding in to try and get to the ball ahead of Kevin Mirallas.

It capped a perfect day for Martínez and his side but while another own goal from Sunderland's Wes Brown extended their winning streak to seven the following weekend, after that the bubble burst with a shock 3-2 home defeat to Crystal Palace and with two more losses in their next three fixtures, the Gunners pulled away from them.

6

Other internationals and representative matches

HERE WE wrap up all the other non-club matches that Goodison Park has staged over the years in the shape of international fixtures in addition to those played at the 1966 World Cup, plus some inter-league games that used to be contested regularly in football's early days.

* * *

Brazil's return to Goodison Park for the 1995 Umbro Cup tournament some 29 years on from their three appearances at Everton's home at the 1966 World Cup was the last full international at the ground.

The South Americans, who had lifted their fourth World Cup the year before in the USA, defeated Japan 3-0 on 6 June 1995.

The original Ronaldo duly led the line in a star-studded line-up alongside the likes of Dunga, Aldair, Edmundo, Leonardo, Rivaldo and Juninho, who would join Middlesbrough later that year.

Roberto Carlos opened the scoring just six minutes in while a 3-0 stroll was completed with a second-half brace from Zinho (51, 63).

With plenty of interest courtesy of late walk-ups to the ground, the official attendance was 29,237, still a figure over 10,000 short of Goodison's capacity.

An estimated 3,000 unfortunate fans were left milling around in the streets outside the ground. The *Liverpool Echo* reported, 'World champions Brazil attracted a huge surge of late support for their game against Japan. That left match organisers at the Everton ground unable to cope. Police decided that no more tickets should be sold on safety grounds.'

Prior to that, Goodison hosted ten internationals in the British Home Championship between 1895 and 1973.

The results were: England 3 Scotland 0 (1895); England 1 Ireland 0 (1907, goal scored by Everton's Harold Hardman); England 1 Scotland 1 (1911); England 3 Ireland 0 (1924); England 2 Ireland 1 (1928, second England goal by Everton's Dixie Dean); England 2 Ireland 1 (1935, Everton's Alex Stevenson scored for Ireland to become the first player to net an away international goal on his club's home ground); England 2 Ireland 2 (1947); England 3 Ireland 1 (1953).

Northern Ireland then replaced Ireland in the tournament but played two 'home' games at Goodison Park in 1973 due to civil unrest in Belfast, the first of which on 12 May was against England, losing 2-1, and then against Wales on 19 May, winning 1-0.

England also played three friendly internationals at Goodison, which included their first home defeat to opponents from outside the United Kingdom when Ireland beat them 2-0 on 21 September 1949.

Con Martin, primarily a centre-half but nicknamed 'Mr Versatility' (his schooling in Gaelic football enabled him to spend prolonged periods in goal for his club Aston Villa), put the Irish ahead from the penalty spot before Everton wing-half Peter Farrell netted to secure the historic victory.

Clifford Webb of the *Daily Herald* used a catchphrase from a popular comedian of the time to bring some gallows humour to the occasion, writing, 'A Tommy Trinder greeting to those players who were overlooked by the FA selectors and did not take part in the Everton soccer debacle England 0 Eire 2 – "You lucky people!"

'This was definitely an occasion on which it was better to be "included out" as the famous film magnate once said.

'Football history – bleak, black history – was made on the Goodison turf for let it be known, this was the first time that any country outside the International Championship has won here.

'Eire, small and weak by soccer standards, triumphed where the great European teams in their pre-war heydays, always failed.

'Before the gloom is too deep upon me, all praise to the boys in green. Brilliantly skippered and set a great example by right-back Johnny Carey [the future Everton manager], they caught England footling and fiddling like a junior girls' hockey side, set about them with keen, swift direct action and flayed the hides off 'em.

'Luck? Sure, there was luck, but it was born of honest endeavour and of the knowledge acquired within a few minutes of the start that victory was well within their grasp.'

The Three Lions returned to defeat Portugal 5-2 on 19 May 1951 and draw 1-1 with Poland on 5 January 1966 when Bobby Moore scored his first international goal.

Goodison has held a quartet of England under-23 internationals: England 3 Scotland 1 (1958); England 0 Hungary 1 (1959); England 2 Wales 0 (1961); England 4 Hungary 0 (1968).

Ex-Everton midfielder Lee Carsley's European champions took part in the last international of any sort at the ground as an England under-21 side captained by Blues centre-back Jarrad Branthwaite defeated their Northern Ireland counterparts 3-0 in front of just 7,890 fans on 21 November 2023, while two decades earlier there had been another England under-21 game with Portugal triumphing 2-1 on 9 September 2003.

The ground additionally staged a couple of under-18 fixtures: West Germany 3 Bulgaria 1 (1983 European Championship) and England 0 Switzerland 0 (1989).

Also, Football League XIs played ten matches at Goodison: 1-1 v Scottish League (1894); 5-1 v Scottish League (1896); 4-3 v Scottish League (1925); 7-2 v Irish League (1929); 10-2 v Welsh/ Irish League (1935); 2-0 v Scottish League (1936); 3-3 v All British XI (1939, wartime representative match); 4-2 v Irish League (1947); 9-1 v League of Ireland (1951); 5-1 v League of Ireland (1955).

Goals galore

MANAGERS AND coaches love clean sheets and nicking 1-0 wins, but fans feed off goals so here are some of the most famous occasions that Evertonians have been treated to high-scoring contests at Goodison Park.

* * *

20 November 1971: Everton 8 Southampton 0 (Scoreboard can't cope with thrashing)

A club of many firsts both on and off the pitch throughout their history, Everton were the first team to install a scoreboard at their ground, but so many goals were netted by the hosts in this game that the device could not cope.

Normally the names of the goalscorers would be displayed at Goodison Park but a lack of space ensured that on this occasion, shirt numbers had to suffice, so instead it simply read 7 9 7 9 8 9 9 7.

The Blues, who went into this fixture in 17th place, had been struggling throughout the season and had already stumbled at the first hurdle in the League Cup – ironically being knocked out 2-1 at Southampton – so despite having beaten Liverpool 1-0 at Goodison seven days earlier, the crowd of 28,718 was just half of the total that had witnessed the Merseyside derby on the previous weekend.

A snowstorm also severely impacted the attendance, but as the headline in the *Liverpool Echo* proclaimed, there was a 'Royle record in Everton avalanche.'

It wasn't just a watershed match for the four-goal homegrown hero playing at centre-forward though.

Nobody could have envisaged it at the time, but this was the last occasion that the man of whom the Gwladys Street chanted 'Who's the greatest of them all? Little curly Alan Ball' would score in the royal blue jersey.

Injuries had ensured that the final time Ball lined up alongside Colin Harvey and Howard Kendall in Everton's most fabled midfield trio had been almost three months earlier for a 1-0 defeat at West Ham United on 28 August.

After this game, he had just one more at Goodison to come – a goalless draw with Stoke City on 4 December – before Harry Catterick made the most controversial move of his managerial career, selling Ball to Arsenal 18 days later.

Just as when Ball had signed for the Blues after a man-of-the-match performance for England in the 1966 World Cup Final win over West Germany, it was a record fee paid to an English club.

Having shelled out £112,000 to Blackpool for Ball, Everton almost doubled their money on him with the Gunners paying £220,000 but that was hardly the point. After all, earlier that year, Catterick had claimed his prize asset's value to be at £1m.

Describing Ball in *Everton: Player by Player*, Ivan Ponting observed, 'Alan's game was a heady mixture of delicate skill and rampant fire, unquestionable bravery and overwhelming self-confidence.

'Physically there wasn't much of him; in terms of talent, commitment and value to the team he was a veritable colossus.'

Not only that, he loved the club, later remarking, 'Once Everton has touched you, nothing will be the same,' and six months shy of his 27th birthday, the tempestuous Lancastrian from Farnworth was arguably still at the peak of his powers.

Typically, Ball was in the thick of the action as Everton tore apart another club he would later play for and also go on to manage, spending his last years in Hampshire before his untimely death aged 61 in 2007, suffering a heart attack when trying to extinguish a fire in his garden.

Michael Charters of the *Liverpool Echo* wrote, 'The worst conditions of the season brought out the best in Everton as they "paralysed" Southampton.'

David Johnson fired the Blues ahead on 13 minutes with a 'fierce low angled shot' while a 'well-placed' effort from Joe Royle doubled their advantage.

Johnson's pace provided the third as he beat Eric Martin 'with ease from 12 yards after he raced through a gap at top speed'.

Royle's second and Everton's fourth five minutes from half-time was a close-range effort but their fifth from Ball just before the break was more spectacular as the midfielder 'raced 60 yards' before sliding the ball past Martin from the edge of the area.

On the hour mark, Royle completed his hat-trick with 'a magnificent shot from 18 yards – a tremendous half volley' while his fourth on 72 minutes was 'a delicate glancing header'.

Despite Charters claiming that 'Everton eased off in these gruelling conditions', Johnson's hat-trick goal five minutes before full-time that completed the rout, was a magical moment in itself.

'Martin came out of goal looking for a backpass from McGrath, but Johnson stepped between them and with the coolest flick shot that I've seen for years, put the ball over everyone and against the far post from where it dropped into the net.'

In terms of the margin of victory, this was as big a win as Everton have ever recorded in the league, along with the 9-1 successes over Manchester City and Plymouth Argyle.

* * *

29 November 2017: Everton 4 West Ham United 0 (Rooney scores from inside his own half to complete hat-trick)

Unfortunately for Evertonians, boyhood Blue Wayne Rooney only bookended his Premier League career at Goodison Park either side of a record-breaking spell with Manchester United but even as a grizzled veteran rather than a dynamic teenage man-child, he was still capable of scoring the kind of goals that most other players could only dream of.

Rooney's long-range missile for the Blues against West Ham United was no fluke.

He had once netted against the same opponents for Manchester United from just inside the opposition half and he would go on to repeat his feat of scoring from his own half against the Hammers for Everton with a similar strike for US side DC United against Orlando City while playing in Major League Soccer.

After defecting from Goodison to Old Trafford when still just 18 in 2004 despite having famously displayed his 'Once a blue, always a blue' T-shirt a couple of years earlier, for a long time Rooney was considered a Judas figure among many Everton supporters and his on-field returns to his former stomping ground were marred by several ugly flashpoints.

As the seasons passed though, there did appear to be a thawing.

Rooney attended the 2009 FA Cup Final against Chelsea as an Everton 'fan' and despite being well on his way to becoming Manchester United's all-time leading goalscorer, when he became a father, he'd dress his sons in both United and Everton replica kits and pyjamas.

He even got to don the royal blue jersey again at Goodison for Duncan Ferguson's testimonial match in 2015 while the following summer, Everton went to Old Trafford to provide the opposition for Rooney's own United testimonial.

By 2017, after winning every honour in club football with Manchester United, the now 31-year-old Rooney was deemed surplus to requirements by manager José Mourinho.

Romelu Lukaku was on the verge of following the Croxteth-born player down the East Lancs Road in a £75m move and although the two deals weren't officially linked, Rooney, granted a free transfer, would return to Everton as a Prodigal Son the day before the Belgian striker sealed his own switch.

Some 13 years had passed since he last played for the club – it was the longest gap of any returning Blues player – but he headed in a goal on his second Premier League debut against Stoke City to suggest there was still some fuel left in the tank.

Rooney would race to ten Premier League goals by 18 December – the only time he hit double figures for Everton – but mostly deployed in midfield by new manager Sam Allardyce in the second half of the season, he subsequently failed to add to that tally.

However, after a 5-1 home drubbing by Atalanta just six days prior to this game, Italian newspaper *Gazzetta dello Sport* lamented of Rooney, 'He is a walking monument. It is sad to see him in this condition.'

But even if the legs had gone, that footballing brain was still razor sharp.

Phil Kirkbride wrote in the *Liverpool Echo*, 'At Goodison there was something old, something new, something borrowed and, in the end, three vital points for the boys in royal blue.

'Against a West Ham side managed by David Moyes, and in front of soon-to-be new boss Sam Allardyce, David Unsworth brought his caretaker reign to an end with an uplifting victory that had the Old Lady singing.

'Wayne Rooney completed his first ever hat-trick for the club by scoring majestically from inside his own half just minutes after a Jordan Pickford penalty save took the wind out of the Hammers' sails before Ashley Williams ensured it became a drubbing when he headed home Gylfi Sigurðsson's corner late on.'

Rooney showed he wasn't that slow off the mark when he was first to the rebound to head in after his 18th minute penalty was saved by Joe Hart, while he stroked home a second ten minutes later after being teed up by a couple of other homegrown heroes, Tom Davies and Jonjoe Kenny.

Kirkbride described Rooney's 59-yard hat-trick goal on 66 minutes as 'picture perfect, struck as if he had used a golf club, flighted sublimely over two West Ham defenders and into an unguarded net with Hart stranded outside the box'.

Rooney would still have time to add a Merseyside derby goal at Anfield to his Everton highlights reel the following month but by the end of the season there was another parting of the ways (along with Allardyce).

His second coming was a gamble that didn't quite come off but as a Scouser surrounded by Blue-blooded kin, he's surely glad he did it.

* * *

30 January 1935: Everton 6 Sunderland 4 (Legendary FA Cup tie settled after extra time)

A ten-goal thriller that went to extra time left many old-timers who witnessed this match claiming it was Goodison Park's greatest-ever cup tie.

What was also remarkable about this incredible game was that despite the ding-dong scoring, home captain Dixie Dean did not find the net in over two hours of play.

The two sides had already played out a couple of crackers over the festive period with hugely contrasting results.

On Christmas Day 1935, Everton defeated Sunderland 6-2 at Goodison Park, but just 24 hours later were then smashed 7-0 at Roker Park on Boxing Day.

Paired together in the fourth round of the FA Cup on 26 January, the Blues fared better on Wearside this time as they cancelled out a 21st-minute goal from Sunderland legend and homegrown hero Raich Carter to earn a replay through Jimmy Cunliffe's effort 16 minutes from the end.

By the end of this contest, the following Wednesday afternoon, it was already being dubbed a classic.

George Green, long-time cartoonist for the *Liverpool Echo*, dubbed it 'The match of a hundred thrills', drawing a couple of stunned fans with one proclaiming, 'Oh it's the best ever,' while his neighbour adds, 'It's much better than that.'

Writing as 'Bee', Ernest Edwards said in the same newspaper, 'I would like to ask whether there has ever been a greater display of skill in the mud in any league or cup match.

'We all keep the memory cells filled with noteworthy sporting occasions, and this latest 6-4 game will top the lot by reason of its two goals in two closing minutes, by the ordering off of a manager of the visiting side, by the multitudinous moments of dramatic thrill and art. It was a pity Sunderland should lose after making a battle of this worthy character.'

He also praised the referee, claiming, 'It was Mr Pinckston's finely judged control that made the greatest of all games possible. He forced the players to "get on with the game".'

Jackie Coulter opened the scoring on 14 minutes, 'The first time Everton's Irish eyes began to smile, a goal was the result, a delicious effort made by one of Alex Stevenson's dodging runs.'

Coulter then scored again to put the Blues 2-0 up after just over half an hour with 'a shot that Jimmy Thorpe could not move to'.

Bert Davis pulled a 'grand' goal back for Sunderland four minutes before half-time but when Stevenson added a third for the hosts from four yards out on 74 minutes, many thought the game was won.

Indeed, 'Bee' provided a pithy footnote given to him by a source dubbed 'Clubmoor' about six Welshmen who had travelled across the border to watch the cup tie but having left early to take the tram back to Liverpool city centre 'thinking it all over with Everton leading 3-1, on arriving at Lord Street, they had to purchase an *Echo* to find the result 6-4'.

With the Cambrian day-trippers now absent, Jimmy Connor made it 3-2 on 78 minutes with 'a fine goal' before a last-minute equaliser from Bobby Gurney, Sunderland's all-time leading scorer, 'an overhead effort', took the tie into extra time.

The additional half an hour, which started with Sunderland manager John Cochrane being ordered off the field, brought four more goals with Coulter completing his hat-trick two minutes in to restore Everton's lead before Connor netted his second on 96 minutes to make it 4-4.

With legs tiring and the light fading, Albert Geldard eventually got the Blues across the line by bagging a late brace with goals on 111 and 119 minutes.

'Bee' wrote, 'It is very wonderful that these trained athletes could last two hours of mud-plugging and kept the game as lively as it had been in the first 90 minutes of play.

'Their stamina was strained but their hearts never grew weary … To everyone concerned, players, officials and police controllers I say, "Well done everybody."'

Everton made it past Derby County 3-1 at home in the fifth round but were beaten 2-1 by Bolton Wanderers in the quarter-finals at Goodison Park.

Sunderland would finish the season runners-up to Arsenal but clinched their sixth and last league championship to date the following campaign despite losing goalkeeper Thorpe in February 1936.

The 22-year-old died four days after being kicked in the head and on the chest after picking up a backpass in a home game with

Chelsea, a tragic incident that would lead to a change in the laws of the game, banning players from raising their feet to goalkeepers who controlled the ball in their hands.

* * *

8 May 1999: Everton 6 West Ham United 0 (On-loan Kevin Campbell's hat-trick takes his goal tally to nine in five games as the Blues secure their top-flight status)

It was a damning indictment of what had gone on before his arrival that Kevin Campbell, who didn't find the net until 11 April, would finish Everton's top scorer in the 1998/99 season, but his goals almost single-handedly saved the club from relegation.

The Blues had struggled to score for most of the campaign – infamously netting just three times in their first 12 Premier League home games and drawing nine blanks in the process – before their 5-0 win over Middlesbrough on 17 February.

For most of Walter Smith's first season, Everton had been teetering just above the drop zone, but a four-game losing streak in the spring saw them plummet into the bottom three on Easter Monday.

Back-to-back defeats to Arsenal (2-0 at home) and Manchester United (3-1 away) prompted Smith to try to bolster his numbers with a couple of fresh faces for the run-in.

He snapped up midfielder Scot Gemmill from Nottingham Forest plus another City Ground old boy, who had departed the East Midlands the previous summer for a stint in Turkey.

Campbell, who initially arrived on loan, was looking for a way out of Trabzonspor following the furore after the club's president branded him a 'cannibal' and would prove to be the Blues' saviour.

It was an inauspicious start for the pair though as they suffered a 3-2 defeat to Liverpool on their respective debuts despite Olivier Dacourt firing the visitors ahead at Anfield after just 42 seconds.

The game was overshadowed by Robbie Fowler's controversial white line 'sniffing' goal celebration that Reds boss Gérard Houllier laughingly tried to dismiss as 'eating the grass' but in truth, Everton had much bigger concerns.

Another loss, 2-1 at home to Sheffield Wednesday just 48 hours later, saw them fall into the relegation places but miraculously Campbell's purple patch was about to begin.

He inspired three successive victories by bagging a brace in each of them: Coventry City (2-0 at home); Newcastle United (3-1 away) and Charlton Athletic (4-1 at home).

Campbell would then draw a blank in a 3-1 defeat at Chelsea, but his goals had been enough to ensure that the Blues could banish any lingering doubts over the drop if they defeated West Ham United at home on the penultimate weekend of the campaign.

The Lambeth-born striker and his team-mates would save their best until last as his hat-trick helped Smith's side to hit the sorry Hammers for six, taking his scoring sequence to nine goals in the space of five matches.

With the purse strings now tightened at the club, though, David Prentice of the *Liverpool Echo* described how there was no guarantee at this point that Campbell, who ultimately did join for £3m, would be remaining with the Blues for the following season despite his already iconic status.

He wrote, 'Walter Smith's begging bowl band of Bosman transfers and homegrown kids wiped the floor with woeful West Ham – and they did it with just one member of the manager's famed "For Sale" list in his line-up. Olivier Dacourt was the player probably saying his Goodison goodbye [he would return to France with Lens just a year after leaving Strasbourg] but even his imminent departure could have a silver lining.

'The Frenchman, booed when his name was read out, could become the pawn who lures "Super Kevin Campbell" to Goodison permanently.'

Campbell's hat-trick came with goals in the 14th, 52nd and 77th minutes. Prentice said, 'If his first goal was a poacher's predatory tap-in, his second and third were clinical strikes. His movement to spin off close-marking defenders was exceptional, although Neil Ruddock and Rio Ferdinand admittedly showed all the mobility of fully laden skips – and his finishing was exemplary.'

Michael Ball struck Everton's second on 25 minutes with their first penalty since he netted in the win over Newcastle when Duncan Ferguson was sold the previous November, while Don Hutchison made it 3-0 on 38 minutes with a 'fierce strike'.

Francis Jeffers, who had struck up an impressive fledgling strike partnership with Campbell, hit the sixth goal three minutes from full time when he headed in from close range after the number nine had flicked on Hutchison's corner.

The result ensured Everton were free of relegation worries going into their final fixture, prompting Prentice to conclude, 'After the traumas of seasons gone by, that's marginal progress.'

Some 25 years on from Campbell's heroics, Evertonians were left distraught by their idol's premature death aged 54 in June 2024 following a short illness.

* * *

30 December 1893: Everton 7 West Bromwich Albion 1 (Six-shooter Jack Southworth)

In Everton's entire history, Jack Southworth is the only player to score a double hat-trick in a single game for either the Blues or their opponents, and the six-shooter's display took his Goodison Park total to ten goals in the space of a week.

Seven days earlier, Southworth had bagged four goals in Everton's 8-1 thrashing of The Wednesday (Sheffield Wednesday from 1929) but although his team-mates could 'only' get seven against the Albion, their centre-forward increased his own personal tally on the day by another two.

Despite the diminutive Fred Geary (who stood at just 5ft 2in) having broken the 20-goal barrier in three of the previous four seasons, following the 1892/93 campaign – their maiden one at Goodison – which had culminated with a 1-0 defeat to Wolverhampton Wanderers in the club's first FA Cup Final (the Blues had been big favourites to win), Everton sought to beef up their attack.

Winger Jack Bell arrived from Dumbarton in April while centre-forward Southworth, already established as a prolific scorer in his hometown of Blackburn for first Olympic and then Rovers – and the First Division's leading marksman in 1890/91 when Everton had been crowned champions for the first time – joined for a handsome £400 fee.

Although the Blues suffered a 7-3 defeat at Derby County on his debut on 9 September, Southworth duly struck his first of 27 goals in 22 matches that season – a haul that would see him finish as the First Division's leading scorer for the second time.

Bell netted first against West Brom, with the *Cricket and Football Field* reporting, 'That artist scored with a beautiful little touch which kept the ball down and gave Joe Reader no chance,' but from then on it was the Southworth show.

Southworth's goal number one, 'Receiving it "with thanks" and popping it through amid loud cheers.'

Number two, 'Bell took a pass from Alex Latta and sent in a slowish shot, with Southworth in full cry after it. Reader dashed out, but ran the ball against the Everton centre, who literally trotted it through.'

Number three, 'Southworth ran right through, and completely beat Reader for the fourth time.'

Number four, 'No sooner had the second half been started than the homesters attacked and put in several warm attempts with which Reader dealt. Presently, however, Latta, Bell, and Southworth got down, and the latter rushed the ball past Reader.'

The visitors then netted their consolation as 'West Bromwich now did their best bit of work so far, for they dashed down in line, and Owen Williams fairly beat' his namesake Richard in the home goal.

Number five, 'Everton was, however, not content, for almost straight away they again ran down in line and Southworth scored with a clever left-footed shot which gave Reader no chance.'

Number six, 'Southworth showed what he could do, for he took a pass from Bell in grand style, slipped the backs, and scored his sixth goal in succession, which feat was duly recognised by the crowd.'

Unfortunately, Everton were only able to enjoy Southworth's incredible finishing prowess for little more than a year with Rob Sawyer reporting in an online article on Toffeeweb that he picked up a serious knee injury in a benefit match for Preston North End's goalkeeper, James Trainer, when he collided with an opposing player. Although he was aged just 27 at the time, he never played another professional match.

Sawyer said, 'The club referred Jack for "special treatment" on his knee by a Dr Whitehead in Manchester which, for reasons not outlined, he declined to attend.'

A brief article in the *Liverpool Echo* on 23 February 1895 stated, 'It is most unfortunate for Southworth that he did not remain an in-patient at the Manchester institution after undergoing the operation by the eminent specialist a couple of months ago.

'We are afraid that his anxiety to get home again has cost him a great deal, and it is not likely that he will be seen on the field again this season.'

Sawyer added that in August 1900, Southworth was listed as Everton's assistant trainer while his playing registration was not expunged by the club until 1903.

However, Southworth's injury did not prevent him from becoming a professional violinist with the Hallé Orchestra and the Royal Liverpool Philharmonic Orchestra after hanging up his boots.

In 1944 the *Liverpool Evening Express* reported that he was still winning bowling competitions in Thingwall, Wirral, aged 77 and Southworth saw out his days at his home in Wavertree, passing away on 16 October 1956, aged 89.

* * *

10 February 2021: Everton 5 Tottenham Hotspur 4 AET (FA Cup goal glut)

In normal circumstances, Goodison Park would have been shaking to the rafters when Bernard netted the decisive ninth goal of the night in extra time but with fans kept out due to the coronavirus pandemic, the defining image of the game was instead Everton manager Carlo Ancelotti calmly blowing into his cup of tea while those around him went berserk.

As is the fashion in the third decade of the 21st century, Ancelotti's cool, understated reaction to the dramatic winner quickly became a social media meme with the boss superimposed against backgrounds depicting the sinking of the *Titanic*, eruption of Krakatoa and even the impending doom of the asteroid hurtling towards Earth that would cause the extinction of the dinosaurs.

At the time, Evertonians, forced like all other supporters to watch the action from television at home, revelled in the Italian's relaxed response.

As Ancelotti's own son and assistant Davide acknowledged when asked what he admired most about his father's managerial style, it was his ability to remain balanced in stressful situations.

After all, here was a super-coach who had secured major honours in all five of Europe's big leagues and taken charge of three Champions League-winning sides – the only man to have achieved that feat but not with a single club.

Ancelotti, who has subsequently now reached five Champions League triumphs, had seen and done it all in the biggest and best dugouts of the continent and Everton fans were delighted to have him.

Unlike Farhad Moshiri's previous appointments, his arrival was unanimously endorsed by the fanbase and almost instantly he had his own terrace anthem 'Carlo Fantastico, Carlo Magnifico'.

Despite seeing his previous stint in England abruptly cut short by Chelsea – at Goodison itself before he'd even left the ground after a 1-0 defeat to Everton, just a year after steering the Londoners to a Premier League and FA Cup double – Ancelotti had penned a four-and-a-half-year contract with the Blues which he'd publicly declared he'd like to extend to lead the club into their new stadium.

But before the 'Grand Old Lady' even had chance to play host to another capacity crowd, Ancelotti had gone, returning to one of his previous posts at Real Madrid.

Perhaps the lure of European football's most successful club side was always going to prove too great or maybe at 62, after seeing his side plummet from being second on Boxing Day and still fifth in March with the chance to jump into the Champions League places if they won their game in hand, to ultimately finishing tenth, Ancelotti figured that time was not on his side when it came to this project?

What this tie did show though was that after some dour, half-baked contests in the early days of football behind closed doors, some games in empty stadia could still produce a thrilling tempo at times.

Phil Kirkbride of the *Liverpool Echo* wrote, 'Three goals in seven first half minutes [Dominic Calvert-Lewin on 36 with a half volley too hot to handle; Richarlison on 38 with a low drive from just outside the area, and Gylfi Sigurðsson's penalty on 43 after Calvert-Lewin was fouled] suddenly had Everton in a 3-1 lead, having conceded in the third minute when Davinson Sánchez profited from generous defending that would linger in the air like a bad smell.

'But the chaos was turned up a notch when more slapstick work at the back allowed Erik Lamela to make it 3-2 just before the break.

'Three-two became 3-3 when Sánchez scored from another corner but with just over 20 minutes left, and with Everton missing the now injured Dominic Calvert-Lewin, Richarlison produced a sublime finish to make it 4-3.

'Defend the lead, protect the lead, keep things tight ... sadly, it wasn't yet the night for that. Harry Kane forced the game into extra time with seven minutes left.'

With legs tiring, those in reserve were making a difference and Kirkbride added, 'It was beginning to look like a battle of the benches. But it was the change that probably seemed the least likely to make a difference, who made the biggest: Bernard.

'Sigurðsson delivered a sumptuous ball over the top, Bernard brought it down and volleyed it home [in the 97th minute].

'Everton had 23 minutes to protect what they had,' but this time they did in 'relatively comfortable' fashion.

Spurs boss José Mourinho, who when in charge of Chelsea back in 2004 had derided Arsenal's 5-4 north London derby win over his future employers as 'a hockey score' and 'disgraceful' in an 11-a-side match, would leave his own post before Ancelotti, sacked on the eve of the League Cup Final against Manchester City, who would also end Everton's FA Cup interest in the next round.

* * *

28 January 1969: Everton 4 Wolverhampton Wanderers 0 (The School of Science at its finest)

Everton would capture their second league championship under Harry Catterick the following season but many of those who witnessed the Blues in 1968/69 reckon this was the side that played the best football they ever had the privilege to watch.

Despite being a manager known for his stealth in the transfer market with a war chest funded by John Moores's fortune, 'The Catt' didn't bring in any new faces ahead of the new season but Alex Young, one of the most revered darlings of the Goodison Park crowd, had departed to take up the position of player-boss of Glentoran in Northern Ireland.

In his place was a centre-forward much more in the traditional Everton mould, in the substantial shape of homegrown hero Joe Royle, but such was the popularity of the 'Golden Vision', it had not always been a popular choice.

Royle had become the club's youngest player at the time when making his debut at Blackpool as a 16-year-old in January 1966, a decision that resulted in Catterick being roughed up by some angry Blues fans outside Bloomfield Road after his side's 2-0 defeat.

By this time though, Royle, who had bagged 20 in 1967/68 and would grab 29 in all competitions in 1968/69, was very much there on merit and only Dixie Dean and the 'other' Alex Young, 1906 FA Cup match-winner 'Sandy', had scored more for Everton by the time he left the club in December 1974 on 119 goals.

While 'Big Joe', from Norris Green, was a classic number nine in terms of being an heir to the likes of Dean, Tommy Lawton and Dave Hickson, those behind him weren't just lumping the ball up to him and the Blues were often at their finest during this period.

Despite losing two of their early First Division matches, Everton then embarked on a 16-game unbeaten run in the competition and although this sequence was finally ended by a 2-1 defeat to Leeds United at Elland Road – where the champions-elect were undefeated all season – on 23 November, the Blues bounced back in style at Goodison Park the following weekend.

Royle plundered a hat-trick as Leicester City were torn apart 7-1 but this 4-0 Tuesday night win over Wolverhampton Wanderers, who also played an easy-on-the-eye style, marked the high watermark for a free-flowing Everton side.

Bristol Rovers manager Freddie Ford – who was at Goodison on a scouting mission ahead of his Third Division side's visit for an FA Cup fifth round tie – and Wolves chairman John Ireland both described it as the finest display either of them had seen in years.

Michael Charters of the *Liverpool Echo* also waxed lyrical. He said, 'Here was a match with so much thrilling, open football that you dare not lose concentration on it for a moment without missing some high-speed constructive touch.'

Royle fired Everton ahead on 21 minutes with an effort that won Charters's approval, as the journalist observed, 'The first was a penalty scored as penalties should be. He thumped the ball with such force from the spot that if Phil Parkes in the Wolves goal had got his body to it, I swear it would have taken him into the net.'

Johnny Morrissey doubled the Blues' lead two minutes before the interval, accepting a pass from Alan Ball 'with the Wolves defence in complete disorder', before a third was added on 71 minutes as Jimmy Husband, 'running with the ball with courage and skill, tormented the Wolves defence, turned sharply on to a Ball pass and hit it just inside the upright'.

Royle, who Charters rated as producing 'the finest performance he has given', bagged his brace eight minutes from the end with 'a magnificent bullet-like header' from Ray Wilson's cross.

This was as good as it got for Everton though. Gavin Buckland pointed out in *Money Can't Buy Us Love* that with a harsh winter ensuring they played just four league matches in ten weeks after Boxing Day, and with a backlog of fixtures to fulfil including nine games in April, 'The finesse and style of the early part of the campaign diluted as the team struggled to score goals.'

* * *

5 February 2011: Everton 5 Blackpool 3 (Louis Saha scores four in Goodison's first 5-3 since Portugal beat North Korea in the 1966 World Cup)

Just say the name Blackpool and for many it immediately conjures up a cornucopia of colourful images in their minds and probably a huge dollop of nostalgia.

From the iconic Tower and its ornate ballroom with Wurlitzer organ to the baser pleasures of kiss me quick hats, sticks of rock and saucy postcards along the Golden Mile plus donkeys and deckchairs on the beach, it's a throwback by the 'bucket-and-spade-full' for a bygone age of the great British holiday.

Blackpool playing in the upper echelons of English football also conjures up memories of days gone by, such as the 'Matthews Final' in the 1953 FA Cup – even though Stan Mortensen scored a hat-trick – and for Everton the Tangerines would provide them with goalkeeper Gordon West and midfielder Alan Ball the following decade.

Colourful West Country gaffer Ian Holloway found the right blend by the seaside in his debut season in charge in 2009/10 and turned back the clock to steer Blackpool into the top flight for the first time since 1971 with promotion via the play-offs, thanks to some help from on-loan right-back Séamus Coleman, who would go on to break the Blues' Premier League appearance record.

When they met for a league fixture at Goodison Park for the first time in almost 40 years and with the Irishman now back turning out for his parent club, Everton and Blackpool produced a scoreline that went even further back as it was the first 5-3 at the ground since Portugal also came from behind to defeat North Korea in the quarter-finals of the 1966 World Cup.

Just as then, the victors would have a four-goal hero with Eusébio's mantle being taken up by Louis Saha in the much wetter conditions of a Merseyside winter.

The Parisian striker, who was already 32 by this point, had been brought to the club in 2008 in a 'pay as you play' type deal due to past injury woes but David Prentice of the *Liverpool Echo* argued that despite David Moyes claiming this was his 'most complete' squad, no Premier League side at this point relied as heavily on one man as Everton did on Saha.

He wrote, 'When Louis Saha is firing, so too do the Blues. When Louis Saha is not fit or not firing, Everton lack the cutting edge to convert all their excellent approach work into victories.

'Injured on the opening day against Blackburn, Louis Saha didn't start a match until November or celebrate a goal until January. And Everton suffered. But the difference that match fitness and confidence brings to Louis Saha's game, and Everton's, is enormous.

'The Blues have lost once in their last seven matches since Saha started scoring again. And here they converted another match with the potential to become a frustrating, if wildly exciting, draw, into a thoroughly deserved three points. The difference, ultimately, was their Gallic charm.'

Saha was on it from the start, and he fired Everton into the lead on 20 minutes with a smart left-footed finish from 12 yards out from Diniyar Bilyaletdinov's low left-wing cross.

Blackpool went into the break level though, as the Blues failed to clear a Charlie Adam corner and after Ian Evatt's shot rebounded off the post, Leighton Baines could only hook the ball into the path of Alex Baptiste who finished from point-blank range on 37 minutes.

With Saha denied another goal before the interval after referee Kevin Friend refused to play advantage, it only took Everton two minutes of the second half to restore their lead with Saha poking in a right-footed shot from Baines's left-wing cross.

However, the Blues temporarily lost their way through a quickfire double blow through unmarked debutant Jason Puncheon

(62) and Adam's diving header (64) after the ball rebounded off the crossbar from DJ Campbell's shot.

Everton, who had seen shots from Marouane Fellaini and Jack Rodwell cleared off the line in the second half, drew level through Saha's hat-trick goal on 76 minutes with a close-range header from Mikel Arteta's corner, completing the 'perfect' treble of right foot, left foot and header.

The goal that restored the Blues' lead three minutes later was sublime as Baines set it up with a delivery on his weaker right foot which was struck sweetly into the net on the volley by substitute Jermaine Beckford.

Saha sealed the incredible win six minutes from the end, picking up the ball from Fellaini in the left-wing position and dribbling inside to clip the ball in with his left foot.

* * *

3 September 1906: Everton 9 Manchester City 1 (Record league win)

Everton's sharp shooters were on fire to melt Manchester City resistance and post the club's record league win as the country basked in sweltering temperatures.

Although later equalled with an identical scoreline against Plymouth Argyle in a Second Division fixture in 1930, in over 130 years this victory remains Everton's largest in the top flight.

It is also a joint record loss for City as one of four occasions in which they have been beaten by an eight-goal margin along with 10-2 v Small Heath (1893); 8-0 v Burton Wanderers (1894) and 8-0 v Wolverhampton Wanderers (1933).

Just why was this contest so one-sided though?

Everton did have a fine side during this era, as after losing to Wolverhampton Wanderers 1-0 in the 1894 final and 3-2 to Aston Villa in 1897, they made it third time lucky in 1906 by eventually lifting the competition's original trophy, defeating

Newcastle United, league champions in 1905 and 1907, 1-0 in front of 75,609 spectators at the Crystal Palace. A goal from Alex 'Sandy' Young on 77 minutes brought the cup back to Liverpool for the first time.

Young, who would later have a stint at Manchester City, had a turbulent life after he hung up his boots, being convicted of the manslaughter of his brother after he shot him in Australia and dying in an Edinburgh asylum after being considered mentally unstable.

Young's record for Everton saw him produce 125 goals over 314 appearances from 1901 to 1911, and he was one of nine members of the FA Cup-winning side from 136 days earlier that lined up at home to City.

The visitors were no mugs though and had finished the previous season in fifth position, six places higher than the Blues.

The mitigating circumstances for their heavy defeat seems to be the heat wave that was baking the country with temperatures recorded as topping 32°Celsius for four consecutive days between 31 August and 3 September.

The 1906/07 season kicked off on 1 September with Everton drawing 2-2 at Middlesbrough while Manchester City slumped to a 4-1 home defeat to Woolwich Arsenal.

The *Liverpool Daily Post and Mercury* carried headlines of 'Football Hot O!, A Warm Kick-Off and Enormous Crowds, Players Collapse' with an editorial declaring, 'The Glorious First, which duly celebrates the commencement of two distinct classes of sport – football and partridge shooting – will long be remembered for its overpowering heat.'

With the trip to Goodison Park coming just 48 hours later and the burning conditions still not abating, the *Liverpool Courier* explained how the visitors had still not recovered from wilting in a Moss Side oven, proclaiming, 'Sympathy was extended to the City by the misfortune which befell them on Saturday, when five of their players were rendered *hors de combat* by the terrific heat.'

Everton in contrast, seemed to produce a supercharged, solar-powered display in this fixture that kicked off at 5.45pm on a Monday.

The *Daily Post and Mercury* observed, 'The inglorious display of the City against Woolwich on Saturday before their own supporters did not suggest a tough job for the Toffees.'

Captain and centre-half Jack Taylor, an early Everton legend who totted up 456 appearances before sustaining serious damage to his larynx in a freak accident in the 1910 FA Cup semi-final, broke the deadlock. The report stated, 'The Blues worked with determination, and gradually forced back the Mancunian defence, until Taylor, finding an opening, put the leather beyond Frank Davies after eight minutes' play.'

Jimmy Settle 'practically unmarked beat Davies easily' to double their advantage, while just moments after the kick-off, Everton regained possession and he netted again, with Davies having 'no chance of repelling his deadly shot'.

Walter Abbott made it four and a fifth goal came before half-time as Young netted his first of four. After the break he made it six by 'beating Davies from Settle's clever pass' before completing his hat-trick with 'a rattling good shot'.

Albert Fisher then netted City's consolation to make it 7-1 but there was still time for the hosts to net twice more through Hugh Bolton and a Young header even though 'the light went very bad long before the finish'.

For the visitors, the sunset and the final whistle must have come as blessed reliefs.

* * *

16 November 1996: Everton 7 Southampton 1 (Gary Speed hat-trick as Blues start gearing up for title 'dark horses' tag)

Following this result, many started to consider Joe Royle's side as dark horses in the Premier League title race but following a day of confusion the following spring the stable door was left open, and the boss had – willingly or not – bolted.

Everton would end the season much closer to the relegation zone than to eventual champions Manchester United, but that spectacular unravelling seemed a long way off back in November.

Even the 'Anfield Iron' Tommy Smith enjoyed the drubbing. Despite his arch Kopite status, Smith regularly attended matches at Goodison Park in retirement and even considered the Blues as his second team, insisting, 'I want to see them win too – unless they're playing against us.'

Remarking on the cries from the home fans of 'Souness, what's the score?' directed at the Southampton manager Graeme Souness who had briefly been his Reds team-mate, Smith admitted in the *Liverpool Echo*, 'I couldn't help it. I had to join in this victory chant!'

Royle had spectacularly revived Everton's fortunes since his return two years earlier. Taking over his former club when they were bottom of the table, he had successfully steered them clear of relegation danger and become the only manager to deliver a trophy in his first season, the 1995 FA Cup.

With the exciting recruitment of Andrei Kanchelskis, Royle followed that up with what proved to be the club's only top-half finish in the Premier League's first decade as Everton came sixth in 1995/96.

More firepower from midfield was added with lifelong Evertonian Gary Speed snapped up from Leeds United in the summer of 1996 and Nick Barmby arriving for a club record £5.75m from Middlesbrough in the autumn.

Both would get on the scoresheet for Royle here, but the main talking point surrounded a couple of other Blues number nines, one past and one present.

The game was Everton's first at Goodison since the death of Tommy Lawton, and David Prentice wrote in the *Echo*, 'Everton honoured their revered and recently departed centre-forward,

Tommy Lawton, in the most fitting manner possible. They reproduced a scoreline which went out of fashion with centre-parts and Brylcreem.

'But there was an irony in among the Blues' irresistible 7-1 slaughter of Southampton. They did it without a big number nine. Duncan Ferguson was the only dissatisfied Evertonian inside Goodison Park on Saturday. He's fit and available for Wednesday's big derby showdown, but there's no way Joe Royle can change a side which swept away the best Southampton sequence for a decade.'

Indeed, Big Dunc had to be content with a second-half substitute appearance in the 1-1 draw at Anfield.

Against the Saints, though, homegrown hero Tony Grant got much of the credit for pulling the strings in midfield.

Prentice wrote, 'His polish and elegance has marked him down as the midfielder Evertonians have craved since Ball, Harvey and Kendall,' before adding the more cautionary note, 'All too often Grant's flashes of brilliance have been followed by frustrating anonymity.'

Graham Stuart opened the scoring on 12 minutes, turning the ball in at the far post after a miss by Kanchelskis, but the Russian international, who Prentice quipped 'got better service than a first-class Concorde passenger', soon added a brace of his own.

On 22 minutes, Stuart fed Kanchelskis on the right and – as he did so many times in a manner of more latter-day 'inverted' wingers – he cut inside to fire into the net with a left-footed shot.

Speed's wand of a left foot brought the third on the half-hour from the edge of the area and he netted again with a diving header just two minutes later while Kanchelskis nodded in the fifth from Andy Hinchcliffe's left-wing cross on 35 minutes.

Despite Egil Østenstad's low drive providing a 39th-minute consolation for the Saints, with the points already seemingly in the bag, Royle made the unusual move at the break to substitute goalkeeper Neville Southall and bring on summer signing Paul Gerrard for his debut.

Barmby netted his first goal for the club on 57 minutes, sliding in at the back post to meet a low right-wing cross from Kanchelskis, while Speed sealed the rout and his hat-trick with a towering header from an inswinging Hinchcliffe corner kick on 72 minutes.

Prentice concluded, 'It was a day when everything went right. Even Speed's cherished match ball was returned – after David Unsworth had booted it clean out of the ground in the 88th minute.'

* * *

31 August 1982: Everton 5 Aston Villa 0 (European Cup winners battered)

Aston Villa's previous game away from Villa Park before this fixture came against Bayern Munich when they were crowned champions of Europe, but 98 days later they were blown away at Goodison Park.

This was an era when First Division sides would regularly conquer the continent and Villa's 1-0 victory over a club that had lifted the trophy in three consecutive seasons in the previous decade was a sixth straight success for English clubs.

It came at the Stadion Feijenoord in Rotterdam where three years later Everton would secure the Cup Winners' Cup but at this stage, little more than a year after Howard Kendall had been appointed manager for the first time, they remained very much a side in transition.

Just about to turn 35 when he returned to the Blues, initially as player-manager – he'd pick himself six times in 1981/82 before hanging up his boots – Kendall, who had originally departed for Birmingham City along with Archie Styles in February 1974 in a deal to bring Bob Latchford to Goodison, had quickly set about reshaping his squad.

Before that first campaign kicked off, Kendall, appointed after an impressive stint at Blackburn Rovers where he'd almost secured back-to-back promotions to the top flight, brought in his 'magnificent seven' new signings but from the group, only Neville Southall was to have a significant long-term impact.

A combination of more acquisitions in the transfer market, including youngsters like Adrian Heath plus old boys returning such as Andy King and David Johnson, were combined with in-house prospects being promoted to the first team to give Everton a very different look.

One of the powerhouses of the pioneering age of professional football under their great patriarch William McGregor, who is regarded as the founder of the Football League, Villa had won six of their seven titles and six of their seven FA Cups by 1920 but emerged from decades of relative mediocrity to clinch their first league championship for 71 years in 1980/81.

They were steered to this success by Birkenhead-born former Everton centre-forward Ron Saunders who had played just three games for the Blues at the start of his career.

Although he would sensationally quit in February 1982 over a contract dispute, defecting to neighbours Birmingham City at a time when his side were in the quarter-finals of the European Cup, his assistant Tony Barton would take over and guide them to the trophy.

Villa's triumphant squad also contained a strong core of players from Liverpool and its environs with captain Dennis Mortimer and Peter Withe – who netted the only goal of the game in the final – both Scousers, right-back Kenny Swain from Birkenhead, Ormskirk-born winger Tony Morley, and Southport native goalkeeper Jimmy Rimmer.

None of them were made to feel at home at Goodison Park though as Everton produced what the *Liverpool Echo* headlined as a 'Super five-star show'.

Adrian Heath, a record £750,000 signing from Stoke City the previous January, put the Blues in command early on by netting the first two goals on seven and 34 minutes.

Ian Hargraves of the *Echo* said that it was 'a vivid demonstration of his golden qualities', adding, 'Since his arrival there have been reservations in one or two quarters about his value. But the way he tore the European champions' defence to pieces left no doubt that here is a genuine international star in the making. Heath's quickness, ball control and marksmanship, were of the very highest class.'

Curiously, 'Inchy' never would be awarded a full cap despite Derek Hatton's memorable backing of his cause on BBC's *Question Time*.

Fan favourite King reacquainted himself with the Goodison crowd with his first goal back on 41 minutes while young Scottish striker Graeme Sharp, who had enjoyed a breakthrough season when finishing top scorer in 1981/82, got himself off the mark for the new campaign by sealing the rout with a late brace, netting on 87 minutes before converting an 89th-minute penalty.

Hargraves concluded, 'It is a long time since I saw an Everton team show so much individual promise or receive such a rapturous reception.'

It took a while for Kendall to get the blend right before the fruits of his labour were to arrive with the club's most successful period – including a chastening 5-0 home reversal to Liverpool just over two months later – but this opening home game of 1982/83 was one of the nights that everything clicked.

* * *

15 January 2017: Everton 4 Manchester City 0 (Pep Guardiola's side blown away by former Barcelona team-mate Ronald Koeman's men)

While Dutch master Ronald Koeman was unable to inspire a Golden Age at Goodison, this game stands out as by far his most aesthetically pleasing piece of work over what proved to be a brief Everton tenure.

It will also have been a result that produced great personal satisfaction for Koeman as it came against his former Barcelona team-mate Pep Guardiola.

As players, the Netherlands international – the most prolific-scoring defender in elite football thanks to his superb long-range shooting, particularly from free kicks – was the greater talent, but as coaches, Guardiola, who subsequently steered City to a Champions League, Premier League and FA Cup treble in 2023, has enjoyed far more success.

Brought in as Farhad Moshiri's first managerial appointment, Koeman was the box-office name the new owner wanted to compete with the other stars on the touchline in the north-west – Guardiola, Liverpool's Jürgen Klopp and Manchester United's José Mourinho – a region the Iranian-born businessman had dubbed the 'Hollywood of Football'.

But other than when Koeman turned out for Barça and there was nowhere bigger to go, he has always been something of a nomad.

He is the only man to both play for and coach all of the 'big three' clubs in his homeland – Ajax, PSV Eindhoven and Feyenoord – and there were always lingering doubts about his commitment to the Blues with what seemed like a cool, businesslike approach from the start.

His unveiling as Everton manager was done from his villa in Portugal rather than cutting short a holiday, and during his time in charge he set up home an hour's drive from Merseyside, tucked away in the affluent Cheshire village of Alderley Edge, where many of the fellow millionaire locals would be less concerned about the red decorations on his Christmas tree than some of the incensed Goodison patrons. Looking beyond the mini festive furore over the hue of his baubles, Koeman's methods were starting to take shape by the turn of the calendar year.

Everton's players lift the club's ninth and last league championship at Goodison Park on 9 May 1987

Andy Gray celebrates with Graeme Sharp after scoring for Everton against Bayern Munich on 24 April 1985

Andrew Johnson reminds fans of the score after he sealed Everton's 3-0 win over Liverpool on 9 September 2006

King George V becomes the first reigning monarch to visit an English football ground at Goodison Park on 11 July 1913

Bob Latchford is mobbed by Everton fans after reaching 30 goals by netting a hat-trick against Chelsea on 29 April 1978

The Gwladys Street goes wild following Duncan Ferguson's winner for Everton against Manchester United on 25 February 1995

Headed by Dixie Dean, the team that won the Second Division, First Division and FA Cup in consecutive seasons at Goodison in 1933

A spectator and policeman wade in as tempers flare between Everton and Leeds United on 7 November 1964

Wayne Rooney celebrates with Kevin Campbell after scoring his first Premier League goal on 19 October 2002

The old Main Stand and a floodlight pylon in view as Dave Hickson fires in a shot against Leeds United on 20 September 1958

Roger Hunt and Ray Wilson carry the World Cup followed by team-mates with the league championship trophy and FA Cup ahead of the Charity Shield game on 13 August 1966

Hollywood star Sylvester Stallone on the Goodison Park pitch ahead of Everton v Reading on 14 January 2007

Eusébio scores his first of four goals for Portugal against North Korea in the World Cup quarter-final on 23 July 1966

An injured Pelé walks off the Goodison pitch following Brazil's World Cup exit with a 3-1 loss to Portugal on 19 July 1966

The Littlewoods Stores clock in front of St Luke the Evangelist Church in the corner of the Main Stand and Gwladys Street End

Graham Stuart is mobbed by Everton team-mates and fans after netting the winner against Wimbledon on 7 May 1994

The new Main Stand rises next to the partially demolished old one as Everton play Crystal Palace on 16 August 1969

'The Toffee Lady' giving out Everton mints to fans, shown here before a game against Sheffield United on 7 January 1961, is a Goodison Park pre-match tradition

Andy Rankin saves Ludwig Müller's shot to give Everton victory over Borussia Monchengladbach in European football's first penalty shoot-out

Jarrad Branthwaite celebrates with Dominic Calvert-Lewin after putting Everton ahead against Liverpool on 24 April 2024

There had already been setbacks with early exits from both domestic cup competitions and a last-gasp Goodison defeat to Liverpool the previous month, but progress was being made and Romelu Lukaku's regular supply of goals was helping keep the side afloat.

Indeed, Lukaku had put Everton ahead against Guardiola's side when they'd met at the Etihad Stadium in October, a game that saw Koeman's fellow Dutchman Maarten Stekelenburg save penalties from Kevin De Bruyne and Sergio Agüero before Nolito earned the hosts a point.

The return match at Goodison was to be a much more one-sided encounter; deploying a 3-5-2 formation, Koeman outthought Guardiola while his Everton players outfought Manchester City on the pitch.

Phil Kirkbride of the *Liverpool Echo* wrote, 'The significance of this victory was not in breaking that long wait to stick four past City, as exhilarating as it felt, but in what it represented for the Blues boss.

'The real meaning was that it left you with the unmistakable belief that this could be the start of something exciting; because when it works like this, as Koeman plans meticulously during the week, then Everton are a match for anybody.

'Don't allow your praise for the Blues be put against a context of Man City's misery and the growing pains of the world's finest manager adapting to English football because this was fully deserved, worked for and earned.

'Never before, under Koeman, have Everton played as close to his instruction as this.'

Lukaku set them on their way on 34 minutes with a left-footed finish from 12 yards after a neat interchange of passes from homegrown heroes Tom Davies and Ross Barkley.

Davies headed a Bacary Sagna header off the line before the break but after the interval the Blues took charge with Kevin

Mirallas doubling their lead on 47 minutes through a low right-footed drive from another Barkley assist.

Man of the match Davies produced a sublime third goal to open his account for the club with the 18-year-old marauding upfield, playing a one-two with Barkley, before dispatching what Kirkbride described as a 'deft, exquisite, cheeky and wholly confident chip' over Claudio Bravo with 11 minutes remaining.

There was enough time left for another teenager to get in on the act as Ademola Lookman, signed from Charlton Athletic earlier that month, came on for his debut on 90 minutes and smashed home a fourth goal in stoppage time after Séamus Coleman had shown greater desire to get to the ball than former Blues player John Stones.

As Kirkbride concluded, 'This, by some distance, was Everton's biggest scalp of the season. It was Koeman's best day as manager.'

* * *

27 August 1988: Everton 4 Newcastle United 0 (Hat-trick hero Tony Cottee's flying start)

With a first goal after 34 seconds and a debut hat-trick, Tony Cottee looked like being an instant hit at Everton but ultimately his time at the club would coincide with their downturn in fortunes.

It's a position they've only reached once again in the subsequent years but after finishing a 'mere' fourth in his first season in charge, Blues boss Colin Harvey embarked on an expensive squad rebuilding programme as he attempted to put his own stamp on the title-winning side he had inherited.

While his former – and future – gaffer and midfield partner Howard Kendall enjoyed a Goodison Park 'marriage' having been brought to the club as a 20-year-old from Preston North End, Harvey had been a lifelong Evertonian.

His selflessness and devotion to the cause in immediately reverting to his previous role as assistant upon Kendall's return as boss in 1990 is testament to that.

Much of Everton's success in the mid-1980s is attributed to Harvey's coaching methods, and the hard-pressing football he implemented a generation before such an approach gained widespread recognition.

When Kendall left for Athletic Club Bilbao in 1987, Harvey, still only 42 himself but with a wealth of experience at the club, seemed the natural choice to succeed him.

Despite conceding just 27 goals in 1987/88 – the lowest seasonal total in the club's history – the Blues suffered a 29-point year-on-year swing against neighbours Liverpool who had finished nine points behind them as runners-up in 1987 but 20 points above them this time around.

After keeping his powder dry in the transfer market on initially taking the reins, Harvey's personnel would now undergo significant change.

Paul Power retired while Gary Stevens, Derek Mountfield, Alan Harper, Ian Wilson and then Adrian Heath, in the autumn, all departed.

In their place came Neil McDonald, Stuart McCall, Pat Nevin and, for a British domestic transfer record, West Ham United striker Tony Cottee.

On this viewing at least, the substantial price tag for the diminutive Cockney marksman looked like a sound investment.

Writing in the *Liverpool Echo*, Ken Rogers enthused, 'Tony Cottee began to repay his £2.2m fee with a dream debut hat-trick as Everton swept aside Newcastle United at Goodison Park.

'To describe Cottee's input as remarkable would be an understatement. He struck after 34 seconds, pouncing after tremendous work by Neil McDonald and Graeme Sharp.

'Former Newcastle right-back McDonald was booed by the Geordie fans when he launched the ball forward following his first touch from Neil Pointon.

'Sharp cracked in a low shot that Dave Beasant was unable to hold and looked for the rebound but Cottee, his new attacking partner, beat him to it to score from six yards and bring the house down.'

The former Hammer brought a new dimension to Everton's attack and doubled their advantage just after the half-hour mark.

Rogers said, 'Colin Harvey got striker Cottee for his explosive pace, and he used it after 31 minutes to secure his second goal.

'Stepping up a gear to leave his marker for dead, Cottee sent a low angled shot which found the net just inside the right-hand post.'

Cottee was 'revelling in the action' and his debut hat-trick was completed on 62 minutes, 'Nevin played the ball into the box and Cottee was on it like a flash, moving wide of Beasant before slotting home an angled shot that brought rapturous applause from the delighted supporters at the Gwladys Street end.'

With his strike partner having secured the match ball, Sharp got in on the scoring act to complete the rout with seven minutes remaining by 'sending a header into the gaping net with Newcastle down and out'.

Despite Cottee's dream start, his First Division tally for that season totalled 13 goals in 36 games – a solid but unspectacular strike rate of slightly better than one in three.

Arriving the year after they won the league championship and departing at the start of the campaign in which they'd lift the FA Cup, in six full trophyless seasons at Everton he would finish the club's top scorer on five occasions but suffered the ignominy of facing his own window cleaner at Morecambe when made to turn out for the Blues' 'A' team (third XI) after falling out with Kendall.

Cottee was stuck on 99 goals for Everton when Mike Walker sent him back to West Ham in September 1994 in what seemed like a feckless part-exchange deal to bring former Liverpool left-back David Burrows to Goodison with the Blues somehow also parting with additional cash.

* * *

24 November 2007: Everton 7 Sunderland 1 (Blues hit a magnificent seven against Roy Keane's side)

Roy Keane has got plenty of anger to dish out in various directions but a lot of his ire over the years has been directed towards Everton which makes you wonder whether memories of this day still haunt him.

With his 'death stare' and withering put-downs, Cork man Keane has earned a reputation as being one of the game's hardest-hitting pundits, but ultimately he's had to carve out a career in the television studio because his managerial career did not hit the dizzying heights of his playing days, although he was no shrinking violet back then either.

Keane, who later clashed with Everton on several occasions while part of the Republic of Ireland national team coaching setup, accusing their players of needing to 'toughen up', later conceded that the 7-1 defeat he suffered at Goodison Park was 'one of the lowest points' of his career, and in many ways it marked the beginning of the end of his time in charge of the Wearside club.

In contrast, the sparkling display represented the culmination of several years' hard work for another fiery Celt in the opposition dugout capable of immobilising you with an icy glare: the long-serving David Moyes.

Having been in charge for over five years by this point, Everton produced some of their most exciting displays under Moyes during the 2007/08 season and this was one of 14 wins in 18 matches between 26 September and 20 December as the side won their UEFA Cup group and advanced to the semi-finals of the League Cup as well as recording notable Premier League victories such as this.

Nine of the starting 11 were Moyes signings, including the club's first eight-figure purchase, Ayegbeni Yakubu, who had joined for £11.25m from Middlesbrough in August.

A proven scorer, the Nigerian international striker became the first Everton player to break the 20-goal barrier in all competitions during the Premier League era by netting 21 times in 2007/08.

Dominic King of the *Liverpool Echo* wrote, 'If Everton keep playing in this way, a wider audience will soon start to see that slowly but surely the seeds Moyes has planted are bearing fruit. Had Arsenal achieved a similar result, pundits would be talking about the display for months.

'If you tried to analyse every magnificent individual performance at the weekend, we would run out of space on this page. Better, then, to detail the bare facts of Everton's magnificent seven.

'Goal one (11 minutes): Tim Howard launched a clearance forward and an afternoon of woe for Paul McShane began as he made a hash of dealing with it. Yakubu reacted instantly, driving a right-footed shot past Craig Gordon via a deflection off Danny Higginbotham.

'Goal two (17): Pick of the bunch. Steven Pienaar picked out Phil Neville, who in turn found Yakubu. His first-time ball sent Mikel Arteta racing clear. He laid a pass on to Neville, whose neat cross found Cahill. The Australian did the rest with a cool right-footed finish.

'Goal three (42): Lee Carsley won possession from Carlos Edwards and fed Nuno Valente, who bombed down the left. An interchange with Steven Pienaar allowed Valente to cross and Pienaar finished the move with a crisp drive past Gordon.

'Goal four (62): A Sunderland attack broke down and Howard rolled the ball out to Joseph Yobo. With plenty of time to look around, he launched an inch-perfect 60-yard pass to Cahill. Brilliant control gave him a shooting opportunity and he made no mistake.

'Goal five (73): With the visitors' defence in utter disarray, they failed to clear a corner from Neville. Arteta laid a chance for Leon Osman to shoot but a deflection carried it into the path of Yakubu. He needed no second invitation to continue the massacre.

'Goal six (79): Was it an aimless clearance or an inspired pass? Either way, Neville's ball forward gave Andrew Johnson the chance to join the fun. He sprinted away from McShane and pushed a smart finish past the crestfallen Gordon.

'Goal seven (85): The coup de grâce. Phil Jagielka rolled a pass to Osman, who had the freedom of Goodison Park to run forward. A nonchalant drop of the shoulder carried him past Higginbotham and McShane and his left-footed drive completed the rout.'

Sunderland's consolation came from Dwight Yorke with a shot from 12 yards out in first-half stoppage time but as Moyes himself proclaimed, 'That was probably the best performance in my time here.'

* * *

26 December 1999: Everton 5 Sunderland 0 (The Blues play their final home game of the millennium and first after Bill Kenwright had taken control)

Perhaps it was poignant that Peter Johnson, the businessman who had made his fortune flogging Christmas hampers, sealed a deal to sell Everton over the festive period, but many Blues fans certainly saw his departure as a welcome present.

Johnson had dreamed big for the club but ultimately failed to deliver and after resigning as chairman the previous year having been accused of selling Duncan Ferguson behind manager Walter Smith's back, his 'getaway car' was accosted by a group of disgruntled supporters.

The Birkenhead-based son of a butcher, Johnson had connections with all three of Merseyside's professional clubs.

A boyhood Liverpool fan, he had shares at Anfield but also spells as Tranmere Rovers chairman either side of his tumultuous tenure at the Goodison Park helm.

In the space of four years controlling Everton they won the 1995 FA Cup, but also had to survive two final-day relegation battles.

The Blues broke their transfer record four times over the period but big stars such as Ferguson and Andrei Kanchelskis were both sold for considerable profits.

Johnson tried to deliver a new stadium in the shape of a 60,000-capacity bowl which fans backed but the potential location was never revealed with far-flung destinations beyond the city boundaries rumoured such as Kirkby Golf Club and even the village of Cronton, which is closer to Widnes than Liverpool.

Merchandising increased with the building of the club's 'Megastore' but there were unpopular experiments with the matchday experience.

It seems sacrilege but Everton's iconic run-out theme from the *Z-Cars* TV show was temporarily dropped for the themes from *2001: A Space Odyssey* and then *Bad Moon Rising* while a bizarre half-man half-toffee mascot named Dixie after the club's most prolific player was also deemed unwelcome in the eyes of many.

While he'd overseen the most successful period in Tranmere's history before going 'across the water', Johnson made such a fudge of his stewardship of Everton that, when the Blues looked on the brink of the drop for the second time in four years in 1998, a banner was unfurled at Anfield ahead of Liverpool's last home game of the season reading 'Agent Johnson: Mission Accomplished'.

If Johnson was always going to struggle to convince Evertonians that he truly understood their needs, the same could not be said for the man who ended up buying the club from him.

Actor turned theatre impresario Bill Kenwright spoke to the *Liverpool Echo* after obtaining an irrevocable undertaking to purchase Johnson's 68 per cent majority shareholding, saying, 'My tummy went to pieces on Christmas Day. I didn't get up. Somebody said to me, "Is this your dream?" Well, my dream used to be to afford to be able to go to somewhere better in the ground than the boys' pen. Then it was to get a season ticket. So, it's much more than a dream.'

The fixture against Everton legend Peter Reid's Sunderland was the last game of the second millennium at Goodison Park but rather than being apprehensive about the Y2K bug, the Blues went into the fixture looking forward to a brand-new dawn and their players responded by giving them something to shout about.

The visitors came into the game in third place, but David Prentice of the *Echo* remarked they were 'annihilated by a wonderful Everton performance'.

Don Hutchison opened the scoring on 16 minutes as he 'sweetly clipped Mark Pembridge's miskick past Thomas Sorensen from the edge of the area'.

Prentice observed, 'With a sense of theatre worthy of the finest hams, Kenwright had just taken his Main Stand seat seconds earlier. He was up and down out of it for the rest of the afternoon.'

Hutchison netted again ten minutes later 'with a stunningly struck 20-yard volley' while Francis Jeffers added a third four minutes before half-time when the 37-year-old Richard Gough 'waltzed upfield like a continental sweeper, carrying the ball deep into Sunderland territory before slipping a wonderful pass into Jeffers's path with the teenager's finish clinical'.

On 61 minutes, Jeffers slid the ball across to provide Pembridge with a tap-in for his first goal for the club while the far more prolific Kevin Campbell finished proceedings on 72 minutes as he 'wheeled before clipping the ball into the Gwladys Street net'.

As Prentice concluded, 'Bill Kenwright has enjoyed many ecstatic afternoons during his lifelong allegiance to Everton, but few will have compared to this one.'

Kenwright, still holding his position of chairman, and then Johnson, would both die during the 2023/24 season just 80 days apart, at a time when the club was in the midst of another takeover bid as Farhad Moshiri failed in his attempt to sell his majority shareholding to the controversial Miami-based private investment firm, 777 Partners.

Decisive defeats

YOU CAN'T win them all in football and while we'd all like to gloss over defeats, some losses are too significant to be omitted from the story of Goodison Park, so they are included here, but *not* Liverpool's 5-0 win in 1982. That would just be masochistic!

* * *

9 August 2005: Everton 1 Villarreal 2 (European Cup football returns to Goodison some 20 years too late)

Pierluigi Collina.

Nothing more needs to be said when it comes to Evertonians.

Like Clive Thomas with an older generation of Blues, the Italian official holds a special place in their hall of shame.

For most football fans across the globe, the distinctive bald head of Collina contained one of the game's greatest refereeing brains.

However, after hanging up his whistle in 2005, he was brought back out of retirement to be the man in the middle for Everton's Champions League third qualifying round second leg in Villarreal.

A headed goal by Duncan Ferguson that would have put the visitors 2-1 up on the night and sent the tie into extra time was inexplicably ruled out for a non-existent push by Marcus Bent.

Blues players were understandably bemused by and livid about Collina's seemingly arbitrary decision but replays just showed the referee, whose performance was described as 'arrogant' by Kevin Kilbane, pointing towards his ear and smiling when Ferguson questioned him.

The following year, after having time to reflect on his controversial call, Collina claimed, 'At that time, I was looking at those players – Bent and his Spanish opponent – and I've seen something that probably television didn't show.'

Catching the Blues on the break, Villarreal would later go down the other end and score again to triumph 2-1 on the night and 4-2 on aggregate but the final scoreline was desperately cruel on Everton who had waited for 35 years to return to European football's premier club competition.

As champions in 1985 and 1987, they had of course been denied their place at the top table because of the post-Heysel ban on English clubs.

A banner carried by one of the huge numbers of Evertonians who travelled to Castellon for the second leg simply read 'Sorry we're 20 years late. Had trouble with the neighbours'.

After miraculously holding out to finish fourth in 2004/05 – 12 months after finishing 17th on 39 points – to secure their highest ever Premier League position, Everton's place in the following term's Champions League was put into doubt by fifth-placed Liverpool winning the competition.

A similar situation in 2000 saw the Royal Spanish Football Association bump fourth-placed Real Zaragoza into the UEFA Cup with that year's European champions Real Madrid, who'd finished fifth domestically, returning to the following season's Champions League.

Given that this was Everton and Liverpool though, and how the Blues had been denied in the past by the transgressions of their local rivals' fans, the FA were in no mood to repeat the trick and it was left to UEFA to give the Reds special dispensation to defend their title, entering at the first qualifying round stage.

But while Rafael Benítez's side were paired with Welsh minnows TNS, Lithuania's FBK Kaunas and Bulgaria's CSKA Sofia en route to the group stages, David Moyes's men fell at the first hurdle against the competition's eventual semi-finalists with his assistant Alan Irvine later revealing that Mikel Arteta had immediately walked out of the club's dining area in disgust when the draw was made.

Understandably, there was a huge release of emotion when Everton did take to the field for the first leg at Goodison Park.

In the *Liverpool Echo*, Nick Coligan wrote, 'Twenty years of frustration were exorcised to the sound of an ear-splitting roar.'

Reflecting on the match itself, his colleague Dominic King added, 'Villarreal may pass the ball at a bewitching pace and boast more recent European experience than Everton. They are not, however, unbeatable. They possess a number of match-winners in their ranks and Everton must learn lessons from both goals they conceded.

'Luciano Figueroa, once of Birmingham City, took his opening goal magnificently in the 27th minute. But Everton were effectively undone by a long, straight ball down the middle that could and should have been dealt with quicker.

'Again, the finish from Josico [45th minute] for the second – a 16-yard diving header – took the breath away and capped a wonderful move fashioned by Juan Riquelme.

'Having just equalised via James Beattie [42] who stabbed home from close range, however, Everton should have been running the clock down in first half injury time.

'It could not have come at a worse time and effectively knocked the wind out of the Blues' sails for the second period. With one cruel sucker punch, a raucous crowd had been flattened.'

Given how galling Collina's decision felt, the one saving grace for the spirited Blues was that, although that Ferguson goal would have left the 'Yellow Submarine' facing some perilously choppy waters, in truth their opponents showed more quality than themselves over the two games.

* * *

3 February 1973: Everton 0 Millwall 2 (End in sight for Harry Catterick with FA Cup humbling)

Seeming to lack the natural charisma of some of the other managerial giants who were his peers, Everton's Harry Catterick asked only to be judged on results so when they started to falter, major setbacks like this would signal the beginning of the end of his long Goodison Park reign.

Succeeding Johnny Carey, the Blues boss sacked in the back of a taxi, and working for the hugely demanding John Moores who would provide him with the kind of funds to break the British transfer record twice and see the club labelled the 'Mersey Millionaires', Catterick knew from the start of the great expectation levels that came with his job.

He'd been an Everton player himself, albeit one who lost a large chunk of his career to the second world war, but after learning the managerial ropes the hard way at Crewe Alexandra and Rochdale before guiding Sheffield Wednesday into the top flight, Catterick would accumulate a higher First Division points total throughout the 1960s than anyone else, including Bill Shankly, Matt Busby, Don Revie, Bill Nicholson and Joe Mercer.

It seems only natural though that with his dislike for publicity – few Everton games were filmed during his reign because Catterick feared it might provide tactical insight to opponents, while one of his biggest managerial assets were his cloak-and-dagger transfer swoops – that he would often be viewed as the antithesis of his extrovert local rival Shankly.

The two men were actually very close and in a surprisingly candid interview after the Scot's death, Catterick admitted, 'I shall miss him. We had many long chats. He was very, very dear to many people on Merseyside. I've never known a character as loved as he was.'

Ruling with a rod of iron across Stanley Park, Catterick commanded great respect rather than affection from players and supporters alike.

Alan Ball, the player Catterick would both buy and then sell for record fees, described him as a 'fearful dictator' but also remarked, 'He did not have the same bubbling personality as Shankly, but he cared just as much about his club and his team.'

Catterick was never afraid to make bold, and sometimes unpopular calls with players.

Mike Trebilcock, a man who totalled just 15 appearances for Everton, rewarded him with two goals against Sheffield Wednesday in the 1966 FA Cup Final when chosen ahead of Fred Pickering at Wembley with fitness doubts over the big-money buy.

The Blues came back from 2-0 down to triumph 3-2 in what Catterick described as 'the thrill of my footballing life'.

Earlier that season he'd been roughed up by his own club's supporters after a 2-0 loss at Blackpool in which he'd dropped fan favourite Alex Young for 16-year-old Joe Royle, while his decision to axe the 'Golden Vision' towards the end of the 1963/64 season also produced the iconic image of the pitch invader being removed from the Goodison turf carrying the misspelt placard 'SACK CATTRICK (sic) KEEP YOUNG' while being escorted away by a policeman.

After over a decade in the hot seat, though, that judgement started to waver.

Ball was sold and new signings proved inadequate. Catterick's health started to fail too, and he suffered a heart attack on 5 January 1972 (he'd die at Goodison after another one 13 years later aged 65).

The writing appeared to be on the wall after this loss, and in the *Liverpool Echo*, Michael Charters wrote, 'Everton's season was shattered beyond recall as they went out of the FA Cup to Second Division Millwall in one of the major upsets of the day.

'Indeed, it was one of the biggest shocks in the history of the club and their overall performance was so poor that I wonder when and where the reconstruction of the team can develop from here.

'I think the repercussions from this cup disaster will be considerable. Chairman John Moores will demand action after three seasons of lack of success.

'The pressures to recreate a side which can restore the glory of Everton will be stepped up.'

When it came to the game itself, Charters mused, 'It was one of those cup ties when physique won the day. Millwall had it, Everton hadn't.

'Millwall scored both goals in isolated raids', with Harry Cripps heading in 'unchallenged' on the hour and another header from Alf Wood two minutes from the end sealing the victory.

Charters admitted, '[Everton] now have to pick themselves up off the floor. The task will be hard and long.'

From 11 April the task would not be Catterick's as he was moved upstairs into an executive role.

* * *

25 August 1990: Everton 2 Leeds United 3 (Neville Southall's half-time sit-down)

Neville Southall won more trophies than any other player with Everton and he played more matches for the club than anyone else, yet decades on from his long and illustrious career with the Blues, the maverick Welsh goalkeeper chooses to use an image of himself from this day as his profile picture on social media.

And why not?

For all those glory days that 'Big Nev' enjoyed with Everton across a record-breaking 751-game spell – 217 more than closest challenger Brian Labone – the photograph of him sat down, deep in thought on the Goodison Park pitch and waiting for the second half to start, would become the defining image of him while wearing the club's colours.

In years to come, Goodison Park goalposts would become the physical platforms for other protesters to hold up Everton games by attaching themselves to them.

Such disruptions in fixtures against Manchester City on 31 January 2012 and Newcastle United 17 March 2022 did not prevent the Blues from securing a couple of important 1-0 victories.

However, Southall, as ever, would be the pioneer in this field, although he insists it wasn't a 'protest' and rather than halting proceedings, he had emerged back from the dressing room ahead of time to do his job.

Evertonians were used to seeing their superstar custodian early – but not like this.

The man from Llandudno who had risen from non-league football, working as a hod carrier, waiter and most famously a binman, was one of the hardest, most diligent trainers in the business and would routinely emerge early from the dressing room long before any of his other team-mates and fling himself around his six-yard box as part of a lengthy and gruelling warm-up regime.

In the 1984/85 season, Everton's most successful, Southall became the fourth, and 40 years on the most recent, goalkeeper to be voted Football Writers' Association Footballer of the Year after Bert Trautmann (1955/56); Gordon Banks (1971/72) and Pat Jennings (1972/73), but while many thought he had reached his personal zenith in terms of performances by around 1990, the team around him had declined.

Southall had put in three rejected transfer requests that year before the 1990/91 season kicked off at home to newly promoted Leeds United and having penned a marathon seven-and-a-half-year contract as recently as December 1988, Goodison Park chiefs valued their prize asset at £3m at a time when Nigel Martyn was the British record signing for a goalkeeper at £1.2m.

With question marks over Southall's future, Everton had even had Egypt World Cup keeper Ahmed Shobair at Bellefield on trial over the summer, but one of the conditions of him being granted a work permit was that the authorities had to be convinced he would come as the first choice and as Ric George wrote in the *Liverpool Echo*, 'Obviously with Southall, the world's best in his position, in Colin Harvey's squad, senior football for the African cannot be guaranteed.'

The game itself saw centre-back Chris Fairclough put the Yorkshire side in front after just eight minutes with a close-range header when the hosts failed to deal with David Batty's long throw-in, and with Everton right-back Neil McDonald firing a penalty wide on 25 minutes, the visitors doubled their advantage through Gary Speed who poked the ball in on 34 minutes after Southall collided with team-mate Martin Keown.

When the number one came out early for the second half and took his spot against the post, television commentator Clive Tyldesley remarked, 'Neville Southall, out of the Everton dressing room, well ahead of his colleagues. Whatever is being said in there, he doesn't feel relates to him.'

Former Everton player Imre Varadi increased Leeds' advantage further 11 minutes after the restart with a close-range tap-in after more calamitous defending by the home side, and although they rallied late on as Pat Nevin poked in substitute Kevin Sheedy's low left-wing cross on 68 minutes before John Ebbrell grabbed his first for the club with a left-footed drive nine minutes later, it was too little, too late.

Southall was fined a week's wages, an estimated £4,000, and reflecting what went on in his autobiography *The Binman Chronicles*, he said, 'At half-time I needed to get out of the dressing room and get my head together, so I left and went and sat down in the goalmouth. People went on about it and said it was a protest, but it wasn't at all.

'At worst it was badly timed, coming around the same time as my transfer request. I certainly wasn't protesting against Colin, who didn't even know about it until that evening.'

Southall would remain at Everton over seven years longer and in 1995 became the only player to win the FA Cup twice with the club.

* * *

27 January 2001: Everton 0 Tranmere Rovers 3 (Humiliation in the 'other' Merseyside derby)

In terms of utter embarrassment, this was arguably Everton's worst-ever day at Goodison Park as Merseyside's third club dismantled them in their own back yard.

The Blues had suffered derby day humiliations at home to Liverpool – notably the 5-0 thrashing in 1982 – but as painful as these defeats were for Evertonians, this was an era in which the Reds dominated not just English but European football.

There had also been other humblings in domestic cup competitions. Over the previous decade, the following lower-division sides had all beaten Everton: (Portsmouth, League Cup 1994/95); Millwall (League Cup 1995/96); Port Vale (FA Cup 1995/96); York City (League Cup 1996/97); Bradford City (FA Cup 1996/97); Sunderland (League Cup 1998/99); Oxford United (League Cup 1999/2000); Bristol Rovers (League Cup 2000/01).

The trail of tears wouldn't end there. While David Moyes stopped the rot in terms of steering the Blues back into the top half of the Premier League, he would oversee the 2-1 FA Cup third round loss at Conference-bound Shrewsbury Town two years later – the first time the club had lost to a side from the fourth tier – but given the geographical proximity of Tranmere, this surely felt like the deepest cut.

Under the controversial future Everton chairman Peter Johnson and with the charismatic former Blues wing-half Johnny King as manager, Rovers came close to joining their two more illustrious neighbours in the top flight for the first time in their early 1990s heyday.

King, always great for a colourful turn of phrase, proclaimed on his arrival at Prenton Park, 'I can't promise anyone success, but I can promise them a trip to the moon.'

On his club's position in the Mersey football hierarchy, King – who loved maritime metaphors – remarked, 'We will never be able to compete with Liverpool and Everton. They're big liners like the *Queen Mary*, but I see Tranmere like a deadly submarine.'

By the time they came to Goodison that day, Rovers – who had lost all three of their previous encounters with the Blues without scoring – were on a relegation depth charge that would see them drop out of the second tier that season, a level they have yet to return to.

However, now managed by their former striker John Aldridge, a lifelong Red and ex-Liverpool player, they had enough firepower to torpedo Walter Smith's side out of the FA Cup.

Indeed, the giant-killing had some fans calling for the Scot's head, but Tranmere's Paul Rideout, the man whose goal secured the FA Cup for Everton in 1995, said, 'About 60 per cent of the side let it go. They let themselves down and let the fans down. I couldn't believe how easy it was.'

The *Liverpool Echo*'s David Prentice also reckoned the fault lay with the players and wrote, 'Rideout's sympathies may lie at Prenton Park now, but he still retains a warm affection for all things Everton, and he seemed more genuinely hurt and distressed by the result than some of the current Blues he was criticising. That was the most alarming aspect of the entire occasion.

'Tranmere thoroughly deserved both their victory and the three-goal winning margin. But too many Everton players didn't seem to care.

'Goodison fans only want to see players who will tackle with relish and close down space exuberantly like the side in white did. They want passion, an enthusiasm to chase the ball; a desire to prove their superiority over more lowly placed local rivals. That was shamefully missing.'

Defender Steve Yates – Tranmere fans still annually celebrate 27 January as 'Saint Yates Day' – broke the deadlock on 22 minutes.

Prentice said, 'Andy Parkinson shouldn't have been allowed to backheel to Sean Flynn. He should have been denied the opportunity to cross, and Yates shouldn't have connected at the far post with a header. All did, however, and the ball looped decisively over the bemused Thomas Myhre's head. Everton fell apart.'

Rovers doubled their lead 13 minutes later as 'Koumas clipped another looping volley over Myhre's head', while on 62 minutes 'Yates headed the third to round it off'.

Having earned a goalless draw at Premier League Southampton in the next round, Tranmere came back from a 3-0 half-time deficit to triumph 4-3 in a Prenton Park replay thanks to a Rideout hat-trick and a winner from another former Blue, Stuart Barlow, before bowing out 4-2 at home to Liverpool in the fifth round.

Another 3-0 FA Cup defeat – this time in the quarter-finals at Middlesbrough in front of a live BBC One audience – would signal the end of Walter Smith's Everton tenure the following season.

* * *

19 April 1975: Everton 2 Sheffield United 3 (Blues blow two-goal lead and title chance)

Despite the bad blood caused by Emlyn Hughes's squeaky voice proclaiming 'Liverpool are magic, Everton are tragic' as the Reds celebrated their first European Cup triumph, the narrative that after 1970 the Blues didn't challenge for honours for the remainder of the decade is actually a gross simplification.

It's true that the Goodison Park trophy cabinet remained bare until 1984, but there were several near-misses and the failure to secure the league championship in 1975 – which would have put Everton back level with Liverpool in title wins had they done so – is surely the most lamentable of opportunities lost.

Three years earlier under Brian Clough, Derby County's players were already on holiday in Majorca when they celebrated the unlikely first title in the club's history – only finding out the following morning after assistant manager Peter Taylor's telephone line to Madrid to get the scores the previous night went dead!

In 1974/75, Everton were top of the table with four matches remaining but somehow ended up finishing fourth.

Three of the Blues' remaining fixtures were away but two of those were against relegated sides Luton Town and Chelsea, while the other was at another club in the bottom half, Newcastle United.

They'd slip up 2-1 at Luton, but Martin Dobson's goal at St James' Park gave them a 1-0 win to keep their hopes alive.

If Billy Bingham's team could beat Sheffield United on the penultimate weekend in what was their final home match of the campaign, then they'd still be in the race going into the last day, but a second-half collapse saw their season's efforts dramatically implode.

Alex Goodman tried to make sense of it all in the *Liverpool Echo*, writing, 'After a season of endeavour it was left to Tony Currie to sink those title hopes with a winning goal for Sheffield United at Goodison Park.

'The goal came just five minutes from the end of an incredible game which ended with United as unbelievable winners.

'They were unbelieving because at half-time it had looked odds on that Everton would finish with at least a four-goal margin in their favour.

'Dave Smallman [in the 24th minute] hit a fine opening goal, his first for the club, hooking the ball at shoulder height past Jim Brown from 15 yards and Gary Jones slotted home the second from the penalty spot after Len Badger brought down Jim Pearson as he lined up a shot [after 30 minutes].

'On top of all that the quality of Everton's football was excellent. It was stamped with championship class as Martin Dobson, Mick Buckley and Jones powered forward from midfield; it was stamped with championship class in the menace of Bob Latchford and Smallman around the goal and there was championship class stamped all over the defence where Roger Kenyon and John Hurst stood rock solid.'

This was the proverbial game of two halves if ever there was one, though.

Goodman added, 'But what a transformation after the break. Within three minutes, Keith Eddy had pulled a goal back and Everton suddenly became a very nervous side.

'On 73 minutes, home goalkeeper Dai Davies jumped with David Bradford but failed to hold the ball which ran out to Bill Dearden for him to crack home the equaliser.

'It was a mistake by Davies, and it was cruelly punished but he did not seek to escape the blame, admitting, "There was no foul. I just dropped the ball."

'After this, Everton threw men forward with both Hurst and Kenyon surging through the middle and Mike Bernard readily overlapping on the right.

'But five minutes from time a fine move that brought the ball out of defence ended with Currie cracking it past Davies from a dozen yards.'

In truth, it shouldn't have all come down to this one game for Everton's title chances. They only won two of their last ten and were guilty of too many draws – 18 in total. It wasn't the only time they'd blow a 2-0 lead either.

After Bob Latchford's header had given them a 1-0 win in what the *Echo* described as a 'dour battle' at Derby on 14 December, they'd gone top of the table and could have stayed there on Christmas

Day had they not surrendered the advantage Latchford's brace had brought them at home to Carlisle United the following weekend in what proved to be a 3-2 defeat.

The Cumbrians would finish the campaign rock bottom but infamously completed a costly league double over the Blues.

Other FA Cup games

AS WELL as staging many famous Everton FA Cup ties plus two finals over the years, Goodison Park has also hosted several other matches in football's oldest competition covered here.

* * *

Kopites might not like the inconvenient fact but Manchester United have attracted a bigger crowd for a 'home game' in the city of Liverpool than Everton's neighbours ever have.

The occasion was an FA Cup fourth round tie between Manchester United and Liverpool at Goodison Park on 24 January 1948 which was watched by 74,721 – almost 13,000 more than Anfield's record gate to date (61,905 for Liverpool v Wolverhampton Wanderers, also an FA Cup fourth round, tie on 2 February 1952).

At the time, Manchester United were playing their home games at neighbours Manchester City's Maine Road ground because Old Trafford had suffered bomb damage during the second world war.

However, with City also being drawn at home in the FA Cup to Chelsea on the same day, Matt Busby's side decided to switch the tie to Goodison.

United triumphed 3-0 with the *Liverpool Echo* reporting that they 'romped' into the fifth round with Liverpool being knocked out by a 'wonder side'.

It's also interesting to note that the report in the *Echo* stated that on a day 'that could have not been more raw', the Goodison terraces were 'packed and swaying' and there was 'a great cheer for Johnny Carey when United came out first'.

United – who played their fifth round 'home' tie with Charlton Athletic at Huddersfield Town's Leeds Road – would go on to lift the FA Cup that season, defeating Blackpool 4-2 in the final at Wembley.

The 1948 clash between Liverpool and their old foes from down the East Lancs Road was just one of several FA Cup ties in addition to finals that took place at Goodison Park involving clubs other than Everton.

The ground staged ten FA Cup semi-finals – four initial ties and six replays. The semi-finals were: Bolton Wanderers 1 Sheffield Wednesday 1 (1896); Bury 3 Aston Villa 0 (1903); Manchester City 3 Sheffield Wednesday 0 (1904); Manchester United 2 Liverpool 2 (1985). The replays were: Burnley 1 Sheffield United 0 (1914); Huddersfield Town 0 Sheffield United 0 (1928); Wolverhampton Wanderers 1 Manchester United 0 (1949); Blackpool 2 Birmingham City 1 (1951); Arsenal 2 Stoke City 1 (1972); Manchester United 1 Liverpool 0 (1979).

In 1974, Goodison Park staged a replayed FA Cup quarter-final between Newcastle United and Nottingham Forest despite the Magpies triumphing 4-3 in the sides' original meeting at St James' Park.

Forest had been 3-1 up through a penalty that saw Newcastle defender Pat Howard sent off for protesting and the home fans had invaded the pitch.

This act led to two visiting players being injured and 23 people taken to hospital due to the ensuing riot with another 103 treated at the ground and 39 arrests made.

Afterwards, Forest protested to the FA and got the result declared null and void.

The authorities made the unprecedented decision to replay the tie at a neutral venue – Goodison – but this match was also marred by a crowd incident with a four-foot metal spear among the objects thrown on to the pitch in a goalless draw.

The sides met again for a third time three days later, on 21 March, again at Goodison, with Newcastle – who would lose 3-0 to Liverpool in the final – triumphing 1-0.

Unfortunately, on this occasion, local troublemakers got in on the act on Scotland Road with the *Echo* reporting, 'Liverpool hooligans stoned buses carrying Newcastle United and Nottingham Forest fans to the FA Cup replay at Goodison Park. The windows of 12 vehicles – more than half the buses being used – were smashed.'

Goodison has also staged a trio of FA Cup first round ties.

Third Division Tranmere Rovers suffered a 1-0 defeat after extra time in a second replay to a Fourth Division Scunthorpe United side featuring Kevin Keegan on 30 November 1970 with Graham Rusling grabbing the only goal on 110 minutes.

The ground was used as a temporary home for a couple of Merseyside football's lesser lights with New Brighton defeating fellow Third Division North side Southport 2-1 in a first round replay on 3 December 1934.

Finally, on 13 November 1993, non-league Knowsley United hosted fourth-tier Carlisle United with the Cumbrians victorious 4-1.

David Bassett of the *Echo* reported that while Carlisle were 'worthy winners', the scoreline was 'scant justice for the battling non-leaguers'.

A crowd of 5,015 saw the Northern Premier League side bow out and their manager Paul Orr said, 'We thought we could get a result and perhaps we were too cocky. We just could not stop them in the first half, but we were not disgraced.'

10

Other Merseyside derbies

THE STORY behind how the city of Liverpool got to have two major football clubs and Everton's move to Goodison Park has already been covered, but the result of those tumultuous events in 1892 – the author believes it is factually incorrect to refer to it as a 'split' as some have done in the past given that Everton relocated almost lock, stock and barrel while their former president John Houlding was forced to form an entirely new entity – has produced one of the sport's fiercest rivalries.

Some have tried to play up a supposed sectarian religious divide between the clubs, like with Rangers and Celtic in Glasgow given that Houlding was a member of the Orange Order while Dr James Baxter, who helped Everton pay for Goodison Park's construction, was a Catholic.

However, even though the Blues had several leading Republic of Ireland players among their ranks in the years just after the second world war, there seems no real credence in such claims – particularly in the modern era – and another of their founding fathers, George Mahon, was the organist at the Methodist church from which the club originated.

Despite the intense level of competition between the two clubs and their fanbases, for many years Everton versus Liverpool was dubbed the 'friendly derby' given the informal lack of segregation in grounds on derby days and early attendance figures suggest that for many decades there was probably a significant overlap in spectator patronage either side of Stanley Park before the game became more partisan and divided on almost tribal lines.

***

9 September 2006: Everton 3 Liverpool 0 (Blues' biggest Merseyside derby win for 42 years)

Jubilant Evertonians hardly needed a reminder of the score but in case any of them were still rubbing their eyes in disbelief, Andrew Johnson's celebratory hand gestures showed them anyway, it was 3-0 against Liverpool.

This was the Blues' biggest victory over their neighbours since they'd triumphed 4-0 across Stanley Park at Anfield back on 19 September 1964, almost 42 years earlier, which made it the most emphatic Merseyside derby success for Everton in living memory for many inside Goodison, including home manager David Moyes who was just a one-year-old when goals from Colin Harvey, Johnny Morrissey, Fred Pickering and Derek Temple sealed a pounding for the Reds on their own turf.

Throughout the intervening four decades, there had been several more 'demolition derbies' in Liverpool's favour – most infamously the 5-0 success at Goodison on 6 November 1982 when Ian Rush struck four times – but such one-sided outcomes in this fixture for the Blues had been a long time coming.

After impressively finishing above the Reds' Champions League winners in 2004/05 to secure fourth place, what had come to be regarded as 'normal service' resumed the following season with Liverpool – who also won the FA Cup – finishing third on 82 points, 32 more than 11th-placed Everton, whose gut-wrenching Champions League third qualifying round second leg defeat to Villarreal proved to be the first of six straight losses.

A 1-0 League Cup exit at home to Middlesbrough at a time when Moyes's men were propping up the table on 26 October 2005 was a ninth defeat in 11 matches – a run that had included a UEFA Cup exit to Dinamo Bucharest barely a month after the pain in Spain.

Although they eventually recovered to climb to a mid-table finish, with just 34 goals scored in 38 Premier League matches it seemed obvious where the team's main problem was.

James Beattie had been unable to replicate the prolific form from his days at Southampton that earned him a club record £6m move to Goodison in January 2005 so Moyes went out and broke the record again to recruit Andrew Johnson from Crystal Palace for £8.6m.

In a summer in which he was able to conduct his business refreshingly early, the Scot was also able to draft in Manchester United goalkeeper Tim Howard – initially on a season-long loan – and Wolverhampton Wanderers defender Joleon Lescott.

The forward planning seemed to bear fruit in the early part of the campaign with Everton unbeaten in their first eight matches, but there was absolutely no doubt over the standout fixture among this impressive run.

Dominic King wrote in the *Liverpool Echo*, 'Everton delivered the kind of performance many have spent years fantasising about. But how many fans will have leapt out of bed yesterday morning with sore heads to buy every paper and watch repeats of *Match of the Day*, *Football First* and *Jimmy Hill's Sunday Supplement* to make sure it wasn't a dream?

'Fear not. There was nothing imaginary about the way Everton systemically dismantled and tormented a side that has visions of challenging Chelsea for the Premier League.

'On this evidence, such claims seem fanciful. Conjuring up a breathless performance that oozed calm and class, the 11 men David Moyes selected for duty secured a result which will be talked about for many, many years to come. Emphatic doesn't really do their efforts justice.'

Of the goals, King said, 'Andrew Johnson did not need a second invitation to wreak havoc. How he took it. Petrified his pace would cause problems, Liverpool simply did not know how to handle Everton's record signing and made a string of errors for which they were ruthlessly punished.

'Playing a key role in the move that led to Tim Cahill [a right-footed finish from seven yards] grabbing the first goal in front of a baying Gwladys Street on 23 minutes, Johnson enjoyed the kind of derby debut that usually appears in the pages of *Roy of the Rovers*.

'Two chances came his way [his first goal on 36 minutes was a cool finish after shrugging off Jamie Carragher's wild challenge] and both were gleefully gobbled up, the second particularly sweet after José Manuel Reina – did the crestfallen goalkeeper earn his second name after the ham-fisted waiter in *Fawlty Towers?* – comically blundered in front of the Park End [Johnson headed over the goal line deep into stoppage time after the Spaniard had made a hash of dealing with Lee Carsley's long-range strike].

'Goodison most definitely has its new hero.'

* * *

20 February 1991: Everton 4 Liverpool 4 AET (Iconic high-scoring derby that ended Kenny Dalglish's reign)

The magnitude of what's at stake often ensures Merseyside derbies become wars of attrition, but this wasn't the case on a night that produced an eight-goal thriller with Everton equalising four times and Liverpool manager Kenny Dalglish subsequently resigning.

This was the third consecutive fixture between the clubs in the space of 11 days. Liverpool had won 3-1 in a First Division home game against Everton on 9 February but then the neighbours played out an FA Cup fifth round stalemate at Anfield on 17 February.

With the action switching across Stanley Park to Goodison, it was time for fans to strap themselves in for a rollercoaster ride.

Neither side was able to deliver a knockout blow, but Ken Rogers of the *Liverpool Echo* compared the end-to-end goal glut to one of boxing's greatest occasions.

He proclaimed, 'I have often wondered what it must have been like to have been in the crowd the night Muhammad Ali and Joe Frazier took each other to the brink of human endurance, exchanging punch for punch, blow for blow in the legendary Thrilla in Manila. Now I know.

'I was one of 38,000 mesmerised football fans who marvelled, gasped and marvelled again at a sporting spectacle of similar heavyweight proportions.

'Everton 4 Liverpool 4 … it was one of those FA Cup occasions we will look back on in years to come and proudly declare, "I was there!"

'We used to do a lap of honour when one goal settled a derby because they were always so tight. But EIGHT – and still no result. It was absolutely unbelievable.

'In the blue corner Everton – fighting like tigers – reeled on the ropes four times but bounced back with the kind of power and passion that suggests they will soon be playing the Glory Game again under Howard Kendall.

'In the red corner Liverpool must surely feel aggrieved and annoyed with themselves for failing to turn the screw.

'The champions used to knock opponents down and keep them down, but these are weird and wonderful times at Anfield.'

Ric George of the *Echo* described the goals. Of Liverpool's 32nd-minute opener, he said, 'Kevin Ratcliffe was dispossessed by Ian Rush who sped goalwards, drew Neville Southall and shot towards an unguarded net. Andy Hinchcliffe's clearance on the line was therefore miraculous but only temporary respite as Rush nodded on the loose ball for Peter Beardsley to rifle home.'

Everton drew level a minute into the second half as 'Hinchcliffe curled in a delicious left-wing cross for Graeme Sharp to power a header which Bruce Grobbelaar could only push on to the inside of his post.'

Liverpool restored their lead on 71 minutes when 'Beardsley cracked a tremendous left-footed shot which flew past Southall'.

The Blues equalised again two minutes later 'as the ever-hopeful Sharp cashed in on a misunderstanding between Steve Nicol and Grobbelaar to slide in'.

The Reds went ahead for a third time on 77 minutes 'when a short corner was worked to Jan Mølby and he clipped over a cross which the inevitable Rush nodded in'.

Everton took the game into extra time with a goal a minute from the end as substitute Tony Cottee – introduced just four minutes earlier – 'pounced on to Stuart McCall's neat pass to score clinically'.

Liverpool went 4-3 up on 102 minutes, as despite earlier Southall heroics 'not even the great Welshman could stop John Barnes scoring with a magnificent curling right-footer from the edge of the area'.

The hosts would hit back again for a final time and 'Goodison erupted six minutes from the end when the alert Cottee shot between Grobbelaar's legs after Glenn Hysén had let Mølby's backpass run on'.

Summarising the night, George remarked, 'Merseyside derbies should come with a government health warning.

'The passion, excitement and unpredictability of these encounters makes it unwise for anyone of a nervous disposition to set foot inside the stadium. This was without question the greatest match I have ever watched – but also the most stressful.'

Indeed, feeling the strain of the aftermath of Hillsborough and the weight of expectation that came with managing the most successful English club side of the era, Dalglish would sensationally quit just 48 hours later.

With Ronnie Moran installed as caretaker boss of the Reds, Howard Kendall's side would triumph 1-0 in the second replay the following week thanks to Dave Watson's 12th-minute strike after some penalty box pinball only to lose their subsequent quarter-final 2-1 at Second Division West Ham United.

* * *

20 March 1988: Everton 1 Liverpool 0 (Wayne Clarke ends Liverpool's 29-game unbeaten run)

Jubilant Evertonians were certainly 'Singing the Blues' this night after Wayne Clarke's goal prevented Liverpool from setting a new top flight unbeaten record.

Everton supporters of course love to belt out their own version of Guy Mitchell's 1956 number one hit song with adapted lyrics whenever their own team triumph and their neighbours are beaten, and it's all the more sweeter for them if those two permutations are achieved from the same fixture.

That's the nature of football fan *schadenfreude* around the world but particularly on Merseyside where some followers of the Reds have in recent years revelled in the self-proclaimed 'Unbearables' tag when it comes to basking in the reflected glory of their own side's successes.

Back in 1988, Liverpool were attempting to become the first team to go 30 games unbeaten from the start of a First Division season.

They'd already equalled Leeds United's 29-match run from 1973/74, prompting *The Mirror* to proclaim that if they avoided defeat at Goodison Park then they would be 'the team of the century'.

Everton knew that 1987/88 would not be their year and that despite being defending champions, the title would be moving back across Stanley Park, for what proved the last time in a sequence of toing and froing that had taken place since 1984.

However, denying the Reds a special place in the game's annals would prove a satisfying consolation prize at least for Colin Harvey's men in his debut campaign at the helm after Howard Kendall had departed for Athletic Club Bilbao.

For match-winner Wayne Clarke, family pride was also at stake ensuring the victory was celebrated with as much relish in West Yorkshire as it was among the blue half of Merseyside.

The Everton striker was the youngest of five brothers to play professional football, alongside Frank, Derek, Kelvin and Allan, who was part of that great Leeds side under Don Revie, and present at Goodison for this game.

Wayne recalled, 'I was pleased Allan was there; I was pleased to score of course but more pleased, really, for him. We hadn't talked before about the game or the record at all during the week but when I met him beforehand, he said he wanted two things from me – a car park ticket and the winning goal.'

The match was played out in front of a huge nationwide television audience on ITV, but it was the parochial nature of the affair that enabled Everton to pull off the famous scalp as they relished their role as Liverpool's party poopers.

The *Liverpool Echo* went with the headline 'Brotherly love! Wayne snuffs out a record run', with Ken Rogers explaining why only the Blues could have pulled off such a feat, 'If Liverpool had been playing any other team in the country, the record would have been in the bag.

'No other side in the land would have had the same incentive to upset the apple cart than Colin Harvey's men. The Evertonians have been forced to eat humble pie of late in the shadows of their arch-rivals.

'Everything was riding on this game in the pride stakes which is why 44,000 partisan fans turned their backs on a free seat in front of a television to help create a very special derby atmosphere.

'Both clubs claimed the record was a meaningless intrusion on a match that was always going to be a no-holds-barred battle, but the voice of ultra-professionalism couldn't hide the fact that both teams had a special incentive.'

Everton's famous winner arrived just 14 minutes into the contest.

Clarke said of his goal, a left-footed hook shot from six yards, 'The chance came from a corner we had to take twice. It was one we've worked on all season.

'We knew that Bruce [Grobbelaar] would come for it, and he couldn't quite reach. Graeme Sharp got a toe on the ball, and it came to me. Looking at the video afterwards, I was surprised at how little space there was to aim at.'

This was one of four meetings between the sides that season with both securing a brace of victories and knocking each other out of the respective domestic cup competitions.

The Blues would finish the season fourth, 20 points adrift of their neighbours, who were denied the First Division and FA Cup double by a shock Wembley loss to Wimbledon.

After this defeat, Rogers remarked, 'Everton must content themselves with a double of a different kind ... two battling victories over the side no other team in the country can master.'

* * *

21 November 1994: Everton 2 Liverpool 0 (By Royle appointment, the Blues are back with a derby win)

At the time of his appointment, Everton were rock bottom of the table and seemingly plummeting out of the Premier League without much of a fight, but this was the night that Joe Royle first unleashed what he came to call his 'Dogs of War'.

With a third of the season already gone and the Blues in 22nd place, having lost eight out of ten Premier League games between 24 August and 22 October (they were also dumped out of the League Cup by second-tier Portsmouth), it was going to be a real dogfight just to stay up despite their last-day escape against Wimbledon in the previous campaign.

Royle's predecessor Mike Walker had landed the Everton job in January 1994 on the back of his work at Norwich City, who he'd steered to third place in the previous season and subsequently pulled off a famous UEFA Cup upset over Bayern Munich.

However, life in the footballing hotbed of Merseyside was a world away from sleepy Norfolk and although he tried to play a cultured brand of football in the best traditions of the 'School of Science', there was no bite and the man nicknamed the 'Silver Fox' during his brief tenure at Goodison Park was unable to halt his side's alarming run of results.

There was a mini revival in Walker's final days, a three-game unbeaten run, including a first win of the season at the 15th time of asking in all competitions – 1-0 at home to West Ham United – but by now chairman Peter Johnson had decided it was time to act and he brought Royle, who had been linked with the job both before and after Howard Kendall's second stint, back home.

Unlike Walker, lifelong Evertonian Royle knew just what was required for Merseyside derby combat and he enjoyed a dream start to his Goodison tenure.

David Prentice of the *Liverpool Echo* wrote, 'Quite simply, Everton wanted the points far more than Liverpool – and once again it was visiting taunts of impending relegation which seemed to light the touch paper.

'Chants of "going down" were followed almost instantly by a 56th-minute header from Duncan Ferguson that set Goodison alight.

'A midfield of Joe Parkinson, Barry Horne, John Ebbrell and Andy Hinchcliffe looked little more than a unit selected to suppress Liverpool's own creative flair. But all four produced thundering performances to out-tackle and outwit and at times even outpass Liverpool as the Blues "went to war" – to use their own manager's words.'

Having broken his scoring duck, this was also the night that Duncan Ferguson began his love affair with the club.

Originally arriving on loan from Rangers, initially he seemed to view the move as a temporary measure to keep him away from the spotlight of Glasgow and his impending court case – he would later be convicted of assault for an on-pitch head-butt on an opponent during his time at Ibrox – but this would prove to be the first of many times he'd rise to the big occasion for the fanbase with which he formed a mutual adoration.

The Scot's aerial threat also prompted Everton's second goal a couple of minutes from the end. Prentice said, 'Ferguson challenged David James who, panic stricken, punched the ball against the Everton striker where it dropped into Paul Rideout's path, and he slid the ball in from eight yards.'

The result sparked a major revival and having secured their Premier League status for another year with a 1-0 win at Ipswich Town in their penultimate fixture thanks to a goal from Rideout, Everton were able to go out and enjoy themselves in the FA Cup Final against Manchester United, defeating Alex Ferguson's side by the same scoreline.

Recalling Royle's impact on the 25th anniversary of that Wembley triumph, Rideout told the *Echo*, 'Everyone knew their job. That was the difference between Joe and Willie [Donachie, his assistant] and the previous manager who had no concept of how to put things right.

'The instructions were to play to a certain shape and if you couldn't do that then you weren't going to play.

'Joe was a no-nonsense boss. If you annoyed him then you'd know all about it because he could be nasty – but in the right way – yet he could also be a really cool guy. He was one of my favourite managers of my career because he was a straight talker.'

* * *

22 September 1962: Everton 2 Liverpool 2 (First league derby in over 11 years)

It's often said that absence makes the heart grow fonder but while there was no love lost between Everton and Liverpool after 11 years and eight months since their previous league derby meeting, the respective sets of players – and their fans – relished the prospect of resuming hostilities.

Everton had been defending champions when the Football League stopped for the second world war in 1939 and then Liverpool won the title in the first season back in 1946/47 but the subsequent postwar years had not been a boom time for Merseyside football.

In 1951, the Blues dropped into the Second Division for only the second time in their history. Before then, other than a solitary campaign in 1930/31, Everton had played in every top-flight season since the Football League began in 1888 but this time it would take them three years to return.

They passed Liverpool going in the opposite direction when they came back up in 1954 with the Reds relegated as the Blues were promoted.

This at least ensured that the city kept up its unique record of being the only location in England to stage top-flight football in every season since the league was founded but Liverpool's spell in the wilderness was even longer and spanned eight seasons until they won promotion under Bill Shankly in 1962.

There had actually been a dozen minor-competition clashes between the pair between 1957 and 1962 in the Floodlit Challenge Cup, Lancashire Senior Cup and Liverpool Senior Cup.

None of these are counted in the records as first-team appearances but three games were watched by crowds of over 50,000, three by more than 40,000, three by over 30,000 and the other three by more than 20,000.

In the 4,264 days since Everton had triumphed at Anfield on 20 January 1951, the sides had met just once in a competitive clash,

Liverpool's shock 4-0 win at Goodison in the FA Cup fourth round on 29 January 1955.

Leslie Edwards of the *Liverpool Echo* chronicled the big match atmosphere and wrote, 'A just verdict – but only just! That, in a sentence, sums up the memorable game at Goodison Park. It was hard, exciting, entertaining, noisy, tense and fluctuating but never a football classic. How could it be, with the atmosphere so charged – with dynamite?

'Many, including those who only go on special football occasions, thought it commonplace; the regulars, of whom I am one, probably rated it as an outstanding meeting of the seniors of our city because it had a thousand agonising twists of fortune: a dozen incidents to keep us talking for weeks as long as there is an Everton.

'Seventy-three thousand people (rather too many, I would say, on the terraces) gave the first league derby for 11 years an extraordinary back-cloth of sound and movement. They were never still, never silent. They swayed, they roared, they cheered, they chanted. Almost from first to last. Ev-er-ton! Liv-er-pool!'

Home captain Roy Vernon put the ball into Liverpool's net less than 60 seconds into the contest, but his effort was chalked off due to a supposed foul on goalkeeper Jim Furnell. Dennis Stevens then thought he'd fired the Blues in front only to be denied by the linesman's flag.

The deadlock was finally broken through Vernon's 29th-minute penalty as he coolly smashed the ball low to Furnell's left after Gerry Byrne had handled.

Kevin Lewis equalised six minutes later with a hooked shot from close range but Johnny Morrissey – transferred from Liverpool to Everton just a month earlier – netted his first goal for his new club with a right-footed drive that Ronnie Moran tried to swipe clear but the ball had gone over the line.

However the Blues would be denied victory by a last-minute equaliser from Roger Hunt as he pounced on Lewis's nod-down to beat Gordon West to the ball and poke home.

When it came to the contentious decisions, Edwards said, 'Just as 73,000 saw all these incidents so there must be 73,000 different versions of what happened and why.

'They will mostly be coloured according to the redness or blueness of the people who hold them. Not being either I think Vernon's goal was probably good, Stevens's position probably offside and Byrne's offence likely to be unintentional.'

He added, 'The breaks, I thought, went Liverpool's way.'

The return match at Anfield on 8 April finished goalless but Everton would go on to secure their first league championship in 24 years the following month.

* * *

11 December 2004: Everton 1 Liverpool 0 (Lee Carsley nets the winner in the 200th derby)

The enduring image of Everton's victory in the 200th Merseyside derby is the one of their players piled on top of each other celebrating Lee Carsley's winner, but the hero of the hour was nowhere to be seen.

Manager David Moyes was so delighted by the photograph – which symbolised his first success against the Blues' neighbours – that he ordered a framed copy for every member of his squad.

However, recalling the match several years later, Carsley told *The Independent*, 'I find it ironic, because I'm still asked to sign that picture of my goal celebrations and I'm the only Everton player not on it.

'That was a great day, people still talk to me about it, but after the goal I fell to the floor, everyone jumped on me and then Tim Cahill piled on top. He is the only one looking into the camera and he's probably signed as many copies of that photograph as I have.'

In a way though, the picture sums up hard grafter Carsley's understated but integral contribution to the Everton cause even if he wasn't necessarily the player who immediately caught your eye with his winner against Liverpool one of just 13 goals in 198 appearances for the club, averaging less than two per season.

The fruitful 2004/05 campaign, in which Everton shocked the football world by going from 17th on 39 points the previous campaign to finishing fourth with their highest Premier League placing to date, was by far Carsley's most prolific on Merseyside as he found the net on five occasions.

Indeed, his form, providing a shield in front of Moyes's defence, was so impressive that many observers speculated that Real Madrid might well have signed the wrong player when they snapped up fellow bald central midfielder Thomas Gravesen in January 2005 as a replacement for Claude Makélélé in the anchorman role.

Despite the Dane's 'Mad Dog' nickname and fist-shaking, eye-popping nature, he was more artist than artisan in the engine room.

Although he subsequently proved himself to be both an erudite columnist with the *Liverpool Echo* and astute coach, steering England to glory at the UEFA European Under-21 Championship in 2023 before a caretaker stint in the Three Lions' top job, Carsley – whose other famous goal celebration shot is one of him sporting a bandaged head against Fulham – was a genuine hard case on the pitch.

It wasn't entirely in keeping with the principles of Goodison Park's fabled 'School of Science' but the Birmingham-born Republic of Ireland international once quipped that when he heard the club's famous *Z-Cars* anthem, 'I want to kill, I want to take someone out!'

Such an uncompromising and committed approach helped Moyes's unlikely band of Blues brothers to climb the table in 2004/05, with the likes of Cahill and Marcus Bent coming in to replace Wayne Rooney and Tomasz Radzinski.

The Goodison success over their neighbours – who would finish the campaign by winning the Champions League – saw Everton move back up into second spot, and they were well worth their win.

David Prentice of the *Echo* wrote, 'Lee Carsley placed an effective restraining order on Steven Gerrard, but elsewhere Everton tried to be as expressive as a team can be under the constricting restraints of a derby match.

'Kevin Kilbane terrorised the hapless Josemi, Leon Osman's constant probings ensured [John Arne] Riise couldn't advance down the opposite flank and Thomas Gravesen took advantage of what rare chinks of space emerged in the midfield area to chisel out openings in the Reds' rearguard.

'But Everton's real unsung heroes were at the back. Alessandro Pistone has always been a Rolls-Royce of a performer, but with a mechanical record of a second-hand Škoda, but in his 19th consecutive performance for the Blues he was polished and precise in everything he did.

'To his right, the redoubtable [Alan] Stubbs and [David] Weir were heroic, the skipper's injury-time challenge on [Neil] Mellor was the stuff of derby day legend.'

The goal came in the 68th minute and Prentice wrote, 'Carsley was a popular goalscorer. After he picked up a loose clearance and curled in a 20-yard drive with the inside of his right foot, he was promptly submerged beneath a battery of ecstatic team-mates.

'There is a newspaper clipping pinned to the noticeboard at Bellefield which says, "Blues chief warns leave cars at home," to which a team-mate has jokingly added, "And play 4-4-2!"

'It is very much a joke, because Carsley's influence on the Everton side stretches far beyond the wickedly clipped right-footed strikes he has weighed in with this season.'

Such was his importance, Carsley himself later chirped that the Blues had to shell out a then club record £15m on Marouane Fellaini to eventually replace him.

* * *

7 December 1992: Everton 2 Liverpool 1 (Peter Beardsley downs his old club in the 'Billy Kenny derby')

On the night, jubilant Evertonians were just delighted to toast Peter Beardsley downing his former club in a comeback victory, but in time they would come to have contrasting regrets over both him and the other hero of the hour, Billy Kenny.

Despite both starring against the Reds, neither match-winner Beardsley nor man of the match Kenny would kick a ball again for the Blues after the 1992/93 season had finished.

That itself is deeply lamentable but the reasons behind their respective Goodison Park exits and subsequent careers are poles apart.

As a Liverpool player, Beardsley had netted six times in matches with Everton, more goals than against any other opponent.

However, following the arrival of Dean Saunders from Derby County in 1991 for an English record fee of £2.9m – ironically under the nose of Blues boss Howard Kendall who had looked poised to land the Welshman's signature – the now 30-year-old Beardsley was deemed surplus to requirements at Anfield and allowed to make a controversial move across Stanley Park.

Graeme Souness wasn't the only Mersey manager guilty of writing off Beardsley prematurely though as Kendall repeated the Scot's mistake.

Netting 20 goals in his first season at Everton, after Beardsley's scoring output dropped to 12 in his second campaign, the Blues allowed him to return to his native north-east to join newly promoted Newcastle United.

Under Kevin Keegan, the veteran striker enjoyed an Indian summer, earning an England recall and continuing in the Premier League for another four seasons.

Despite growing up in an era when a hard-drinking culture prevailed in the game, Beardsley's teetotalism was often cited as one of the reasons behind his footballing longevity.

In contrast, the gifted protégé who Beardsley dubbed the 'Goodison Gazza', having played alongside Paul Gascoigne during his first spell at the Magpies, would have done well to follow his senior colleague's lessons in sobriety.

At 19, local lad Billy Kenny seemingly had the world at his feet but after his dominant display bossing the engine room in the heat of Merseyside derby combat, his fortunes took a rapid downward spiral.

Issues with drink and drugs would see Kenny sacked by Everton barely 15 months after his sparkling display against Liverpool and then out of football full stop at just 21 years of age.

The Blues went into the derby just a point above the relegation zone after a rotten run that had seen them lose seven of their previous nine Premier League matches, picking up just one win in the sequence.

However, the visit of their local rivals saw them rise to the occasion – eventually.

Ken Rogers wrote in the *Liverpool Echo*, 'Somewhere down on a pitch swamped by a royal blue invasion, 11 Everton heroes revelled in a dramatic revival that turned a night of potential disaster into a full blown Goodison carnival.

'There have been better derbies and more impressive victories, but it is a long time since a win over the old enemy was quite so sweet.

'Everton's season has been little short of a nightmare, which is why the Blues went into this derby as undoubted underdogs.

'Liverpool were so confident their main sponsors Carlsberg took a tongue-in-cheek advert out in the *Echo* which included a special form to mark down the goalscorers. The Blues had just one line, the Reds five. To adapt a famous advertising slogan, it was "probably" the biggest *own goal* ever committed prior to one of these fiercely contested clashes.'

At first, proceedings appeared to be following the form book as Liverpool centre-half Mark Wright opened the scoring on 62 minutes 'with a soaring header from a well-struck Mike Marsh corner'.

However 'the visitors were still celebrating when Maurice Johnston grabbed the equaliser, turning on a sixpence before curling a left foot shot into the far corner' of Mike Hooper's goal.

From then on, Everton started to take the game to Liverpool with Kenny probing at every opportunity.

Kendall revealed that the youngster had penned a new contract just hours before the game and said, 'I thought the lad was absolutely tremendous. He had earned it and he fully justified it on the night, passing the ball superbly and looking a top-class prospect.'

The winner, a low drive from outside the area, came five minutes from the end with Rogers remarking, 'Enter Beardsley to send home spirits soaring as high as the satellite that beamed the game live to the nation [Sky coverage was still a novelty in the Premier League's debut season]. Christmas had come early for everyone wearing blue.'

* * *

9 April 1909: Everton 5 Liverpool 0 (Blues' record Merseyside derby win, later equalled)

In over 130 years of Merseyside derby combat, this result remained Everton's biggest victory over Liverpool at Goodison Park.

The Blues would later equal the record with a 5-0 win at Anfield on 3 October 1914, en route to their second league championship in the wartime 1914/15 season, but on home turf they would never overcome their local rivals by such a scoreline again.

Despite Everton's status as the senior club in the city, Liverpool had quickly established themselves on an equal footing.

By the time of this fixture, both sides had two major honours to their name: Everton the 1890/91 championship and 1906 FA Cup while Liverpool had a brace of titles in 1900/01 and 1905/06.

The Reds' crowds were by now also comparable to the Blues'. Although Everton enjoyed the highest average attendances in the whole Football League for its first decade, gates either side of Stanley Park were now similar in numbers and Liverpool's figures were slightly higher in both the 1902/03 and 1905/06 seasons.

However, it seems highly likely there was a significant crossover in spectators during this period with many older fans attesting to the widespread practice of watching matches at Goodison and Anfield on alternate weekends.

Derbies at both grounds would typically attract the biggest crowds of the season from the start though and 45,000 crammed in to watch this one.

The *Liverpool Courier* reported of 'Everton's splendid victory' that, 'The struggles of Everton and Liverpool are always a source of unbounded interest, and on these occasions, partisanship runs exceedingly high, but when the meeting occurs on Good Friday; football excitement in the city is at an unusually high pitch.

'It was a game which bristled with good points and in which both sides were hard triers, and very often the football was of a high-class order.

'Such a wide margin as five goals to nothing with which Everton managed to win, was not generally expected, although no one will begrudge the Blues their success, as they earned it by a style and standard of play which was superior to that of Liverpool.

'There was scarcely a weak spot in the home 11, all of whom worked together with thorough understanding, with the result that for the greater part of the game they more than held their own.'

Everton took the lead on 15 minutes as 'The centre [Bertie Freeman] cleverly tipped the ball to John Coleman, who ran though, and [with goalkeeper] Sam Hardy running out, the inside-right tipped the ball into an untended goal.'

Freeman himself, whose 38 goals made him the First Division's leading goalscorer that season, doubled the Blues' advantage on 35 minutes.

The report stated, 'Freeman snapped up a pass, and beating Crawford, ran well towards goal. Hardy came out, but as he collided with the Everton centre, Freeman touched the ball into the net.

'Freeman, Hardy, and Robert Crawford were all on the ground, and the Liverpool goalkeeper evidently received a bad shaking, as he had to receive attention before he was able to resume.'

The Blues' further goals came after the break, but the timings are not recorded.

Wattie White made it 3-0 when he 'scored with a fine drive in the top corner of the goal' after 'tricking Harrop'.

It was 4-0 when 'a splendid movement by Everton resulted in Bob Turner scoring with a brilliant cross shot just after White had hit the post', while Freeman completed the rout 'from a good run by Sharp after Hardy had saved twice'.

Everton had been early pacesetters at the top of the table in the first half of the campaign and remained at the summit until 23 January, but they'd fall away badly.

Although they'd finish runners-up to champions Newcastle United, they finished seven points adrift of the Magpies and this was one of only five wins from their last 20 fixtures.

Liverpool's slump was even more alarming. Sitting fourth in the table as late as 27 February, this was the fifth of six straight defeats for them in an eight-game winless sequence in the First Division, and they'd end the season in 16th place, just two points clear of relegated Manchester City.

Indeed, some eight and a half decades before Everton's great escape against Wimbledon, the Reds had to dramatically beat title winners Newcastle at St James' Park in their final fixture to avoid the drop with former Magpie Ronald Orr netting the only goal of the game 12 minutes from the end.

* * *

4 February 2009: Everton 1 Liverpool 0 AET (Dan Gosling scores the greatest derby winner never seen by many as ITV pulls the plug early)

Everton youngster Dan Gosling's dramatic extra-time goal that knocked Liverpool out of the FA Cup was the greatest Merseyside derby winner than many armchair fans never saw.

After almost two hours of pulsating but goalless action at Goodison Park and the prospect of a first penalty shoot-out between the local rivals looming, ITV accidentally cut away from the game to an advertisement break.

The television blooper ensured many viewers were being shown commercials for Volkswagen cars and Tic-Tac sweets instead of 19-year-old Gosling's curled shot going in off Martin Škrtel's leg in the 118th minute to secure a thrilling victory for the Blues.

Some just managed to catch the goal after several ITV regions and digital channels returned to the game seconds before Gosling's strike but for others the adverts continued, and the first fans knew of the goal was when they cut back to the Everton celebrations.

It is understood an automated system for broadcasting adverts, which should only be used on 'regular schedule' nights, not live events which can overrun, kicked in as the game continued in extra time.

Anchorman Steve Rider apologised, saying, 'Well, it was a dream strike from Gosling and Liverpool's goose was cooked, and technically I'm afraid it came at a pretty bad time for us as well. If you missed the goal, our apologies for the technical problems we had at that time.'

It was the third meeting between Everton and Liverpool in just 17 days and the first time in almost five hours of football they could be separated.

The first game, in the Premier League, finished 1-1 at Anfield on 19 January as Steven Gerrard's 25-yard blockbuster midway through the second half was cancelled out by a glancing header from Tim Cahill three minutes from full time.

The Blues then crossed Stanley Park again for the first FA Cup fourth round encounter six days later.

This time it was the visitors who drew first blood, through Joleon Lescott's close-range strike on 27 minutes, before Gerrard earned a replay with a 54th minute shot that squirmed through Tim Howard's hands.

The Goodison clash was even tighter but with the Reds reduced to ten men after Lucas's second booking 14 minutes from the end of normal time, Dominic King of the *Liverpool Echo* described the dramatic finale, 'As the seconds ticked down in extra time, seemingly taking us ever nearer to penalties, the mind could not help but wander back to those shattering nights against Villarreal and Fiorentina when massive opportunities were ripped from Everton's hands.

'Another Fiorentina, for example, would have been too much for some to take and one shudders to think what might have happened to the direction of the campaign had Liverpool been victorious via the lottery of a shoot-out from 12 yards.

'Now, thanks to Gosling, a fresh momentum has surely been added; his 118th-minute strike must leave Everton's players feeling they have taken another step nearer to closing the gap with the top four and reaffirmed the faith in their abilities.

'Everton will definitely play better than they did here in the future, and it would be wide of the mark to say this was their best effort of the season. It wasn't. Moments of inspiration and genuine skill were all too scarce from both sides. But who cares?'

Of the goal itself, King added, 'Apart from a big engine, Gosling also has his share of skill and the composure he showed to take a cross down under pressure before dispatching a shot past Pepe Reina – Liverpool's star man alongside Jamie Carragher – had the hallmark of quality.

'And what of the man who served up the chance? There is no logical reason why [Andy] van der Meyde has such a following on the terraces, given some of his escapades in recent years, but finally he has provided a moment of sheer delight.'

Two more Goodison ties then saw David Moyes's men dispatch Aston Villa 3-1 and Middlesbrough 2-1 before a tense penalty shoot-out victory over Manchester United in the semi-final after a goalless draw.

Before that Wembley clash against Sir Alex Ferguson's side, Moyes confidently predicted, 'This Everton team will win a trophy soon,' but he would ultimately leave Goodison empty-handed after over 11 years in charge.

The 2009 FA Cup was the only final he reached and despite the Blues going ahead after just 25 seconds - at the time the quickest goal in cup final history - even the eventual scoreline of 2-1 flattered Everton on an afternoon in which they wilted in the heat of the capital.

* * *

24 January 1981: Everton 2 Liverpool 1 (Imre Varadi's humble pie for the Reds in the FA Cup)

Everton hero Imre Varadi said that scoring what proved to be the winning goal in an FA Cup Merseyside derby had him licking his lips, if only to wipe away the meat and potato pie supposedly flung at his face by an irate Liverpool fan.

Recalling the incident in which the savoury staple of British football terraces was chucked in his direction after he netted at the Park End, the striker told the *Liverpool Echo*, 'I was so excited I ran around the back of the goal not realising it was full of away supporters. I incurred the wrath of an angry Liverpool fan who chucked a meat and potato pie straight into my face … I can still taste it now!'

Whereas the modern Merseyside derby is the Premier League fixture to have produced the most red cards, encounters of yesteryear

– particularly FA Cup meetings like this – were notoriously brutal affairs with a greater toleration of a physical approach.

Varadi, who was just 20 at the time, acknowledged they were a different sort of game to the type of football we're now used to.

He recalled, 'I still have that game on tape and if I get it out to show people, they all say there would have been about ten sendings off if it was played today. Some of the challenges were bordering on GBH.

'I remember Steve McMahon topping Phil Neal with one tackle which sent Neal somersaulting right up in the air – and he got away with it! It was like a war. Unbelievable.

'The atmosphere, the passion, the speed ... it was an incredible experience.'

At one point tensions threatened to boil over when Liverpool substitute Jimmy Case caught Martin Hodge after going in studs showing on the Everton goalkeeper, prompting a mass melee before controversial referee Clive Thomas – who had infuriated Blues with his inexplicable decision to disallow what would have been a winning goal for Bryan Hamilton in the 1977 FA Cup semi-final against the Reds – stepped in.

Everton's opener on 17 minutes was credited to Peter Eastoe but appeared to be an own goal by Avi Cohen.

The pace of Eastoe's flicked shot was dulled by a save from Ray Clemence who had come rushing out, but the ball was still goal-bound before Phil Neal attempted to clear it off the line only for it to ricochet into the net anyway off his Israeli team-mate.

Varadi's goal on the hour was a close-range effort into the roof of the net after he was picked out by Eamonn O'Keefe, who had tried to round Clemence but had been taken wide.

Case's left-footed finish from six yards with 14 minutes remaining had Everton nerves jangling but Varadi still had time to miss a sitter with his shot off target after dribbling his way past Clemence.

It was a particularly sweet day for the hosts' Blue-blood captain Mick Lyons who – after missing the 1978 'Andy King derby' – tasted victory for the first time in 20 matches in the fixture.

Ian Hargraves wrote in the *Echo*, 'At long last, Evertonians can walk tall again. Against all form and expectation, they outran and outfought a side generally regarded as the best in the country and were full value for that success.

'Indeed, so dominant were they on the day, they could have easily doubled the winning margin. As Sir John Moores [Everton's former chairman who would celebrate his 85th birthday the day after the game] remarked, "After years of having our noses rubbed in it, it is some solace to have beaten them at last."'

Like many a good story, this 'pie in the sky' tale has perhaps become embellished somewhat in the subsequent decades.

Television footage from the game does show an object that could well be the infamous flying savoury snack being aimed at Varadi, but it appears to hit his back.

However, when it comes to the subject of food and drink, what isn't in doubt is the moniker given to the celebratory tipple that Evertonians toasted this victory with.

Varadi said, 'We all went out celebrating that night. We ended up in a place called Snobs in the city centre. People were going to the bar and ordering Varadi and Cokes instead of Bacardi and Cokes! It was a great night. Ever since then I've drunk Bacardi and Coke. I love the stuff now. But that was the first time I'd ever drunk it.'

* * *

18 October 1997: Everton 2 Liverpool 0 (False dawn for Howard Kendall's third stint and teenage prospect Danny Cadamarteri)

The 1997/98 season was arguably Everton's grimmest of the early Premier League era but among all the Goodison Park gloom, teenager Danny Cadamarteri – for a fleeting spell at least – sparked some raw energy into what appeared to be a sinking side, and this was his finest hour.

The Blues' preparations for the campaign were messy to say the least – if not downright shambolic.

After Joe Royle's strange exit back on 27 March it had taken chairman Peter Johnson three months to find a successor.

He told fans that he had been 'pleasantly surprised' by the high level of interest in the job and proclaimed he would be hiring a 'world-class manager' but ended up choosing Andy Gray, who despite being a fans' favourite from his playing days, possessed no managerial experience.

The Scot then turned down the job in favour of a lucrative new contract at Sky Sports where he worked as a pundit and Johnson was forced to go back to Howard Kendall, who despite being initially overlooked for Gray, took the reins for a third time.

Kendall himself said, 'I know I wasn't first choice, but that is not a concern.'

However, Johnson seemed less convinced and with the owner unwilling to release major funds for new signings, the returning legend was forced into some difficult horse-trading in the transfer market.

His once shrewd eye for a bargain now seemed to elude him though. David Unsworth, brought back the following year for £3m by Walter Smith, via a bizarre short spell at Aston Villa, was swapped for West Ham's Danny Williamson, whose injury-plagued time at the club amounted to just 17 games.

Kendall then raided his previous club Sheffield United to exchange Graham Stuart for Carl Tiler and Mitch Ward while other new arrivals such as Tony Thomas from Tranmere Rovers and Manchester United's John O'Kane also failed to convince.

Big names departed from the dressing room with the club's record appearance maker, most-decorated player and undisputed best-ever goalkeeper Neville Southall playing his 751st and final game in a 2-0 home loss to Tottenham on 29 November with Everton rooted to the foot of the table.

While time had finally caught up with the 39-year-old, fellow Welshman and captain Gary Speed, at 28, was still at the peak of his powers at the time of his acrimonious January exit which remained shrouded in mystery.

Even the team's kit wasn't right. Along with it being a lighter hue than the deep royal blue traditionally worn by Everton, an eagle-eyed fan spotted that the blue, white and yellow band along the centre of the shirt was upside down on the replica shirts compared to those sported by the players.

Embarrassed manufacturer Umbro was forced to act quickly and conveniently insisted that it was the team's kit that was wrong, not the thousands already sold to fans!

Among this chaos, Everton somehow managed to pull off a memorable Merseyside derby scalp, just three days after Kendall had been involved in an on-field spat with some of his players after he'd asked them to warm down following a 4-1 League Cup exit at Coventry City.

David Prentice wrote in the *Liverpool Echo*, 'A respectful handshake, offered before the final whistle, isn't what you expect from a Merseyside derby match. But Neil Ruddock's magnanimous gesture to substituted Everton hero Danny Cadamarteri was in keeping with the rest of an astonishing afternoon.

'The wag who sent [the theme from] *Tales of the Unexpected* booming out of the Goodison public address system five minutes after the final whistle summed up the afternoon perfectly.

'Everton stepped out as the biggest underdogs since Joe Royle's first match as manager. They ended it as top dogs in the city once again – after spectacularly rediscovering the passion and spirit which had been so missing in midweek. It was an amazing transformation.'

The Blues got the break they needed when they went ahead on the stroke of half-time as 'David James fisted the ball against a startled Ruddock and in for an own goal.'

However, it was the youthful vigour of Cadamarteri that sealed the win 15 minutes from the end. Prentice said, 'He smuggled the ball away from Bjørn Tore Kvarme, charged purposefully forward before cutting inside Ruddock, ignoring the better-placed Duncan Ferguson and crashed a right-footed shot into the net.'

It was his fifth goal in a seven-game purple patch, but he wouldn't net again all season.

* * *

28 October 1978: Everton 1 Liverpool 0 (Andy the King for the Blues)

Everton scratched the seven-year itch after going 15 Merseyside derbies without victory before their number seven Andy King netted a memorable match-winner against Liverpool.

Luton-born King, who was a real fan favourite with the Goodison Park crowd, infamously had an attempted touchline interview with *Grandstand* abruptly cut short by a policeman who insisted that both he and the reporter 'get off the pitch', but once he did get to speak after the crowd had gone home, he remarked, 'It is beyond a dream.'

The Blues hadn't beaten the Reds since David Johnson – a man who would go on to net winners for both sides in Merseyside derbies – scored in a 1-0 victory at Goodison on 13 November 1971.

Back then, Everton were level with Liverpool, Manchester United and Arsenal at the top of the English football food chain with seven titles apiece but in the subsequent years their local rivals had dominated both at home and abroad with Phil Thompson admitting he was 'as sick as a parrot' to relinquish the seven-year unbeaten record in the fixture.

Despite the one-sided nature of derbies over several seasons, both teams went into this top-of-the-table fixture in fine form with Liverpool at the summit and Everton undefeated.

Writing in the *Liverpool Echo*, Charles Lambert explained just how much the result meant to long-suffering Evertonians, 'Very rarely over the last few years have Liverpool been the bridesmaids rather than the bride, but that was their lot at Goodison Park.

'Seven years is an awfully long time for a club in such a football-mad area as Merseyside to wait for a victory over their rivals.

'Jimmy Case said, "You would think that Everton had won the league, the way they are celebrating," and he was quite right. But in a way this was, for Everton, the equivalent of winning the league. The result meant not only can they once more call themselves top dogs on Merseyside, but the tide of football fortune is slowly turning in Everton's favour.

'I don't mean that so much in the context of local rivalry as in relation to Everton's standing in the football world as a whole. The years of decline after 1970 ended when Gordon Lee took over. But although Everton improved, they still fell short of their own aspirations.

'They reached the League Cup Final – and lost. They reached the FA Cup semi-final – and lost. They even had their runners-up spot in the league snatched away from them – by Liverpool. Signs of promise were dogged by the seeds of frustration.

'But Bob Latchford's 30 goals last season gave Goodison something to sing about, and how they revelled in that moment of triumph. And now, by beating the Liverpool jinx, Everton have taken another step up the ladder that leads to the top.'

King's match-winner was a sweet half volley from inside the D after Martin Dobson had nodded down Mike Pejic's lofted ball into the box but rather than the victory being any kind of smash-and-grab raid, Lambert maintained that the Blues showed throughout the game they had no inferiority complex despite their recent struggles against their neighbours.

He added, 'Over the previous 18 months Everton had proved to the rest of the country that they could play. Now they have proven it to the other half of Merseyside as well.

'The teamwork and commitment engendered by Mr Lee paid off handsomely. This time there were no psychological problems.

'That, perhaps, was Everton's biggest satisfaction. Nowhere, not even in their hearts or their innermost thoughts, do they feel the slightest trace of inferiority.

'They went out convinced that they could beat the best team in the country. The world now knows they were right.'

Opposition manager Bob Paisley bemoaned that it was Liverpool's worst performance of the season, but Lambert observed, 'Credit must go to Everton for not allowing them to play. It's not very often that Liverpool are hustled out of their stride by any team.'

Indeed, on *Match of the Day* that evening, host Jimmy Hill quipped, 'If they'd have had matches like that in Roman days, they could have made do without the lions!'

Ultimately Lee would fail to end the Blues' trophy drought, but Evertonians showed their enduring appreciation for King, who had two spells at the club, by turning out in great numbers to line the streets around Goodison for his funeral at St Luke's Church in 2015.

* * *

24 April 2024: Everton 2 Liverpool 0 (Blues end hoodoo during incredible week to survive against the odds)

The 2023/24 season was the most testing campaign beleaguered Blues had ever known as Everton were handed two separate points deductions, but they overcame those setbacks to ensure their final year at Goodison Park would be in the Premier League with a first Merseyside derby win on home turf since 2010 pushing them towards survival as part of a hat-trick of successes in an incredible week.

Everton's single breach of the Premier League's Profit and Sustainability Rules governing permitted financial losses resulted in them being handed an immediate ten-point deduction on 17 November 2023, which at the time was the most severe sporting sanction in 135 years of English top-flight football.

Blues supporters – and influential figures such as politicians – immediately started a vociferous campaign of protests with a furious backlash against the Premier League but although Everton got the deduction reduced to six points on 26 February 2024 following an appeal, they had already been hit by a second charge for a new time period on 15 January.

This would result in a deduction of a further two points on 8 April, leaving the Blues with a final total of eight taken off for the season, and again the club immediately announced its plans to appeal but that process was later dropped after results like this enabled the team to save themselves on the pitch.

A wonder goal from Alejandro Garnacho had cruelly taken the wind out of Everton's sails in their first game after their initial deduction as Manchester United triumphed 3-0 at Goodison Park but the Blues, who went into their next fixture at Nottingham Forest bottom of the table, then embarked on a four-match winning run.

The sequence ended with a penalty shoot-out defeat at home to Marco Silva's Fulham in the League Cup quarter-final, and the hangover saw the team endure a club record 13 Premier League fixtures without victory, a period stretching beyond Christmas to Easter.

That wretched run was finally ended with an ugly 1-0 home success over Burnley on 6 April but a 6-0 thrashing at Chelsea next time out proved a painful watershed moment as manager Sean Dyche told his players he was staying and fighting.

To mark the fresh start, Dyche swapped his usual shirt and tie for a tracksuit and his squad responded with three league victories at Goodison Park in a single week for the first time since April 1904 as they defeated Nottingham Forest 2-0 and Brentford 1-0 either side of the derby delight.

Facing their title-chasing neighbours at Goodison on the anniversary of the Bayern Munich game some 39 years earlier, Everton were emphatic winners despite having not beaten Liverpool at the ground since they triumphed by the same scoreline some 13 and a half years earlier.

Although they were denied an early penalty after Dominic Calvert-Lewin was brought down by visiting keeper Alisson only for a VAR check to show the Blues striker was offside, Dyche's men dominated throughout and there was added poignancy in the backstory of their two scorers.

Centre-back Jarrad Branthwaite, who was the team's breakthrough star of the season having returned from a loan spell at PSV Eindhoven looking like a potentially generational talent, broke the deadlock on 27 minutes after some penalty box pinball as he stretched out one of the long legs in his 6ft 5in frame to hit a left-footed shot that was too hot for Alisson to handle as it squirmed through the Brazil international's hands and into the net.

Centre-forward Calvert-Lewin, who had seen Dyche's methods cure the injury issues that had restricted him to just 18 games in both of the previous seasons after what the Yorkshireman called 'a factory reset', went on to play 39 times in 2023/24 but despite having become just the fourth player to break the 50-goal barrier for the club in the Premier League earlier in the campaign, he then endured a 23-match scoring drought.

Nevertheless, he sealed this win with a classic Everton number nine's header in front of the Gwladys Street as he nodded home Dwight McNeil's right-wing corner at the back post on 58 minutes.

Joe Thomas of the *Liverpool Echo* said, 'After so many years, so many disappointments in this fixture, and so much heartbreak and heartache, it was an emotional one.

'This is a club and a fanbase that has suffered their lowest as their biggest foes have ridden the crest of a silverware-laden wave.

'All those taunts, all those jibes, all that devastation – all now a thing of the past. The underdogs bit back, roared on by a crowd that has deserved far more nights like this in recent years.

'"You lost the league at Goodison Park" was the cry that rang out as this game entered stoppage time [departing Liverpool manager Jürgen Klopp, previously unbeaten against Everton in front of fans, went into the match with only goal difference keeping his side off the top of the table]. This was not just a win, it was an exorcism. It was the night a tormented fanbase banished some of its most spiteful ghosts.'

* * *

11 March 1967: Everton 1 Liverpool 0 (105,000 watch Alan Ball's FA Cup winner in two grounds)

Thanks to large screens being installed at Anfield to relay the action from Goodison Park, a record-breaking 105,000 fans watched Everton triumph against Liverpool in this historic FA Cup fifth round tie.

Pathé News produced a short film on how the experiment by ABC Television was deemed a success.

Their engineers fought against 45mph gales to erect eight 30ft by 40ft screens around Anfield, costing £500 each, with tickets for a 40,149 crowd selling out within 36 hours of going on sale.

Other than one of the screens being lifted for a few seconds by a gust of wind, the action from Goodison, where 64,851, including Howard Kendall who had joined the Blues the previous day, watched Alan Ball net the winner on the stroke of half-time, was viewed clearly, even if the outcome didn't please Kopites.

One well-told tale from the day surrounds celebrity Liverpool fan Jimmy Tarbuck trudging out of Anfield after the full-time whistle with the usual gap-toothed grin wiped off his face by the result, only to be told by a fellow comedian, 'Don't worry Jimmy – it's only a film!'

The *Liverpool Echo* reported on how, after some initial teething problems, those watching at Anfield were given quite a show, writing, 'The cameras came on shortly after 6.30pm [it was a 7pm kick-off] and there were some good-humoured cheers when the picture proved extremely unreliable. However, things soon settled down to normal and the crowd were entertained by a brief film of last year's FA Cup Final [Everton's 3-2 comeback victory over Sheffield Wednesday after trailing 2-0].

'The cheers which greeted Everton's three goals showed that plenty of their supporters had strayed across the park but the loudest applause of all was for the now famous incident when two supporters were removed by policemen.

'This was followed up by a film of Liverpool's Wembley triumph of 1965 [winning the FA Cup for the first time, beating Leeds United 2-1] which was naturally much to the liking of the crowd.'

As often happens with so much at stake on these occasions, the game itself failed to match its billing with the winds that had impacted on Anfield's big screens also hampering the football being played at Goodison.

Michael Charters of the *Echo* was damning about the quality both on show that evening and in Merseyside derbies in general.

He remarked, 'I suppose it was too much to expect that Saturday night's cup derby would produce the epic everyone had hoped, the soccer spectacular everyone wanted to see.

'The pre-game ballyhoo blinded us all to the fact that we haven't seen a really top-class derby for years and the latest clash, with tension built up to an unprecedented pitch, was very much in the usual run.

'The electric atmosphere, the packed Goodison Park, the TV relay to Anfield, all made it one of the great occasions in Merseyside sporting history, but the football content was so inadequate that I felt sorry for the thousands of people who had struggled so hard to get a ticket, struggled through the traffic to get there, and had to watch a game ruined by a gale and the inability of both teams to sustain any sort of smooth attacking play.

'The reaction of the 64,000 crowd was the best possible illustration of what they thought of it. Apart from the tremendous din at the start and the end, the only time they were able to let themselves go was when Alan Ball, with superb opportunism, scored the goal that put Everton through to the quarter-finals.'

Although Charters scolded 'even that developed from a mistake' as Liverpool's Gordon Milne misjudged the pace of a backpass to his goalkeeper Tommy Lawrence, he conceded that the way Ball, who had been snapped up by the Blues in the aftermath of their 1-0 defeat to Liverpool – also at Goodison Park – in the Charity Shield the previous August, 'cleverly hooked it past his chin into the net' meant his effort was 'a brilliantly taken goal'.

Everton would lose their quarter-final at Nottingham Forest 3-2 but almost half a century later Lawrence, unlike Tarbuck, would be able to look back on this game with a smile when asked by a BBC reporter, unaware of his identity, whether he remembered the big match, as he replied, 'I played in it.'

* * *

23 November 2013: Everton 3 Liverpool 3 (One of the greatest Merseyside derbies)

It might sound somewhat cringeworthy, but football was the winner following one of the most open and entertaining matches in Merseyside derby history as both managers adopted an expansive approach to an often-attritional fixture more traditionally associated with blood and thunder.

David Moyes's penchant for a safety-first philosophy in games against Liverpool had prompted opposite number Rafael Benítez to make his infamous 'small club' jibe after an Anfield stalemate in 2007 – a remark for which the Spaniard had to do some serious back-pedalling to explain when he controversially became the first manager to have taken charge of both Merseyside giants some 14 years later.

The Scot's successor, Roberto Martínez, was considerably more cavalier in his footballing philosophy though and when coming up against fellow former Swansea City manager Brendan Rodgers for his first Merseyside derby, the pair created a footballing feast seldom seen on such occasions, with BBC Sport's chief football writer Phil McNulty proclaiming it to be 'the finest meeting between these two sides in years'.

Twice Everton came from behind to equalise but despite finally getting themselves ahead, they would ultimately have to be content with a share of the spoils.

Greg O'Keeffe of the *Liverpool Echo* mused, 'Perhaps it was fitting that the words of Paul McCartney's famous ode to acceptance echoed around Goodison Park before a half of derby football which was both heart-warming and heart-breaking in equal measure. "Let It Be" sang the choirboy on the pitch during the break, and Everton were duly forced to be philosophical after a contest which promised so much, but in the end succumbed to the seemingly inevitable.

'There was a feeling of déjà vu for the home supporters when Daniel Sturridge levelled for Liverpool with a minute of normal time remaining.

'Having battled back from going behind twice, Everton had dominated the midfield and suggested a thrilling victory was on the cards. Then Liverpool did what they so often do and delivered the sucker-punch square in the gut.

'But it would be wrong to label this a "same-old" derby. They might have had to be content with a point, but for Everton there was a promising newness about the afternoon.

'The Toffees more than played their part in a classic between two ideologically similar managers, each advocates of the continental passing approach, and ultimately they produced the braver, more entertaining football.'

O'Keeffe was glowing in his appraisal of the Blues' homegrown hero name-checked in their new 'School of Science – it's on its way back terrace anthem'.

He said, 'Ross Barkley was outstanding. Imagine how good he will be when his rough edges have been erased. Decision-making and concentration are perhaps his only minor flaws, but what he offers in contrast is significant.

'Barkley will learn from his lapses, like the momentary neglect when he switched off and allowed Philippe Coutinho [5th minute] to plunder a gallingly early lead for Liverpool from a corner.

'Even then, faced with such an early setback, Evertonians becoming accustomed to Roberto Martínez's style might have known an equaliser was due.

'It was Kevin Mirallas [8] who delivered, tellingly from a Barkley nod-down, and the Belgian's timing was spot on.'

On Liverpool's second goal, O'Keeffe said, 'Fine margins in football account for much, hence why Steven Pienaar's slack positioning in the wall allowed Luis Suárez [19] to peg the Blues back again from that exquisite free kick, but even trailing at the break, there was a sense Everton were always going to come back.'

The action cranked up a notch after the break and O'Keeffe added, 'The ever-impressive James McCarthy showed good awareness on the back of a mature display to tee up Romelu Lukaku [72] to level again.

'Then the big striker showed why luminaries such as Duncan Ferguson and Andy Gray talked about him in such glowing terms by scoring a barnstorming header [82] which would have made both proud.

'Like Barkley, he too must improve his decision-making, but he still shone like a beacon in the second half.

'Liverpool's goalkeeper Simon Mignolet had to be in inspired form, and even though Sturridge [89, with a header from a Steven Gerrard corner] delivered that late slap in the face, it was the visitors who must have celebrated like they had won.

'Afterwards both managers puffed out their cheeks and acknowledged a derby to remember, perhaps on par with the renowned 4-4 of 1991.

'That was a game which saw an Everton side at the end of an era. This time, with four players aged under 21 on the pitch at the end, they're only just beginning.'

* * *

12 February 2025: Everton 2 Liverpool 2 (James Tarkowski saves Everton in the last seconds after over 130 years of Goodison derby combat)

After 120 matches across more than 130 years, an explosive volleyed goal with virtually the last kick by captain James Tarkowski ensured Everton didn't finish with a losing record against Liverpool in Merseyside derbies at Goodison Park.

Incredibly, after facing off against each other since 1894, Everton and Liverpool went into Goodison's final derby with 41 victories apiece at the ground.

However, while the all-time record was delicately poised ahead of a fixture that has been delayed by a couple of months due to a postponement in December when 60mph winds from Storm Darragh were battering Merseyside, ensuring David Moyes had now replaced Sean Dyche in the home dugout, the returning Blues boss acknowledged that there was now a gulf between the two sides and he faced a big task trying to bridge that gap.

Backed by deafening roars from the moment that they took to the field to the strains of *Z-Cars*, Everton started brightly and took the lead on 11 minutes. Joe Thomas of the *Liverpool Echo* wrote, 'Jarrad Branthwaite seized on the ball, took a quick free kick and threaded a pass behind the away defence for Beto to latch on to. He coolly finished past Alisson to send Goodison wild.'

That joy was short-lived, however, as just five minutes later Liverpool netted an equaliser out of nothing, with Thomas remarking, 'As Salah chipped a cross into the box Alexis Mac Allister was an underdog in a fight that should have pitched him against Branthwaite, Tarkowski or Jake O'Brien, all of whom tower above him. Somehow he drifted between all three and glanced in to level.'

Everton kept probing and, just moments after Abdoulaye Doucoure had spurned an inviting opportunity at the other end, it seemed particularly cruel when Mohamed Salah fired Liverpool ahead on 73 minutes.

Thomas wrote, 'It was Liverpool that delivered what looked set to be the knockout blow. Tarkowski half-cleared a cross that could have been swallowed up by Jordan Pickford and Branthwaite blocked the shot that followed into the path of Mo Salah. Of course he scored.'

For all Everton's efforts, both on the night and over the previous 13 decades, it appeared as though Liverpool would have the last and longest laugh at the Blues' long-time home.

Their travelling fans who had previously been drowned out for most of the game certainly thought so as they belted out 'You'll Never Walk Alone' and 'We won the league at Goodison Park'.

With just seconds remaining though, they would be silenced with a glorious Goodison moment that will live for Evertonians forever.

Paul Joyce of *The Times* summed it up as he wrote, 'In years to come, when a new generation of supporters asks what made the Goodison derby stand apart so often, they will be pointed to the chaos and carnage of this final instalment.

'The answer lay in the closing act. The Liverpool supporters had just cleared their throats, having sung for the first time this season about winning the Premier League, when the unrelenting drama that this fixture so often delivers conjured one more episode.

'Everton launched one last attack, Tim Iroegbunam flicked on Vitalii Mykolenko's cross and James Tarkowski, of all people, thundered home a volley at the back post to equalise.

'Suddenly those chants were washed away by a guttural roar, a wave of emotion sweeping around this old stadium.

'There was the inevitable delay as VAR checked for offside, and then whether Ibrahima Konaté had been fouled, but the goal stood and, with that, the blue touch paper was lit on the final neighbourhood tussle in this patch of L4.

'Everton's new stadium at Bramley-Moore Dock has much to live up to when this febrile rivalry is resumed there next season.'

Tarkowski's goal, which Thomas wrote 'took the roof off this sporting colosseum', was greeted with wild scenes of jubilation from Everton supporters, including one wielding the corner flag in delight and the centre-back remarked, 'I had an 80-year-old grabbing me and then a five-year-old kid pulling me to the floor, there were stewards everywhere, it was chaos, but it shows what a moment it is.'

A hectic postscript to what was the 38th derby draw at Goodison saw four red cards shown after the final whistle to Abdoulaye Doucoure, Curtis Jones, Liverpool head coach Arne Slot and his assistant Sipke Hulshoff, but other observers concurred with the Blues skipper.

Andy Hunter of *The Guardian* remarked that it was 'a final kick worthy of the grand old stadium'.

Oliver Holt of the *Daily Mail* concluded, 'It felt like the old ground, which has always been a bear-pit at its best, could scarcely have had a better send-off. This was Goodison's night. Its honour and its memory were preserved at the last.'

11

Dixie Dean

IF ONE player has come to symbolise Everton it is Dixie Dean, the most prolific goalscorer in the history of the club and in any single season in English professional football.

A lifelong Evertonian, Dean was plucked from Tranmere Rovers as a teenager and at the age of just 21 he set a never-to-be-beaten record of 60 league goals in a season – a figure set in the top flight that also leads the way in all four divisions.

His 383 goals for Everton are the most by any individual for a single English club and are more than double the total any other player has ever netted for the Blues, with Graeme Sharp next up among the seven other triple-figure marksmen on 160.

* * *

5 May 1928: Everton 3 Arsenal 3 (Dean hat-trick secures 60-goal league scoring record)

History was made in dramatic fashion by Dixie Dean on what was surely the most glorious afternoon in Goodison Park's 133-year history.

Everton had already secured a third league championship so all eyes were on their centre-forward to see if he could score his seventh First Division hat-trick of the season to break the Football League record of 59 set by Middlesbrough's George Camsell in the Second Division a year earlier.

The Blues' title win had not been straightforward though.

After the penultimate weekend of the season, leaders Everton were three points clear of second-place Huddersfield Town, but the Yorkshire side had two games in hand, wins in which could see them climb to the summit.

However, the Terriers – who had won three championships in a row from 1924 to 1926 – suffered a late collapse, losing consecutive fixtures, 1-0 at home to Sheffield United on the Monday and 3-0 at Aston Villa on the Wednesday to ensure the crown went to Goodison with a game to spare.

Incredibly, when Dean had missed Everton's 2-0 win at Sunderland on 31 March, he was still 15 goals shy of breaking Camsell's record with just seven games to go but a late spring scoring spree saw him reel in the target as he netted in all the remaining fixtures.

His sequence going into the final day went as follows: Blackburn Rovers, 4-1 at home, two goals; Bury 1-1 at home, one goal; Sheffield United 3-1 away, two goals; Newcastle United 3-0 at home, one goal; Aston Villa 3-2 at home, two goals; Burnley 5-3 away, four goals.

Although Arsenal were a mid-table side that season, they had beaten Everton twice already having knocked them out of the FA Cup; their own legendary centre-forward Charles Buchan was playing the final game of his career and did not want to be upstaged by the young upstart who was his opposite number.

A report from 'Bee' in the *Liverpool Echo* attested to the 'electric start' to the Arsenal match that saw the visitors take a second-minute lead in controversial circumstances through James Shaw 'after handling the ball and getting away with it'.

Dean restored parity a minute later as he 'headed it to the extreme left-hand corner' after George Martin had turned Ted Critchley's corner on to him.

Referee Lol Harper then gave another debatable decision on six minutes when he pointed to the spot after 'an accidental collision' when Dean was crossed by Arsenal's 'long-legged' centre-half Jack Butler.

The Everton hero drew level with the record as he 'was able to rise from the ground and take the penalty kick successfully and well'.

Even though there were still another 84 minutes left for Dean to break the record, time started to ebb away, and nerves jangled when Arsenal drew level ten minutes before half-time as Everton left-back Jack O'Donnell 'turned the ball over his own goal line' after a mix-up with goalkeeper Arthur Davies.

Frustration was growing and 'for long spells, Dean was crowded out, or received an unwise pass'. His magic moment would come though, eight minutes before full-time, 'Alec Troup took the corner kick and out of a ruck of probably 14 players, Dean with unerring accuracy, nodded the ball to the extreme right-hand side of the goal.

'There has never been such a joyful shout at Everton. It was prolonged for minutes and went on until the end of the game.

'The crowd never stopped cheering for eight solid minutes, and Dean was hugged by all his comrades, and indeed there was a threat of the crowd breaking on to the field of play.

'In fact, two men rushed across through the barrier of police, and the referee had to bundle one man off, and out of the way of trouble.'

Such was the mayhem, even another home defensive blunder resulting in Shaw's second goal of the game for Arsenal on 86 minutes after collecting a rebound when Davies had failed to make what should have been 'an easy save', failed to dampen Blues' spirits.

While Dean's record has rightly been revered by Evertonians for almost a century now, some observers away from Goodison have misguidedly tried to make out that scoring was somehow not very difficult in his era.

Although he and Camsell both took advantage of a relaxation in the offside law in 1925, the fact is that no other top flight-player before or since has got closer than being 11 goals shy of Dean's total with his nearest challenger being another son of Birkenhead, Tom 'Pongo' Waring, who netted 49 for Aston Villa in 1930/31.

***

28 March 1925: Everton 2 Aston Villa 0 (Dean's first Everton goal on home debut)

Dixie Dean's record-breaking scoring spree started here.

Christened William Ralph Dean, preferring Bill but known to the football world as 'Dixie', the most iconic player in Everton's history was born at 313 Laird Street in Birkenhead on 22 January 1907.

He'd been a Blue since childhood having been enthralled by his first visit to Goodison Park when taken by his father William Dean senior during the 1914/15 title-winning campaign, but he started his professional career at his hometown club, Tranmere Rovers.

After netting 27 goals in as many games for a struggling Tranmere side who would finish second bottom of the Third Division North in 1924/25 – they weren't even Wirral's top team that year with the now long-since defunct New Brighton finishing above them in third place of the same division – Dean was one of the game's hottest properties.

Newcastle United, Arsenal, Bolton Wanderers and Aston Villa – ultimately his first victims in an Everton shirt – all supposedly coveted the 18-year-old's signature but he is reputed to have turned them all down as he kept waiting for his beloved Blues to call.

In the 21st century, deadline-day transfers can of course be frantic affairs.

Alex Iwobi was on a boat during a family holiday in Dubai when he joined Everton in 2019 while manager David Moyes vividly recalled the mad dash he personally embarked upon to ensure Marouane Fellaini became the club's record signing in 2008.

The Scot told the *Daily Mail* how he endured a 'terrifying' ride across the English Channel in a tiny aircraft – an action later brought into sobering focus by Cardiff City signing Emiliano Sala's tragic crash in 2019 – before struggling to locate Fellaini, one of football's most distinctive figures, in a seemingly incomplete hotel.

He then had to watch club secretary Dave Harrison 'scream down the phone to the FA', trying to explain that the fax machine was broken as they tried to send over the relevant documentation in time.

Back on 16 March 1925, a young Dean didn't even know it was transfer deadline day and went to the Scala cinema in Birkenhead to watch a silent film called *Rupert of Hentzau*.

On returning home, his mother told him that Tom McIntosh had called to try and sign him, and such was the centre-forward's enthusiasm to make the switch, he immediately ran the two and a half miles to the Woodside Hotel where the Everton secretary was waiting for him.

The deal was sealed for £3,000 and although Dean was expecting his family to receive a ten per cent cut, they were instead given just a tenth of that figure and received a mere £30 with Rovers manager Bert Cooke insisting, 'That's all the league will allow.'

He made his debut in a 3-1 defeat at Arsenal just five days after signing but subsequently broke his duck against Aston Villa the following weekend in the first game he played at Goodison.

It seems that Dean was already an instant hero before the Blues faithful, whose side were 20th in the First Division at the time, had even seen him kick a ball.

'Stork' reported in the *Liverpool Echo*, 'Dixie Dean, who made his debut at home, came in for a special little cheer all to himself.'

Dean broke the deadlock on 27 minutes, but it was not with a trademark header. Under the subheading 'Dean makes good', the article continued, 'The Villa adopted offside tactics, which is most unlike them, but that it did not avail them anything was proved when Fred Kennedy bamboozled the Villa defence into the belief that he would allow the ball to go over and so claim a corner, instead of which he hooked the ball back to Dean, who slammed it clear into the net.

'Never was there a more popular goal scored at Goodison. While Dean must be praised for his shot, Kennedy must take the plum for his astuteness.'

David Reid's goal midway through the second half sealed the win for Everton, after Alec Troup 'placed a corner kick so well that he simply had to let drive', but much of the attention was already on his new teenage team-mate.

Other observations of his play stated, 'Dean had done remarkably well. Not only was his goal a gem, but he had ideas of what was required by his flank men,' plus, 'Dean headed like a veteran, and he had hard luck when he directed Troup's centre just over the bar.'

The Dixie Dean legend had begun.

* * *

8 October 1927: Everton 5 Manchester United 2 (Five-goal Dean single-handedly destroys United)

Five-star displays like this from Dixie Dean had helped Evertonians to spin the yarn that their legendary centre-forward had been boosted by having a metal plate inserted under his forehead after a motorcycle accident had threatened to end his career.

In the summer of 1926, at the end of his first full season at Goodison Park, Dean came off his bike in Holywell, North Wales, fracturing his skull and jaw and leading doctors to fear he might never play again.

Dean of course was a true warrior though and having already recovered from the enforced removal of a testicle while on the receiving end of a heavy challenge in a reserve team game for Tranmere against Altrincham, he battled back to score – with a header – on his return at Elland Road on 23 October that year, setting the Blues on their way to a 3-1 win.

The following season, 1927/28, would be both his and English football's most prolific in terms of individual goalscoring with the visit of Manchester United his most fruitful day of the campaign.

Everton centre-forward Jack Southworth's double hat-trick at home to West Bromwich Albion in 1893 is the only instance of a player scoring six goals in any game involving the club.

However, of the subsequent five occasions that Blues players have scored five in one match, three of those were by Dean and he'd repeat the feat twice in consecutive months in 1931/32 at home to Sheffield Wednesday (9-3) and Chelsea (7-2).

The other two times were not in top-flight matches with Tommy Eglington netting five in a 7-1 Second Division victory at home to Doncaster Rovers on 27 September 1952 and Bob Latchford in an 8-0 League Cup second round win over Fourth Division Wimbledon at Goodison on 29 August 1978.

Manchester United were no great shakes in this era – they did not win any trophies during the interwar period – and would, along with six other clubs including Liverpool, finish just a point above the relegation zone this season but Dean's personal destruction of them, taking his goal tally to 17 from the first nine games, in which he'd scored in all, was remarkable.

In the *Liverpool Echo*, 'Bee's Notes on Sport' waxed lyrical about how Dean's display was the crowning glory of his incredible comeback to date.

He wrote, 'It is very difficult to know what to say next about this young, breezy man Dean. William is himself again; a year ago we were going about the clubhouse, one lot saying he would never play again; another lot saying "you can't keep a good man down" and declaring that Dean would be back before Christmas.

'I remember the director, Mr Andrew Coffey, telling me he believed Dean would be back with the football task in October, and I thought it a sort of fatuous optimism.

'Yet Dean came back to his side in October and is gaining strength every day. He is not putting on weight, and indeed his poundage is somewhat similar to that of years ago; he touches 12st 4lb and touches the hearts of all who like to see big heavyweight men capable of being dainty in their movements. Not until January does he touch manhood's estate, 21 years of age.'

For a blow-by-blow account of Dean's goals we must turn to the *Athletic News* which wrote, 'Manchester United were overwhelmed at Goodison Park, where Dean scored all five goals for his side.

'Everton's toll would have been doubled but for the alertness and resource of goalkeeper Lance Richardson, who was called upon to tackle finishing efforts, the high standard of which have not been seen in any game on Merseyside this season.

'In the first minute Critchley took a Forshaw pass to provide Dean with his first goal, and seven minutes later it was the inside-right who gave Dean his second chance.

'After 30 minutes had gone by Forshaw took the ball ahead for Dean to send it into the net with his head, and after Joe Spence [in the 35th minute] had reduced the lead, Dean went off on his own [43] whilst the United defenders were clamouring for offside.

'The Everton leader obtained his fifth goal after 20 minutes in the second half and from a free kick against Jack O'Donnell, before Ray Bennion ended the scoring seven minutes from time.'

The best was still yet to come for Dean as what would prove to be a record-breaking seasonal tally took Everton to their third league championship the following spring.

* * *

27 December 1930: Everton 9 Plymouth Argyle 1 (First of two 9-1 wins in two months as Everton match record league win)

For almost a quarter of a century, Everton's 9-1 thrashing of Manchester City in 1906 stood as their record win but the Blues were to equal that scoreline twice in a single season in 1930/31.

For the first time since the Football League had begun in 1888, Everton were competing outside the top flight.

The Blues missed Dixie Dean badly during his injured spells in the previous campaign and had finished rock bottom of the First Division just two years after being crowned champions.

As a result, the most prolific marksman in English top-flight history got to terrorise Second Division defences for a season, and it hardly seemed fair.

After the debacle that had seen Everton relegated, there were calls at the shareholders' Annual General Meeting for the board to be sacked and for the club to appoint a manager like so many other teams had done, but both suggestions were dismissed.

With Dean mostly fit again, the Blues proved a class apart among their humbler surroundings and they bounced straight back up by romping to the Second Division title.

They plundered 121 goals in the process with 76 at Goodison Park alone, having flown out of the traps and netted 48 times in their first 16 matches.

Bagging eight goals in his previous four games, including another four-goal haul at Goodison against Oldham Athletic, Dean had his eye in for this encounter as the visitors were ruthlessly punished ahead of what in those dark days between Christmas and New Year's Day would have seemed like a very long trip back to Devon.

However, such was the scoring spree on this occasion that four-goal Dean had to share top billing with left-winger Jimmy Stein.

Indeed, writing in the *Liverpool Echo*, 'Bee' put the visitors' sluggishness down to their journey up to Merseyside, declaring, 'Plymouth had travelled all night and had that train deadliness that comes with hours of being tucked up in the corners of the woodwork, instead of tucked up in the rolls of blankets and sheets.

'The men landed here at 6am which I may tell you who do not know that hour in December is a ghastly black washout; cold and miserable.'

He added, 'The Plymouth players went straight to bed, and stayed there until the middle of the day, when they were greeted by a big crowd, some sunshine, and a wealth of mud in the middle of the field that caused the referee to spin the coin on the far side of the pitch instead of on the centre line.'

The report of the first goal read, 'Ted Critchley showed a wise foreknowledge of where Dean would be. Dean leapt high and beat the goalkeeper with a header that was a winner from the moment it touched his head. One minute, one goal.'

Dean's second goal on five minutes 'followed a shot by Jimmy Dunn that struck the upright'.

Tommy Johnson netted the third on 15 minutes via a rebound with 'his task being easy, because Critchley had slipped through space and had trapped a shot that goalkeeper Harry Cann was content to punch away'.

Stein got his first goal on 32 minutes 'with a shot into the right-hand corner of the net' and it was 4-0 at the interval.

It was reported that Everton were seen to 'ease up' early in the second half, enabling Sammy Black to pull a goal back on 55 minutes, having previously twice gone close but his consolation merely spurred the Blues on to a second wind.

On 63 minutes, Stein made it 5-1 as he 'cracked it into the net with his best left-footed drive – a truly enormous shot'.

The Scottish outside left completed his hat-trick five minutes later, when he 'went up to make a perfect header of Critchley's best centre'.

A minute later, Dean bagged his treble as he was 'allowed to go on and dribble to his heart's content' before finishing.

Two minutes after that he made it eight as he 'timed a Stein centre in such a manner that Cann had no chance'.

Stein completed the rout to equal Everton's record with his own fourth of the day, three minutes from the end with 'another ferocious drive'.

The amazing win set the Blues off on a run of 14 consecutive victories in all competitions – including another 9-1 home success against Third Division North Southport in the FA Cup quarter-finals – before their sequence was finally ended with a 1-0 defeat to West Bromwich Albion, who finished runners-up behind them in the Second Division, in an FA Cup semi-final at Old Trafford.

* * *

14 November 1931: Everton 7 Chelsea 2 (Five from Dixie, including a ten-minute headed hat-trick)

A 10-minute hat-trick of headers from Dixie Dean among a five-goal spree in a 7-2 home win over Chelsea was the highlight of an amazing scoring sequence from Everton late in 1931.

Having come straight back up as Second Division champions after their first season outside the top flight, the Blues became one of five clubs in English football history to be crowned league champions in their first season after promotion along with neighbours Liverpool (1906), Tottenham Hotspur (1951), Ipswich Town (1962) and Nottingham Forest (1978).

They were particularly potent on home turf, netting 84 goals at Goodison Park alone at an average of four per game, and between 17 October and Boxing Day they scored at least five goals in six consecutive home victories: Sheffield Wednesday 9-3, Newcastle United 8-1, Chelsea 7-2, Leicester City 9-2, Middlesbrough 5-1, Blackburn Rovers 5-0.

Dean netted 20 goals himself during this purple patch, including another haul of five against Sheffield Wednesday to set off the sequence.

'Stork' reported the action in the *Liverpool Echo*, 'Everton wanted an early goal. They had been used to one and it was forthcoming exactly on five minutes. When Jimmy Stein made his centre, it went to where Dean thought it would come, and with a perfect header, Dean sent the ball well wide of Sam Millington, to score a perfect goal.

'The crowd rose to Dean like one man, and after a spell by Chelsea the same crowd went nearly frantic when Dean notched his second goal in the eighth minute.

'It was another brilliant header, even more brilliant than the first goal, for when Tommy Johnson's pass came over, Millington was standing close by, but Dean, with the side of his head, glanced the ball away from the goalkeeper and into the net.'

Just 15 minutes in, Dean completed his ten-minute headed hat-trick.

Stork wrote, 'There was pandemonium around the ground, and it was not surprising, for such brilliant ball control, especially with the head, was uncommon. When Ted Critchley gave Dean his chance, the Everton leader, by nodding down instead of up, made difficulties for Millington, who could not get across to prevent Dean's header from striking the inside of the upright and going into the net.'

All five of Dean's goals came in little more than the first half an hour.

Dean got his fourth goal on 24 minutes – the fourth in 19 minutes – but it was Johnson who was mainly responsible, for it was following his shot, which Millington appeared to push out, that Dean was given his chance, and it was interesting to note that he scored this goal with his foot.

His fifth, on 32 minutes, equalled his career-best totals, both set at Goodison Park against Manchester United in 1927 and Sheffield Wednesday, less than a month before this game.

'Stork' said, 'For this goal I will give the laurels to Critchley as it was his massive drive which rattled the crossbar and rebounded into play, placing Dean in an almost unassailable position.'

George Mills pulled a goal back for the visitors on 38 minutes as both he and Ted Sagar went for the ball together with the Chelsea man 'just beating the goalkeeper to the punch'.

It was 5-1 at half-time and the Dean show was complete, but Everton added two more goals after the break.

'Stork' observed, 'The teams did not leave the field in the interval and within five minutes of the restart Everton increased their bag of goals to six.

'Johnson, who had returned to his rightful position, beat Millington with a cross-shot which was too strong and accurate for the Chelsea goalkeeper to attempt to make a save.

'At the hour Chelsea suffered their seventh blow, and it was due to a misunderstanding on the part of Peter O'Dowd and Millington.

'The Chelsea goalkeeper pushed out an effort by Stein, and O'Dowd should have completed the clearance, but each left it to the other and Stein, who had followed up, took the ball from them and planted it safely in the net.'

Alex Jackson pulled a goal back for the Londoners five minutes from the final whistle as he 'cleverly guided the ball past Sagar' from Jackie Crawford's centre but there was still time for Dean to almost bag a double hat-trick and equal Jack Souththworth's individual game record from 1893 as 'just at the end he was right through again but shot outside'.

Everton secured their fourth championship with two games to spare on 30 April when a single Dean goal at home to Bolton Wanderers was enough to clinch victory.

* * *

2 September 1936: Everton 3 Sheffield Wednesday 1 (Dean overhauls Steve Bloomer's career scoring record)

Steve Bloomer, the most prolific goalscorer in English football before the Great War, had no Everton connections as a player but he does hold the distinction of being the man who inspired the 'School of Science' nickname.

In 1928, the same year as Dixie Dean's 60 and the Blues' third league championship, Bloomer, who originally hailed from the Black Country village of Cradley, was credited with rather eloquently observing, 'We owe a great deal to Everton. No matter where they play, and no matter whether they are well or badly placed in the league table, they always manage to serve football of the highest scientific order. Everton always worship at the shrine of craft and science, and never do they forget the standard of play they set out to achieve.'

In earlier years, Bloomer, who was widely considered to be the game's first true superstar, had let his football do the talking.

As well as having an even better goal ratio for England than Dean with 28 in 23 games compared to 18 in 16, he netted 391 goals in 655 games and remains the all-time leading scorer for Derby County with 332; well over a century on from his last game for them, the Rams now run out to the song 'Steve Bloomer's Watchin''.

The esteemed record held by Bloomer that Dean overhauled against Sheffield Wednesday was his Football League total of 352.

In this respect, the 29-year-old Everton man had the edge having eclipsed a figure that Bloomer had played until the age of 40 to reach.

Dean had moved level with Bloomer when he netted in a 3-2 defeat at Arsenal on the opening day of the 1936/37 season and would go past the old master just three days later.

In an era before floodlights, 31,586 were present for a 6.15pm Wednesday fixture against the Owls and Dean provided the moment they were all waiting for just shy of the half-hour mark.

Writing in the *Liverpool Daily Post*, 'Stork' enthused, 'At 6.45 last night a great cheer rent the air at Goodison Park. Dean had broken a record which has stood the test of time for many years.

'All the supporters had gone to Goodison Park in the hope of seeing the famous Everton centre-forward and captain beat Steve Bloomer's record of 352 goals.

'Every time Dean bobbled up, the crowd were expectant, and when he at last nodded the ball from Jackie Coulter's corner kick beyond the Sheffield Wednesday goalkeeper at the 29th minute hardly one person remained in a sitting posture.

'Cheer after cheer broke the air, and Dean's colleagues dashed up to their captain, an old school chum of Dean's also grasped his friend's hand and added to Dean's great reception.

'It was a happy moment for the Everton crowd, for never in the history of the club has there been such a popular member.

'Dean has done practically everything there is to be done in this game of football. He still holds the league record for the highest number of goals in a season, and strange to say the goal that made his highest was a very similar point to the one which beat Bloomer's record. It came from a corner, from the same wing, and in the same manner.'

For the record, Charlie Luke equalised for Wednesday on 37 minutes, 'a simple task', before Alex Stevenson restored Everton's lead five minutes later, 'For so small a man [5ft 5in] Stevenson can put astonishing power behind his shot, and I am sure Jack Brown only saw the ball as it burst beyond him and into the far corner of the net.'

Torry Gillick sealed the Blues' victory on 72 minutes 'with a shot which barely had legs to travel beyond the prone Brown'.

Although Dean was now the leading goalscorer in Football League history, 1936/37 – his last full campaign with Everton – would mark the beginning of the end for him as a top-flight footballer.

The following January, the Blues recruited 17-year-old Tommy Lawton to be his long-term successor.

Arriving in Liverpool from Burnley, Lawton recalled that he was greeted by a tram conductor with the comment, 'You'll never be as good as Dixie!'

However, Dean himself was more welcoming, mentoring the youngster for almost a year. The pair played alongside each other on nine occasions (losing seven and winning just one) before Dean was sold to Third Division South Notts County after making his 433rd and final Everton appearance in a 1-1 draw at home to Birmingham City on 11 December 1937 with just 17,018 inside the ground.

12

Non-football events

WHETHER IT'S been other sports or a couple of historic royal visits, Goodison Park has also staged some significant non-football events over the years and they are documented here.

* * *

Life imitated art when Tony Bellew defeated Ilunga Makabu at Goodison Park on 29 May 2016 in what was the first outdoor boxing event in Liverpool since 1949.

Lifelong Evertonian 'Bomber' Bellew had played 'Pretty' Ricky Conlan, who fought a fictional fight against actor Michael B. Jordan's character Adonis Creed in the film *Creed* the year before, with Goodison the supposed venue thanks to real footage taken during an Everton match against West Bromwich Albion.

Over the years, Goodison also hosted several other notable non-football sporting events; including four rugby league matches involving touring Antipodean sides between 1908 and 1921.

During the 1908/09 Kangaroo tour of Great Britain, Australia defeated a Northern Union XIII 10-9 on 18 November 1908 before England beat Australia 14-7 on 3 March 1909.

The 1911/12 season saw Australasia (a combined team of Australians and New Zealanders) overcome a Northern League XIII on 25 October 1911 before 1921/22 witnessed Australasia's 29-6 victory over Lancashire on 30 November 1921.

Baseball was even played at the ground between the 1920s and the 40s. Danny Bloyce's *Baseball in England* recounted how Goodison was one of two English stadia (the other being Chelsea's Stamford Bridge) used in this country during the 1924 world tour by Major League outfits Chicago White Sox and New York Giants.

Their exhibition match on Merseyside only drew in a crowd of 2,000 but one of the players managed to hit a ball clear of the large Goodison Road Stand.

Steven R. Bullock's *Playing for Their Nation: Baseball and the American Military During World War II* records that a game between two Army Air Force baseball teams attracted an 8,000 attendance at Goodison, which had been commandeered by the military during the second world war, raising over $3,000 for the British Red Cross and St John Ambulance fund.

Liverpool Trojans' history documents that they and Formby Cardinals were the last two teams to play baseball at Goodison in the 1948 Lancashire Cup Final.

In May 1997, BBC One religious programme *Songs of Praise* broadcast an episode from Goodison Park – after curiously choosing Manchester United's Old Trafford, home of the Red Devils, for its inaugural visit to a football ground in 1994 – and two of the biggest crowds at Everton's long-time home haven't been for sporting contests at all but royal visits.

On 11 July 1913, Goodison became the first English football ground to be visited by a reigning monarch when King George V and his wife Queen Mary – whose statues mark the Liverpool entrance to the Queensway Tunnel underneath the Mersey to Birkenhead after they opened it in 1934 – attended.

This trip was combined with the royal couple opening the Gladstone Dock, the biggest in the world at the time, in Bootle.

Writing in his *Jubilee History of the Everton Football Club 1878–1928*, Thomas Keates recalled their visit, 'The arena was a riot of colour and animated charm; 1,920 elementary school children, prettily attired, sang the national anthem as the royal party drove round the ground, escorted by a squadron of King Edward's Horse [a cavalry regiment].

'Ascending a platform, the royal party witnessed a musical drill, physical exercises (executed with artistic precision) and a detachment finally formed a living model of a Union Jack.

'The King and Queen seemed to find the display a restful delight after an exhausting day. The enthusiastic cheering everywhere, added to the plethora of ceremonial and speech making at every stoppage, must have made the day an unusually tiring one. Goodison Park really seemed to be a restorative.'

Almost 25 years later, on 19 May 1938, King George V's son King George VI and his wife Queen Elizabeth, the future Queen Mother, were at Goodison Park.

As Duchess of York the latter had presented the FA Cup to Everton captain Dixie Dean in 1933, and when told by Lord Derby who the player was, she was reported to have replied, 'Even I know Dean!'

Their visit was to present the new colours to the Liverpool-based 5th Battalion, King's Regiment and the Liverpool Scottish (Queen's Own Cameron Highlanders) and there were an estimated 80,000 people inside Goodison for the military parade, which if accurate would be an even greater attendance than Everton's biggest gate of 78,299 against Liverpool on 18 September 1948.

A report in the *Liverpool Echo* captured the excitement on the streets from the people of Merseyside for the royal visit, stating, 'Tumultuous scenes were witnessed when the King and Queen departed from the Town Hall for the Everton football ground.

'Thousands of voices took up the cry, "We want the King! We want the Queen!" Followed by more cheers.

'The route to the football ground, Dale Street, Byrom Street, Scotland Road, Kirkdale Road, Everton Valley, Walton Lane, Goodison Road, was lined with cheering crowds.

'One of the best views of the procession was obtained by a gang of workmen engaged on a house chimney in Kirkdale Road, who used the scaffolding as a grandstand.'

13

Battling displays

EVERTON'S LATIN motto *Nil Satis Nisi Optimum* (Nothing but the best is good enough) is a proud aspiration to try to live up to, but in reality, given the manner that football is structured now and the way the Blues have slipped down the food chain compared to the game's powerhouses with greater resources, it can be a lofty ideal these days.

During recent battles near the wrong end of the table, loyal but long-suffering Evertonians have simply called through banners for the team to 'fight for us' and while the Goodison Park crowd has always appreciated stylish play, the one thing they take as a given from their team is desire and this chapter documents the occasions that such a quality has come to the fore.

* * *

7 May 1994: Everton 3 Wimbledon 2 (The Great Escape Part 1)
James Hunt, the Formula One world champion of 1976, once declared, 'The closer you are to death, the more alive you feel.'

While Mike Walker's side weren't putting their actual lives on the line this day like motor racing drivers such as Hunt – who died in Wimbledon aged just 45 less than a year before this game – for Evertonians and their proud boast of being the club with the most seasons spent in the English top flight, this felt like the football equivalent.

Not only was this possibly the most nerve-racking day Goodison Park ever experienced in terms of high drama, but the way it all unfolded was like a real-life *Roy of the Rovers* type story.

At the time of Howard Kendall's resignation on 4 December 1993, Everton were 11th but they were left to drift over the festive period, losing six out of seven games during caretaker boss Jimmy Gabriel's winless tenure.

Despite starting with a 6-2 home thrashing of Swindon Town in his first Premier League game in charge, Walker was unable to stop the rot and having lost seven out of ten in the run-in, the Blues went into the final game of the campaign in the relegation zone for the first time all season.

Everton knew they needed a result to avoid the drop but even that might not be enough as they also depended on their rivals not triumphing elsewhere.

On the *Match of the Day* commentary that night, as the sides took to the field to a truly tumultuous reception, Barry Davies remarked, 'A full house at Goodison and a welcome fit for champions from Everton supporters not knowing if they've come to praise or to see their team buried.'

This was an era in which Wimbledon's 'Crazy Gang' were known for their on-pitch intimidation of opponents, but they were given a hot reception on Merseyside with Davies adding, 'Wimbledon's coach was burnt out last night at their team hotel in what the police are describing as "suspicious circumstances". The kit was on board, but it was rescued in time … if a little smoky.'

It was the home side that appeared nervous though in the opening exchanges and disastrously found themselves 2-0 down within 20 minutes.

First, they conceded a penalty just four minutes in after a handball by Anders Limpar. David Prentice of the *Liverpool Echo* wrote, 'Dean Holdsworth fired it low to Neville Southall's right,' and although he 'got a firm touch on the ball' he couldn't keep it out.

Wimbledon's second goal was even more calamitous from an Everton point of view. Prentice said, 'A cross into the Everton penalty spot saw Dave Watson and David Unsworth both challenging for the ball together.

'The ball still appeared to be drifting wide until Gary Ablett tried to clear the danger and hooked the ball into his own net.'

The Blues looked down and out but arguably their most spectacular comeback since the 1966 FA Cup Final, when they also recovered from 2-0 down to defeat Sheffield Wednesday, ensued.

Just four minutes after Wimbledon's second goal, the hosts were awarded a penalty of their own when Limpar went down under a challenge from Peter Fear.

Despite it looking at first like keeper Southall might take the kick as he strode upfield with the ball under his arm, 'Graham Stuart showed coolness to strike the ball to Hans Segers's right and into the corner of the net.'

While Stuart's strike in front of the empty skeleton of the mid-rebuild Park End stand – allowing ticketless fans to watch from the trees in Stanley Park – gave Everton hope, Barry Horne's outrageous 25-yard half volley to equalise midway through the second half threatened to take the roof off.

Prentice described it as 'one of the best goals seen at Goodison for years' as he 'crashed a magnificent shot into the top left-hand corner of Segers's goal before being swamped by team-mates and supporters alike'.

The winner arrived nine minutes from the end as Stuart exchanged passes with Tony Cottee before 'he lunged in light-footed and sent the ball crashing beyond Segers amid scenes of delirium'.

Evertonians didn't even know whether the victory had been enough to save their side when they swamped on to the pitch in great numbers at the final whistle but eventually news started to filter through that they were safe with Joe Royle's Oldham Athletic and Sheffield United, who had led 2-1 against Chelsea at Stamford Bridge until 14 minutes from the end – a result that would have relegated the Blues regardless of what they did – going down along with the already-doomed Swindon Town.

* * *

7 December 2019: Everton 3 Chelsea 1 (Duncan Ferguson's first game as caretaker manager)

This was the day that Duncan Ferguson showed he was a lover as well as a fighter. Like many of Big Dunc's opponents over the years, Evertonians were feeling battered and bruised as they went into the fixture but their team's former centre-forward restored their faith in his first game as caretaker manager.

Previous boss Marco Silva had appeared to be a dead man walking ever since members of the home crowd joined in with Norwich City fans' taunts of 'You're getting sacked in the morning' during a 2-0 defeat to the Premier League's bottom club at Goodison Park on 24 November.

However, the beleaguered Portuguese gaffer limped on for another two fixtures, a last-gasp 2-1 defeat at Leicester City when the home side's stoppage-time winner, initially ruled out for offside was given after a VAR check, and a humiliating 5-2 Merseyside derby thrashing by champions-elect Liverpool, which left the Blues languishing in the relegation zone.

Despite an unsuccessful attempt to hire him before predecessor Sam Allardyce's appointment, Silva's credentials for the Everton job had always looked dubious, particularly based on his track record in England.

Although he had won the domestic cup in his native Portugal with Sporting CP and the Greek league with Olympiacos, his Premier League experience amounted to a five-month stint in which he failed to keep Hull City up and then little more than half a season at Watford before being sacked.

Despite starting with a farcical 22-0 friendly win in the Austrian Alps against minnows ATV Irdning, the Goodison hot seat ultimately proved too big for him and the day after the chastening result at Anfield, club owner Farhad Moshiri eventually relieved Silva of his duties during a lengthy visit to Finch Farm.

It was on this personal trip to Everton's training complex that Blues icon Ferguson was handed the reins on a temporary basis.

While Silva appeared a somewhat impersonal character throughout his 18-month tenure, unable to inspire his side to a single come-from-behind win in the Premier League, Ferguson's in-your-face passion was the shot in the arm that both players and fans alike needed.

Reverting to the 'old-school' 4-4-2 formation that was prevalent in his own playing days, he engineered a real throwback performance reminiscent of when he would terrorise the top flight's big guns himself.

Phil Kirkbride of the *Liverpool Echo* wrote, 'Everton went back to the future with Duncan Ferguson in the dugout. The Blues jumped out of the bottom three and are looking up after a performance dug up from a different time on an emotionally charged day at Goodison.

'Ferguson made no secret that his intention was to get his club back to basics and to see a display that he recognised as quintessentially Everton. In riotous fashion, that was delivered and rammed down Chelsea's throats.

'Big Dunc would sport a suit and tie but in a deliberate nod to the past, he wore his famous sweatband on his wrist and his regular rallying of the crowd, and charging celebrations down the touchline, ensured the temporary boss had what he asked for – a "proper" Goodison atmosphere.

'Ferguson had also listed his other demands ahead of kick-off, saying he wanted "tackling, scrapping, running, showing for the ball and always looking to help your team-mate next to you", and the players delivered that in spades.'

The 47-year-old was racing down the touchline in celebration just five minutes into proceedings when Richarlison headed his side in front, and then he swung a ball boy in the air when Dominic Calvert-Lewin doubled Everton's lead four minutes into the second half.

The hosts' nerves jangled just three minutes later when Mateo Kovačić pulled a goal back for Frank Lampard's men with a long-range effort, but the points were secured six minutes from the end as Calvert-Lewin proved sharpest in the box during a goalmouth scramble to fire the ball through Kepa Arrizabalaga's legs after the world's most-expensive goalkeeper had given up possession with a poor clearance.

Afterwards, Ferguson said, 'It was an unbelievable atmosphere for myself, but it's the players who need to take the pride and the praise.'

A 1-1 draw at Manchester United and penalty shoot-out defeat to Leicester in the League Cup followed under his stewardship but by the time Everton were back in Premier League action at Goodison for a goalless stalemate with Arsenal on 21 December in what proved to be Ferguson's last match in charge, Silva's replacement Carlo Ancelotti, whose arrival had been confirmed before kick-off, was watching from the stands.

Over the subsequent 18 months, the Italian with the stellar CV, and Blue Blood Ferguson, installed as his assistant, proved to be the 'Odd Couple' tasked with reviving Everton's fortunes before Ancelotti went back to Real Madrid, leaving his number two to work alongside Rafael Benítez.

* * *

14 February 1953: Everton 2 Manchester United 1 (Dave Hickson comes back on despite head wound to net FA Cup winner)

With the amount of blood gushing out of Dave Hickson's head wound during this FA Cup tie, Goodison Park looked as though it was hosting a Valentine's Day massacre but on the annual date for lovers, the Everton idol showed just how much playing for the Blues meant for him.

Despite suffering a horrendous gash above his eye, a patched-up Hickson returned to the field to net the winner and secure a famous FA Cup scalp for his Second Division side against the reigning league champions.

Hickson was an extremely humble man – he would later serve cups of tea to Goodison visitors on stadium tours – but in the eyes of the Gwladys Street, he was Everton royalty.

Perhaps the only surprise for his adoring fans was that the blood spilled for the cause wasn't blue!

Speaking on the BBC's *The Official History of Everton FC* video in 1988, Hickson, one of the few footballers to turn out for Everton, Liverpool and Tranmere Rovers, remarked, 'I'd break every bone in my body for any club I play for, but I'd die for Everton.'

On this occasion he might have come as close as he ever did to putting that claim to the test with the kind of bravery that endeared him to his fans, but would these days be considered a foolhardy and downright reckless act by both the player and his team alike.

Although scoring 111 goals in 243 games for the club, and a swashbuckling centre-forward in the best Everton tradition, Hickson played for the Blues during one of the fallow periods but the 'Cannonball Kid' was just the kind of warrior the fanbase could relate to throughout these lean years.

With Cliff Britton's side out of the First Division, big FA Cup ties like this provided rare opportunities for glory and Hickson certainly rose to the occasion.

Some 77,920 packed into Goodison for this fifth-round match which looked to be going with the form book when Jack Rowley put Manchester United ahead on 27 minutes.

'Ranger' reported in the *Liverpool Echo* that Rowley 'lashed the ball into the net from six yards' after home goalkeeper Jimmy O'Neill could not gather a shot by Johnny Berry.

Tommy Eglington equalised for Everton seven minutes later, 'The start of the movement was a very clever pass by George Cummins to Hickson who quickly transferred the ball to Eglington, who came in to round left-back John Aston and then score with a grand right-footed shot from ten yards' distance.'

However, five minutes before half-time, Hickson retired injured after he 'flung himself at the ball in a praiseworthy effort to score but came in contact with an opponent's outstretched boot and blood poured from his eyebrow', ensuring he 'was led off by trainer Harry Cooke with a pad of cotton wool held to his face'.

Patched up with five stitches, the number nine would make a dramatic return early in the second half, 'Although Hickson was not in his place when the teams lined up for the restart, he trotted out a minute later to the accompaniment of a resounding cheer. He carried a handkerchief in his hand, which now and again he applied to his eye.'

Even with the stitches and hankie, the blood continued to flow, 'Hickson's eye was obviously giving him trouble again and the referee appeared to be suggesting that he should go off. Hickson however, indignantly waved away any such suggestion.'

His courage was rewarded with a winning goal on 63 minutes, 'Chasing the ball, Hickson beat one man, sidestepped another, and then screwed back an oblique shot which Ray Wood failed to reach.'

The centre-forward reopened the wound when he headed against the post late on and despite his face being caked by blood, 'When the final whistle went, O'Neill dashed half the length of the field to throw his arms around Hickson, the hero of a wonderful win, but one which was shared equally by all 11 players.'

Speaking at Hickson's funeral in Liverpool's Anglican Cathedral in 2013, Everton chairman Bill Kenwright paid a glowing tribute to his own boyhood idol.

He said, 'What gives us that feeling of overwhelming love for our club? For me it's two words, "Dave Hickson".

'For shy, timid postwar kids in Liverpool he gave us the courage to dare. He made us feel safe. You cannot fool an Evertonian. They saw in Dave Hickson something honest and something special.'

* * *

10 May 1998: Everton 1 Coventry City 1 (Gareth Farrelly to the rescue in the Great Escape Part 2 – sequels are seldom as good)

Back in 1994 when Everton stayed up by the skin of their teeth against Wimbledon, the *Liverpool Echo* carried a banner headline screaming 'Never again … please'.

Over the next couple of years, the Blues would win the FA Cup and record their only top-half finish in the first decade of the Premier League but somehow in 1998 it was Groundhog Day at Goodison Park.

The difference was, while the class of 1994 had been underachievers – just 12 months later, eight of the starting 11 against Wimbledon defeated Manchester United to taste Wembley glory – Dave Watson, the man who lifted the cup that day, and Wembley substitute Duncan Ferguson were the only survivors from then to face Coventry City.

Although teenage homegrown hero Michael Ball, who went against his physio's advice to bravely battle on in this game, would go on to be an England international, many of the supporting cast just weren't good enough and it's no surprise that they found themselves in relegation danger again going into the final fixture.

Unlike in 1994 when five clubs were in the mix for going down on the last day, this time around it was a straight shoot-out between Everton and Bolton Wanderers, managed by former Blues defender Colin Todd.

With one game to go, the Trotters were a point better off but Howard Kendall's Everton had a superior goal difference.

Once again, the Blues' destiny was not in their own hands, and they had to better Bolton's result at Stamford Bridge against a Chelsea side who would be playing a European Cup Winners' Cup Final in Stockholm against Stuttgart just three days later.

Having been through the gut-wrenching experience so recently before, many Evertonians didn't have the stomach to do it all again.

There was talk of Kopites parading a royal blue coffin down Bullens Road while an Everton shirt hanging up at Stanley Dock market that morning had an additional letter G placed next to the sponsors' logo, so it read 'GOne 2 One' – a reference to the imminent threat of relegation to the First Division.

The tension proved all too much for Blues legend and former captain Brian Labone, who was famously photographed wearing his club tie and blazer, pacing up and down the pavement on Goodison Road in the shadow of the Main Stand as the action unfolded inside.

Also, in contrast to four years earlier when Everton stayed up in a blaze of glory after a wretched start, on this occasion they got their noses in front early on, only to proceed to make life difficult for themselves.

Just as Barry Horne had proven an unlikely goalscorer from midfield against Wimbledon, up popped Gareth Farrelly seven minutes in.

The Irishman had netted just once in 27 games in his debut Blues season until that point – in a League Cup tie at Scunthorpe United back in September – but David Prentice of the *Echo* wrote,

'Farrelly has been readjusting his sights at the Park End goal all season. This time he lined up his right foot beautifully and the ball soared into the top corner.'

Clinging on for most of the match – and with Gianluca Vialli putting Chelsea ahead against Bolton on 73 minutes – Everton had the opportunity to wrap things up six minutes from the end when they were awarded what Prentice considered an extremely fortunate penalty.

He said, 'Coventry bossed the possession and looked much the likelier scorers – until referee Paul Alcock made a decision quite astonishing in its ineptitude. Paul Williams's tackle on Danny Cadamarteri was beautifully timed. The defender prodded the ball to safety but the official ludicrously pointed to the spot.

'Nick Barmby '98 assumed the Graham Stuart '94 mantle but Magnus Hedman made a superb save.'

Things then went from bad to worse. Prentice added, 'If Barmby was distraught in the 84th minute, in the 88th minute he was desolate.

'David Burrows swung over a cross from the left flank, Dion Dublin rose unimpeded and directed a header which Thomas Myhre flapped into the net. Just one more goal from Coventry – or Bolton – would have dumped the Blues into the First Division.

'Instead, the only other goal of an amazing afternoon came from Chelsea [Jody Morris in the 90th minute]. That was enough to bury Bolton. Everton had survived because of another club's inadequacies rather than their own efforts. It was a grimly fitting way to end a season which has stumbled from one catastrophe to another.'

* * *

11 February 2006: Everton 1 Blackburn Rovers 0 (Backs-to-the-wall victory after early sending-off for keeper Iain Turner)

While Evertonians like to affectionately refer to Goodison Park as the 'Grand Old Lady', she could often be more like a belligerent battleaxe than a sweet grandmother and Hell hath no fury like a woman scorned.

Many visitors have commented on how difficult it was to come to Goodison when you're not a Blue and it's that intimidating bear pit atmosphere that Dan Meis and his team of architects were tasked with replicating when it came to designing the new stadium at Bramley-Moore Dock.

Sir Alex Ferguson said, 'It is always a nightmare going there and it wouldn't matter whether it was Dixie Dean playing for us, the atmosphere is fantastic,' while José Mourinho claimed, 'I love to play Everton, especially at Goodison Park, where the atmosphere is magnificent.'

Liverpool have a global reputation for European nights at Anfield but Arsène Wenger insisted, 'Everton's ground is a lot more aggressive than Liverpool's. It's one of the noisiest I've been to. It has a great atmosphere,' with Paul Scholes concurring, 'I never found Anfield intimidating. Goodison Park had the better atmosphere.'

It's not just opponents who have felt the heat. Howard Webb took charge of a World Cup Final but admitted that for him Goodison was 'the hardest place to referee in the Premier League'.

Like all grounds there could be quiet moments but when Everton's passionate supporters were packed to the rafters, Goodison could flick like a light switch into a bubbling cauldron, with Phil Neville's bone-crunching challenge on Cristiano Ronaldo in 2008 a prime example.

Whereas that tackle on his former Manchester United team-mate roused Blues fans to life, things would also go up several notches when a decision riled the home faithful.

That's just what happened here in what in normal circumstances would have been something of a run-of-the-mill February fixture between a couple of mid-table sides but ended up being described by one press box sage as 'the maddest game' he'd ever seen at Goodison.

The first flashpoint came when Everton goalkeeper Iain Turner was sent off just nine minutes into his Premier League debut with Dominic King of the *Liverpool Echo* observing, 'Strictly adhering to the letter of the law, referee Peter Walton had no choice other than to brandish a red card to the young Scot after he handled outside the area. But did Turner prevent the visitors a clear goalscoring opportunity? Hardly.

'While many expressed fears that the writing was on the wall for Everton from then on, the opposite was true. Brave, bold and bellowed on by a belligerent crowd, Blackburn were left bewildered as the Blues set about them.

'When Goodison Park bounces as it did at the weekend, there are few more intimidating arenas in the country. The noise levels appeared to frighten the life out of Mark Hughes's men and meant their attacking threat was negligible.

'John Ruddy, the 19-year-old keeper who came on to take over from Turner between the posts, could not have asked for a better game in which to make his debut. Thanks to the efforts of the men in front of him, he only had one save to make.'

Despite Everton having three efforts disallowed as Tim Cahill (twice) and Alan Stubbs were adjudged to be offside while James McFadden had earlier missed an open goal, former Blackburn trainee James Beattie netted the winner for the hosts on 33 minutes, with what King described as a header that 'bulleted past Brad Friedel' from Mikel Arteta's free kick.

David Prentice of the *Echo* tried to make sense of the madness by writing, 'The name Mr Philip Walton will resonate around Goodison Park for years.

'The referee left the pitch with a reputation somewhere between Anne Diamond and Vlad the Impaler's. But, in truth, he should be saluted. Yes, really. Because the eccentric performance of Mr Walton and his two out-of-shape assistants was responsible for one of the more memorable matches of recent years.

'The record books will carry the bare statistic: Everton 1, Blackburn 0. But the real story is so much more colourful, so unpredictable, so wildly improbable.

'And it was fired by a sense of injustice which came from the officials. Three disallowed goals, one inexplicably; a contender for miss of the season; a red card for a home debutant goalkeeper and two yellow cards in front of a disbelieving crowd.

'What an opening 16 minutes! An incendiary atmosphere never wavered for a minute after that as home fans reacted with incredulity to what they were witnessing.'

* * *

7 November 1964: Everton 0 Leeds United 1 (Infamous 'Battle of Goodison Park' with the teams taken off to calm down)

Arguably the most memorable scene from *The Damned United*, the 2009 film adaptation of David Peace's bestselling novel, is Brian Clough's abrupt address to his stunned players on succeeding Don Revie as Leeds United manager when he tells them to throw all their medals into a dustbin, 'Because you've never won any of them fairly. You've done it all by cheating.'

Both the book and big screen versions of the work proved hugely controversial with members of the Clough family and the Leeds players because they portray a true-life story of the manager's tumultuous 44-day reign at Elland Road in 1974 through a largely fictionalised dialogue. However, the infamous 'dustbin speech' is one of the few moments that those present at the time agree is shown in largely accurate terms.

Just what maverick football genius Clough was trying to achieve through undermining his long-serving predecessor and rival Revie – a fellow son of Middlesbrough – in such derogatory terms, only he will have known, but given his inflammatory opening gambit to one of the game's most close-knit and competitive dressing rooms, the fleeting nature of his tenure hardly seems surprising.

While admired for their footballing prowess under Revie, the club were still known to the rest of the country as 'Dirty Leeds', and it was a reputation accrued over a prolonged period.

The infamous 'Battle of Goodison Park' against Everton came almost a decade before Clough signed his own death warrant in West Yorkshire with his ill-judged team talk.

Such was the ferocity of the match between the Blues – who seemed to give as good as they got – and their newly promoted opponents that, in an unprecedented move by the referee, both sets of players were taken off the field for a period so they could calm down.

Michael Charters of the *Liverpool Echo* reported on the brutal encounter by remarking, 'Goodison Park was the scene of one of the most explosive incidents in Football League history when referee Ken Stokes of Newark stopped the Everton-Leeds United game for ten minutes and every player followed him off the pitch.

'The first half had been full of incidents which were a disgrace to football. Only five minutes after the start, Everton's Sandy Brown was sent off for a foul on Johnny Giles, and then followed foul after foul with so many free kicks that there was no continuity in the game.

'After the referee had halted the game – many in the crowd thought he had abandoned it – an announcement was made that he *would* abandon the game unless the crowd stopped throwing missiles on the pitch. The game resumed after an 11-minute delay.'

Brown went for his (very) early bath after tangling with Giles just outside the penalty area.

Charters admitted, 'I didn't see the actual incident as I was following the ball on the opposite side of the field, but the referee was in no doubt of what he had seen, and off went Brown.'

The tit for tat petulance continued with a former Everton captain, the 5ft 3in Bobby Collins, showing he was not afraid to mix it with the big boys, 'After this explosive start, the temper of the crowd did not lessen when Collins fouled Roy Vernon in midfield.'

And so it went on, 'With these various incidents already and the referee blowing up for a series of fouls on both sides, the football seemed to be forgotten.'

There was one piece of free-flowing play which enabled Leeds' Willie Bell to net the only goal of the game on 14 minutes as the full-back 'came racing in unnoticed by Barry Rees and headed the ball at top speed past Andy Rankin'.

Following a collision between Derek Temple and goalscorer Bell – on a stretcher and carried off respectively – the referee took both sides off.

Charters said, 'Fights were breaking out in the crowd while they waited for the game to resume, and this incident was the most-sensational I have seen in my years of watching football.

'The Leeds players were first back on to the pitch, and before the Everton team appeared, the crowd started a chant of "Dirty Leeds", but in all fairness, it must be repeated that the Brown sending off incident had started this disgrace, and it had been players of both teams who had carried it on.

'It had not been one-sided by any means.'

* * *

9 December 2012: Everton 2 Tottenham Hotspur 1 (Late, late show as Everton recover from 1-0 down on 90 minutes to win)
With his deadly first-time finishing, Nikica Jelavić was an instant hit at Everton but after a prolific start with the Blues, the Croatian striker proved to be something of a flash in the pan.

After registering his first goal in the corresponding fixture at home to Tottenham Hotspur the previous season, a 1-0 win on 10 March, he'd go on to net 11 times in 16 games.

Even though this last-gasp strike against the same opponents would complete a dramatic late comeback, it also marked something of a watershed in Jelavić's Everton career as he'd register just one more goal in the Premier League in 2012/13.

On retiring in 2021, he recalled, 'The first eight months with Everton was the best period of my career. After that goal against Tottenham, everything seemed so easy. It was amazing, whenever I shot, it was in. I was so relaxed and confident. I was like, "I don't care who I play against, they have to care about me."'

However, the confidence spilled over to become complacency and Jelavić admitted, 'I thought, "I can go a little bit easier and still play well." You need to slow down just one step and you're gone – and this is what I did.'

David Moyes had searched for so long to find a reliable frontman to spearhead his attack and take his teams on to the next level but would often be thwarted in his efforts.

He spent big in trying to rectify the problem, smashing the club's transfer record on three occasions to bring in James Beattie for £6m from Southampton in 2005, Crystal Palace's Andrew Johnson for £8.6m the following year, and Ayegbeni Yakubu for £11.25m from Middlesbrough in 2007.

Beattie never replicated his prolific Southampton form – he failed to find the net from open play in 35 games in 2006/07, his final season at Everton – with both his goals coming from penalties.

In a similar vein to Jelavić, Johnson got off to a flying start but couldn't keep it up while Yakubu became the first Blues player since Peter Beardsley in 1992 to break the 20-goal barrier in a single season but then became a shadow of his former self after rupturing his Achilles tendon at White Hart Lane.

Following his £5.5m signing from Rangers in January 2012 – the Glasgow giants' last big sale before their financial meltdown forced them to reform and start again in the fourth tier of Scottish football the following season – Jelavić, for a time, looked like he finally might be the answer.

Although his scoring touch was already starting to elude him by this point, Greg O'Keeffe of the *Liverpool Echo* highlighted how this last-gasp winner proved to be an early present for Evertonians in the festive period.

He wrote, 'In Everton's recent Christmas video a young supporter excitedly unwraps his gift to find Nikica Jelavić beaming at him inside. It's a smile that has been missing from the striker's face for the last five weeks when he has found little fortune of his own in front of goal.

'But whether it's on a YouTube clip or at Goodison Park, Jelavić always has the potential to surprise in the box – and he delivered his own festive gift in style yesterday to rocket Everton up to fourth in the Premier League.

'David Moyes had barely finished celebrating what seemed like another draw when his centre-forward pounced, to squeeze the last drip of drama from an absorbing contest.'

The game had been locked in a stalemate until Clint Dempsey looked like he'd nicked it for Spurs on 76 minutes.

O'Keeffe said, 'Tom Huddlestone had only been on for a few minutes when he slipped a short pass to the American who spotted that his compatriot Tim Howard had strayed from his line and took advantage with a shot that looped over Everton's goalkeeper and into the net.'

As for the grandstand finale in stoppage time, he added, 'It seemed like the familiar tale of being left to rue missed chances was unfolding. Yet to their credit the Blues remained calm and were rewarded spectacularly.

'Coleman crossed after good work from Naismith, and Steven Pienaar arrived late to score an opportunistic header. It was Everton's 1,000th Premier League goal, and they didn't have to wait long for their next.

'Star man Darron Gibson aimed a ball at Apostolos Vellios and while the Greek striker fell attempting an overhead kick, Jelavić pounced on the loose ball and rifled it gleefully past Hugo Lloris. Cue pandemonium as Goodison erupted and Moyes celebrated on the pitch.'

* * *

25 February 1995: Everton 1 Manchester United 0 (Duncan Ferguson overcomes Alex Ferguson at Goodison: Part 1)

Alex Ferguson would dominate English football with Manchester United for much of his namesake and compatriot Duncan's two spells at Goodison Park but if there was one thing Everton's tartan talisman loved to do, it was giving the biggest teams in the land a bloody nose.

Initially brought to the club on a three-month loan to escape the Glasgow goldfish bowl as he awaited a police charge for head-butting Raith Rovers' Jock McStay (an on-field offence he'd later be jailed for), Ferguson seemed to have little idea of the football romance that lay ahead for him on Merseyside when he first arrived.

Asked in a Bournemouth hotel bar ahead of a League Cup tie at Portsmouth by David Prentice of the *Liverpool Echo* if he'd be staying long-term, he replied in his broad Stirling accent, 'I wouldnae thought so.'

However, something changed very dramatically in the months ahead for Ferguson and Everton.

Under Mike Walker, the manager who initially brought him to the club, the Blues played pretty but ineffectual football yet the 6ft 4in target man would thrive when new boss Joe Royle, a former centre-forward at the club himself, started playing to his strengths.

While adored by the Gwladys Street, there remained a frustration that Big Dunc could not always produce the super-human displays he reserved when rising to the occasion against many of Everton's more illustrious opponents.

Although unplayable on his day and a long-standing fan favourite, Ferguson would net double figures in just two of his 11 seasons at the club.

This was one of *those* days though as he terrorised the reigning Premier League champions.

After Ferguson had stunned Manchester United, the headline in the *Echo* asked, 'Is this the new Dixie Dean?' It was added that Blues fans were 'smitten by an outbreak of Fergie fever'.

Prentice reported, 'Two thoughts will be mulling through Evertonian heads this weekend – one stimulating, one appalling.

'Firstly, could Duncan Ferguson really become as revered a centre-forward as Dixie Dean? And more worryingly, will other strikers be tempted into copycat imitations of the Scot's [shirtless] goal celebrations?

'The thought of Micky Quinn or Peter Beardsley performing the dance of the seven veils, half-naked around a Goodison corner flag is a bone chilling one.

'So too was the prospect of relegation three months ago. That is receding all the time now, although still a long way from being completely banished – and one of the leading lights in that renaissance has been Ferguson.

'Comparisons with Dean are inappropriate, if not irrelevant, but it was easy to see just what manager Joe Royle meant when he said after the defeat of Manchester United that Ferguson could become "the biggest thing here since Dixie Dean. He's that popular".

'The big Scot scores regularly at home – especially in the big matches. The enthusiasm which manifests itself in outrageous goal celebrations is almost Andy Gray-like and lapped up by the fans.'

Kick-off was delayed by 20 minutes after travelling United fans were delayed by congestion on the M62, but, pumped up for challenge, Everton's number nine was quickly moving up the gears and causing trouble for his opposing centre-backs from the start.

Prentice wrote, 'Ferguson easily won his first two aerial challenges against Steve Bruce and Gary Pallister, and afterwards in the tunnel, the latter would acknowledge a simple but sincere, "Well played, big man."'

The Blues had earned a fearsome reputation under Royle for the danger posed from inswinging corners from Andy Hinchcliffe and sure enough it was from such a set piece that they'd net the only goal of the game on 58 minutes.

Prentice remarked, 'Hinchcliffe's excellent corner was missed in the air by Peter Schmeichel and Ferguson buried a header at the far post before tearing his shirt off and charging towards the home fans to celebrate.'

The abiding memory of Everton's 1994/95 season was their victory over the same opponents by the same scoreline 85 days later in the FA Cup Final, but the trip to Wembley would have seemed futile if the Blues had not secured their Premier League status.

Despite Royle's arrival in November, defeating Liverpool 2-0 in his first game in charge when the then on-loan Ferguson broke his scoring duck and the striker subsequently making his move from Rangers into a permanent switch, the Blues had to wait until their penultimate fixture before Paul Rideout's goal at Ipswich Town finally banished any lingering relegation fears.

Along with the derby delight to set the ball rolling, this was Ferguson and Royle's other standout scalp of the campaign.

* * *

19 May 2022: Everton 3 Crystal Palace 2 (Blues fight back to secure top-flight status)

A year earlier, Everton had been managed by the most successful coach in Champions League history but after Carlo Ancelotti defected to Real Madrid, Blues endured the hiring of a former Kop idol as his replacement and then a fight just to remain in the Premier League in a rollercoaster of a season that ended with a dramatic comeback.

After the artificial-feeling, surreal and sanitised environment of games mostly being played behind closed doors or if they were lucky, in front of severely restricted attendances during the 2020/21 season because of the unprecedented restrictions on public gatherings due to the global coronavirus pandemic – a setting that produced several shock results such as Everton's first win at Anfield since 1999 and only success at Arsenal's Emirates Stadium to date but also Fulham's first league victory at Goodison Park – Evertonians were given a huge dose of reality when spectators returned en masse at the start of the 2021/22 campaign.

It wasn't so much the welcome return of capacity crowds up and down the country – there was a raucous atmosphere as the Blues kicked off a new era by coming from behind to triumph 3-1 at home to Southampton on the opening day – but the fact that following Ancelotti's abrupt exit at the end of the previous season to begin a second stint in the Spanish capital, Farhad Moshiri had picked Rafael Benítez to succeed the Italian.

The majority shareholder's choice – despite warnings from chairman Bill Kenwright and director of football Marcel Brands – was the most controversial appointment in the history of the most passionate city in English football.

In many Evertonians' eyes it felt bad enough that Benítez was a former Liverpool manager, but it was more than that given that during his time as Reds boss, he petulantly branded Everton 'a small club' just because his opposite number David Moyes had the tactical nous to earn a goalless draw at Anfield in 2007 through a solid display, rather than go across Stanley Park and get battered 4-0 as happened twice to his successor Roberto Martínez.

While coming to Everton was a convenient move for the Spaniard, who had retained his family home on Merseyside and previously shown he was willing to court controversy by taking the reins at Chelsea, a bright start quickly eroded and things came to a head following a 4-1 home defeat to Liverpool on 1 December when visiting Kopites rubbed salt in the wounds by chanting their old favourite's name before Brands was involved in a heated verbal exchange with an angry Blues fan following the final whistle.

The Dutchman quit his post before Everton's next fixture and Benítez followed him out of the exit door after a 2-1 loss at bottom club Norwich City on 15 January, sacked due to what Kenwright would later aptly describe as 'unacceptably disappointing' form rather than his previous employment with the neighbours.

Frank Lampard was chosen to pick up the pieces and try to restore a fractured club but a 2-0 loss in the next derby at Anfield plunged the Blues into the relegation zone and while that was followed by back-to-back victories over Chelsea and Leicester City, the team went into their final home fixture of the season with their top-flight status yet to be secured.

Having blown the chance to get themselves safe by losing 3-2 to Brentford at Goodison Park four days earlier, Everton were 2-0 down at half-time against Crystal Palace following Jean-Philippe Mateta's 21st-minute header and Jordan Ayew bundling in a close-range finish 15 minutes later.

However, following some tactical tweaks at the break and roared on by their passionate fans, the Blues repeated their trick from the final day against Wimbledon in 1994.

Centre-half Michael Keane started the comeback with an audacious half volley with the outside of his weaker left foot in the 54th minute before Richarlison capitalised on some penalty box pinball to float a left-footed effort into the far corner on 75 minutes.

Dominic Calvert-Lewin sealed the remarkable recovery with a classic Everton diving header to meet a Demarai Gray free kick just five minutes from the end.

Joe Thomas of the *Liverpool Echo* wrote, 'The Grand Old Lady rocked and bounced, it erupted and exploded, it was a chaos of noise and emotion and by the end the air stung with the taste and smell of the smoke bombs that have come to symbolise the passion and desire of a fanbase that refused to give up.

'After Dominic Calvert-Lewin – a striker whose personal despair has been entwined with his club's agony during a wretched season of injury for the talisman – sealed one of the most dramatic, and important, comebacks in Everton's modern history, the sky turned blue.'

***

12 March 2016: Everton 2 Chelsea 0 (Romelu Lukaku's brace downs his old club to send Everton to Wembley as new majority shareholder Farhad Moshiri watches on)

In years to come, Farhad Moshiri's legacy at Everton could be that he was the man with the vision to build the club's new stadium, even if most of all the other things he attempted went badly wrong.

The Blues' new majority shareholder watched on for the first time having had his initial 49.9 per cent controlling stake in the club, which was gradually increased to 94.1 per cent, approved by the Premier League.

Moshiri pledged to tackle the issue from the start, declaring on the eve of the FA Cup tie, 'We will also be looking at the best options in relation to our stadium. Goodison Park has served the club extremely well, but we need to make sure the club has a suitable stage to perform on for the future. We will review the best options and how to finance, especially as it is likely to cost a little more than the £3,000 it apparently did back in 1892.'

He proved to be a man of his word.

After various aborted attempts to leave Goodison, including Peter Johnson's bowl at an unspecified location, the previous waterside project at King's Dock that would ultimately become the indoor arena, Destination Kirkby and the short-lived suggestion of Walton Hall Park, Everton are finally moving to an iconic new home on, as the old terrace anthem goes, the banks of the 'royal blue' Mersey.

Moshiri's presence in the directors' box for the game against Chelsea would signal the beginning of the end for England's first purpose-built football ground – in the guise it existed in for 133 years.

Over the coming years, the Iranian-born businessman would provide the financial muscle to enable the Blues to splash out on numerous extravagant signings, only to be left apologising to fans with the admission of 'we have not always spent large amounts of money wisely' when the Profit and Sustainability Rules breaches that would ultimately lead to points deductions loomed on the horizon.

Here it was their existing record signing, Romelu Lukaku, a player who would accumulate almost £300m in combined transfer fees throughout his career, who proved the match-winner against his former – and future – club on this occasion.

Phil Kirkbride of the *Liverpool Echo* captured the mood by writing, 'As convincing as chairman Bill Kenwright's sales pitch will have been, nothing could have sold the Everton dream to Farhad Moshiri as well as this.

'The Blues' new majority shareholder said he had been taught what it means to be a fan of the club but now, after experiencing a special night at Goodison Park, he will have felt it course through his veins.

'After two quickfire goals from Romelu Lukaku sliced through the tension and sent Roberto Martínez's side to an FA Cup semi-final at Wembley, Moshiri left his seat in the directors' box with a beaming smile and shaking hands with jubilant supporters.

'Goodison was shaken to its foundations. The walls of this wonderful old ground reverberated to the sounds of triumph, of fight and of harmony.

'Everton and their home haven't been easy bedfellows of late, there has been a lack of unity and togetherness, but this FA Cup tie under the lights proves the bond is not broken.

'And as he reflects on his first game at the Old Lady, Moshiri will now understand that bit better just how much of a wrench it would be to leave this sacred place.'

It took a special solo goal from Lukaku 13 minutes from the end to break the deadlock.

Kirkbride wrote, 'Lukaku came into this tie having scored 59 goals for the Blues but not one of those was against his former club Chelsea. But with a moment of world-class forward play he changed all that.

'Moshiri will have been deafened by a noise that could be heard all along Wembley Way. Lukaku twisted César Azpilicueta and Branislav Ivanović one way, John Obi Mikel another, and sent Gary Cahill's head spinning before firing a low drive past Thibaut Courtois. Ricky Villa eat your heart out.'

Diego Costa, for appearing to bite Gareth Barry, then the Everton midfielder himself for picking up a second booking for a foul on Cesc Fàbregas, would be sent off in the latter stages but not before Lukaku had sealed the win by bagging his brace.

Kirkbride said, 'Lukaku's second, five minutes later, was far more straightforward, yet it was decisive. His drive, after latching on to Ross Barkley's through ball and fired through the legs of Courtois, was like a dagger through Chelsea hearts.'

As Phil McNulty of BBC Sport concluded, 'While Moshiri confirmed the issue of Everton's ground is high on his agenda, he sampled this glorious old arena at its finest – a bear pit from first to last and resounding to raucous sounds of victory at the final whistle.'

* * *

20 April 2005: Everton 1 Manchester United 0 (A decade on, Duncan Ferguson does it again against United to boost Blues' top-four hopes)

A decade on from when he first felled Manchester United, Duncan Ferguson repeated the trick to earn a result that put Everton on their way to securing their highest Premier League finish.

The Blues' march to fourth place in 2004/05 was remarkable considering how they went into the campaign.

There was talk that manager David Moyes had lost the dressing room when Everton slumped to finish 17th with just 39 points the previous season despite getting themselves safe at Easter and not being in any kind of realistic relegation battle all year.

Over the summer, the club's homegrown hero Wayne Rooney went on to play a starring role at the European Championship but, all of a sudden, he went from being Everton's Wayne Rooney to England's Wayne Rooney and the 18-year-old new national treasure was soon on his way to Manchester United for £27m – a world record fee for a teenager at the time.

Fellow striker Tomasz Radzinski had also departed and in their place came journeyman Marcus Bent and a prospect from the championship in the shape of Tim Cahill for barely £2m combined.

A season of struggle seemed to lie ahead after the Blues were beaten 4-1 at home to Arsenal on the opening day but five wins out of their next six Premier League games saw them climb to third in the fledgling table.

Indeed, the Merseyside derby win at Goodison Park in December saw them rise to second and while there was something of a post-Christmas slump with seven losses in 13 matches, they were still clinging on to the final Champions League qualification spot above eventual winners Liverpool.

Ferguson might not have developed into the latter-day Dixie Dean he'd been compared to by Joe Royle a decade earlier but after returning to his beloved Blues in 2000 – having been sold by chairman Peter Johnson, behind Walter Smith's back according to the manager, in 1998 – he remained the darling of the Gwladys Street.

By now, the 33-year-old had become an effective Plan B off the bench for Moyes with the likes of Bent and then new record signing James Beattie usually leading the line at the start.

Some 29 of Ferguson's 35 Premier League appearances that season came as a substitute but, perhaps alive to the 'Braveheart' spirit for the grand occasion that his old warhorse possessed, Moyes chose to pair him with Bent against Sir Alex Ferguson's men and left Beattie on the bench.

Scott McLeod of the *Liverpool Echo* was in no mood to play down the importance of the encounter and wrote, 'Superlatives cannot do last night justice. Even before you take into consideration the wider context, it equates to one of the most thrilling nights Goodison has witnessed for many years. Bayern Munich, 1985, anyone? As with that famous night, the mix was perfect. The crowd were rocking, the players were outstanding, and the outcome was ridiculously satisfying.'

He added, 'There was even something poetic about the identity of the man who proved Everton's talisman on the evening. Only Alan Shearer has scored more goals against United since the Premier League came into being than Duncan Ferguson.

'It was one of those goals which provided Everton with their last league victory against them before last night – way back in 1995.

'That was when Ferguson was in his prime. In recent times he has been a shadow of the player who waltzed his way into the hearts of Evertonians all those years ago. But here he was gargantuan.

'His monumental frame cast a shadow over the most successful English team of the modern era – and made Rio Ferdinand look more like a £120-a-week player than the £120,000 one his agent claims he should be.

'Ferguson towered over the England man, winning more battles in the air than Douglas Bader. And he left Ferdinand in his slipstream for the 55th minute header beyond Tim Howard which secured the victory.'

While Ferguson's head brought Everton the win, United lost theirs as Gary Neville and Paul Scholes were sent off in the second half.

As for finishing the job at hand, McLeod said, 'There is humility within the Goodison ranks which prevents them from blowing their own trumpet too loud. But this performance illustrated beyond any doubt that such humility is masking an unwavering belief they are more than good enough to keep hold of fourth place.'

* * *

5 November 2017: Everton 3 Watford 2 (Bonfire Night fireworks with first Goodison comeback from 2-0 down since Wimbledon in 1994)

Talk about Bonfire Night fireworks – this spectacular at Goodison Park crackled with all the whiz-bangs, rockets and explosive action anyone could ever stomach.

A first 3-2 victory on home turf for Everton after trailing 2-0 since the 'Great Escape' against Wimbledon in 1994. Check.

Thirteen minutes of added time after a goalkeeper went off injured. Check.

The Blues securing their winner with a penalty in injury time before Watford had the chance to equalise with a spot-kick of their own only for a Goodison old boy to miss. Check.

Throw into the heady mix that this was also caretaker manager David Unsworth's first victory since Ronald Koeman was sacked and it came against a future Everton boss Marco Silva with future Everton player Richarlison opening the scoring, then there is plenty to digest.

Everything unravelled quickly for Koeman in his second season in charge at Goodison.

So much so that when the Dutchman was dismissed following a 5-2 home defeat to Arsenal on 22 October, owner Farhad Moshiri seemed unsure who to turn to.

Unsworth, the Blues' under-23 manager, was therefore given time to stake his claim having been handed the reins on a temporary basis.

The former Everton defender started with a hat-trick of away defeats though, so the man affectionately known as 'Rhino' by the

Gwladys Street during his playing days was in desperate need for some home comforts by the time this fixture came along.

Phil Kirkbride of the *Liverpool Echo* tried to make sense of the chaotic scenes, writing, 'Quite where Everton, fragile of confidence, lacking in ideas and needing to do something the club hasn't done since 1994, found the spirit to launch a fightback as remarkable as this from 2-0 down, is anyone's guess though you suspect, finally, it was Unsworth's passion finally rubbing off on them which made the difference.

'This game wasn't won because it suddenly clicked for the Blues, or because Everton stylishly cut through Watford and banished the misery of the past few months with a razzle, dazzle display, but because when things became really bad – 2-0 down and facing the prospect of being second bottom going into the international break – they used what the caretaker boss has given them.'

That all looked a long way off when Everton came back out in sluggish fashion after a goalless first half.

Kirkbride said, 'Less than 60 seconds after the restart, Watford gave Everton a nudge as Richarlison was the man to profit from clueless defending before Christian Kabasele made it 2-0 just past the hour mark, shaking off Phil Jagielka to power home a header.'

In between the visitors' two goals, though, they lost their experienced goalkeeper Heurelho Gomes after he collided with Oumar Niasse, and while at 32 his replacement Orestis Karnezis was a seasoned pro himself, this was a baptism of fire for him in English football.

Niasse would help spark the comeback because as Kirkbride observed, 'If nothing else, he runs. And so, when racing on to Ademola Lookman's ball over the top, he nicked the ball past Karnezis, went down under José Holebas's foul in the six-yard box but his momentum, and shoulder, knocked the ball over the line.'

Game on and come 74 minutes, Everton had their equaliser, 'Hope had been plucked from the wreckage and Dominic Calvert-

Lewin, chucked on in place of Wayne Rooney, headed home Leighton Baines's corner to level the game.'

There was more to come, 'With five minutes left, Aaron Lennon was Everton's last throw of the dice and when he went down under Holebas's clumsy challenge, referee Graham Scott pointed to the spot. Baines obliged to make it 3-2.'

However, there was still plenty of time for a dramatic postscript.

Kirkbride said, 'When the fourth official's board brought up 12 minutes of time added on [largely due to lengthy breaks in play due to Watford injuries] everyone knew this wild second half was far from done.

'An uncharacteristic mistake from Jordan Pickford saw the ball drop at Richarlison's feet and in a desperate attempt to make amends, he fouled the Brazilian.

'Tom Cleverley stepped up, the former Blue ready to deliver a cruel blow to his struggling old club, but he sent his penalty wide of Pickford's right-hand post.

'Unbridled joy, relief and confusion greeted the miss before Goodison erupted at the final whistle.

'It's been far too long since it has.'

* * *

11 September 2010: Everton 3 Manchester United 3 (Blues net twice in stoppage time to earn a point and almost go on to win it)

Incredibly, Everton went into stoppage time 3-1 down to Manchester United but following the final whistle, David Moyes still raced on to the pitch to complain to the referee that his side were denied a winner.

Whatever we all might say about the various positive and negative elements of Moyes's long first Goodison Park reign, a determination to keep battling to the end was often one of the hallmarks of his sides with the fitness and spirit the Scot instilled in his players ensuring they'd seldom throw in the towel without first putting up a fight to the finish. That was exemplified in this six-goal thriller.

Greg O'Keeffe of the *Liverpool Echo* wrote, 'There was a time when the only morale boost David Moyes could rely on from old friend Alex Ferguson was a glass of expensive red wine after another routine defeat.

'But recent campaigns have seen Manchester United emerge as perfect opponents when the Toffees are in search of a season-defining moment.

'Two seasons ago it was Phil Neville's crunching tackle on Cristiano Ronaldo which kick-started a faltering term and sent the Blues on a run which culminated in fifth place in the league and a cup final.

'Last time around, United were sent back down the M62 with their backsides smarting after a 3-1 rout which gave Everton the confidence to end their season in scintillating form.'

While that latter result was only their second Premier League success under Moyes against Alex Ferguson's men, they were first out of the traps in this early kick-off too as Steven Pienaar fired them into a 39th-minute lead.

O'Keeffe said, 'Mikel Arteta latched on to a defence-splitting Tim Cahill ball, sprinted past Gary Neville, and drilled a shot at Edwin van der Sar.

'The Dutchman parried, and Leon Osman's cultured football brain saw him resist shooting and instead slip a delicate pass to Steven Pienaar who stroked it home.'

However, Everton's lead lasted just four minutes, 'Goodison rocked, but the delirium was short-lived. A trademark slick United phase of play saw Paul Scholes's free kick set in motion a move involving Ryan Giggs and Nani, neither closed down quickly enough, before Darren Fletcher finished with aplomb.'

Things got worse two minutes after the break as United started to take control, 'With Everton defending deeper and deeper, the exemplary Paul Scholes slipped the ball back to Nani from a corner, and the Portuguese midfielder's cross split Sylvain Distin and Phil Jagielka and met the forehead of Nemanja Vidić.'

When the visitors added a third midway through the second half, it looked all over, 'Scholes lofted a sumptuous pass towards Dimitar Berbatov, and with Distin wrong-footed and ball watching, he burst past him and finished calmly.'

However, a couple of substitutions would help turn the tide again – eventually – as they netted twice in stoppage time.

O'Keeffe said, 'Moyes tried to revive Everton's early verve by introducing Séamus Coleman and asking Yakubu to provide an unlikely dash of inspiration.

'David Moyes will have been thrilled at how his side kept patiently trying to create a way back into a game which looked finished, and with Marouane Fellaini's calm, assured footwork in the box, the Belgian shuffled it out to Baines, whose perfect first-time cross was typically met by Tim Cahill.

'The goal seemed likely to serve only to give Alex Ferguson something to grumble about in the away dressing room, but what came next might have tempted him to whip out the hairdryer.

'Baines crossed again, Cahill headed it down, and Arteta launched a rocket which was diverted in off Scholes. The late controversy over whether Martin Atkinson should have blown for full time as Everton broke again, (he shouldn't), was largely irrelevant. Goodison sensed a turning point had been reached.'

Moyes, who was fined £8,000 for his post-match pitch invasion but escaped a touchline ban, was furious that the referee denied his side the chance of a winner when he blew for full time just as Phil Jagielka was about to shoot at the visitors' goal.

Van der Sar saved the shot, but the Blues boss grumbled, 'It is a spectator sport with people coming to watch the game and not for him to be the main man.'

* * *

28 May 2023: Everton 1 Bournemouth 0 (The Great Escape Part 3)

For the third time in their history but the first occasion in 25 years after near-misses in 1994 and 1998, Everton went into the final day of a Premier League season fighting for survival yet still managed to complete a hat-trick of 'Great Escapes'.

Ultimately the Blues would record what was the club's lowest equivalent points total in 135 years of Football League and then Premier League action but unlike those previous late Houdini acts when the team had also been playing at Goodison Park on both occasions, their fate was at least in their own hands.

Despite manager Frank Lampard steering the Blues to safety in their final home game of the previous campaign and having the prospect of climbing to ninth if they'd beaten Leicester City at Goodison on Bonfire Night, the team went into the unprecedented seven-week mid-season break for the first ever Northern Hemisphere winter World Cup finals in Qatar on the back of a hat-trick of major reversals.

A 2-0 defeat to the Foxes saw Brendan Rodgers' side climb out of the drop zone and leapfrog them in the table while the Romford-born boss then made 11 changes for a League Cup tie at Bournemouth with a 4-1 loss being followed by 3-0 beating in the Premier League back at the Vitality Stadium just four days later.

The downward spiral continued after Everton returned to action by being beaten 2-1 by bottom club Wolverhampton Wanderers on Boxing Day.

Having lost eight of his last nine games in all competitions, Lampard was axed following a 2-0 defeat at West Ham United on 21 January – the club where he started his career and where his namesake father was a legend – with majority shareholder Farhad Moshiri having turned up at the London Stadium to watch his first

Blues match since the 5-2 capitulation at home to Watford under Rafael Benítez 15 months earlier.

With the team joint bottom of the Premier League, Sean Dyche, who had previously been in charge of Burnley for almost a decade – even having a pub named after him in the east Lancashire town after he guided the Clarets into European football for the first time since the 1966/67 season – took the reins and started with a 1-0 win over table-topping Arsenal at Goodison Park.

Although a second consecutive home win, against Leeds United, saw Everton climb out of the relegation zone a fortnight later, they yo-yoed in and out of the bottom three and were back down there in the final month before a sensational 5-1 victory at Brighton & Hove Albion on 8 May shook things up and provided a platform towards safety.

The Blues knew that if they beat Bournemouth on the final day then there was nothing their rivals could do but they went into the fixture without a recognised striker as winger Demarai Gray spearheaded the attack, while with no available full-backs, midfielder James Garner and winger Dwight McNeil were forced to play as wing-backs in front of a back three.

Leeds, who fell behind after just two minutes in a 4-1 home loss to Tottenham Hotspur, were on the back foot all day but with Leicester 1-0 up at home to West Ham United from the 34th minute in a game they'd win 2-1, Everton were heading for a first relegation in 72 years until Abdoulaye Doucoure, who had been frozen out in Lampard's final days after a dispute, lashed in a half volley from the D outside the area in front of the Park End on 57 minutes.

Joe Thomas of the *Liverpool Echo* wrote, 'It was a goal that came from nothing but meant everything. And how fitting that it came from Abdoulaye Doucoure, the player Sean Dyche brought in from the cold to inspire a team bereft of confidence and goals.

'Doucoure now has five of them, along with two assists, meaning the 30-year-old has contributed to more than one fifth of Everton's goals this season in the 15 matches he has played since Dyche arrived with him training away from the first team.

'It was the goal that saved Everton and it sparked celebrations so loud inside Goodison Park they could be heard on the other side of the River Mersey. A flurry of fireworks added to the cacophony.

'It was just as fitting that the goal was inspired by a fanbase that somehow roused itself for one final battle dance after two seasons in which Everton's supporters have proved more effective than anything this club has been able to muster on the pitch.'

14

Quirky

WE'VE HAD the likes of title pushes, historic occasions, goal fests, Merseyside derby ding-dongs and other memorable battles throughout this book, but some matches deserve to be included for their distinctive, sometimes unique, or even downright odd nature. Welcome to the gloriously eclectic 'miscellaneous' section.

* * *

9 March 1985: Everton 2 Ipswich Town 2 (Kevin Sheedy's twice-taken free kick)

When Kevin Sheedy wrote his autobiography it was given the title *So Good I Did it Twice*, and in the eyes of Evertonian readers, no more explanation was needed.

Sheedy's twice-taken free kick against Ipswich Town – both of which ended up in the net but only the second effort counted – has gone down in Blues folklore as a magic moment that exemplified the genius of the player widely credited as having the best left foot in Everton history.

It's somewhat apt that Sheedy sits at number 11 – his usual shirt number – on Everton's all-time scorers' list but all ten of the players above him were forwards and his 97 goals in 369 appearances make him the club's most prolific midfielder, which is incredible considering the future Republic of Ireland international was plucked from Liverpool's reserve team after just five games in four years at Anfield.

But in 1984/85, the Blues' most successful season, Sheedy wasn't the only non-striker chipping in and this FA Cup quarter-final – the only one of 15 Goodison Park fixtures that Howard Kendall's side did not win following the turn of the calendar year in that glorious campaign – was rescued by another regular scorer from further back on the pitch.

Derek Mountfield's 85th-minute equaliser earned Everton a Portman Road replay that they would triumph 1-0 in four days later en route to the final and was one of 14 goals from the centre-back that season, the same total as talismanic striker Andy Gray.

With the Blues fighting for honours on three fronts both at home and abroad, this game kicked off a mere 65 hours after another Goodison quarter-final in the European Cup Winners' Cup as Dutch side Fortuna Sittard had been dispatched 3-0 by Gray's second-half hat-trick in the first leg.

The hosts started quickly and from a lofted left-wing Sheedy cross they had already seen a back post headed goal from Gray disallowed by referee Alan Robinson a minute before the free kick drama.

Robinson, from Fareham in Hampshire, was the same referee who also denied Everton what looked like clear-cut penalties against Liverpool at Wembley in both the 1984 League Cup Final (Alan Hansen using his hand to steer a goal-bound shot from Adrian Heath off the line) and 1986 FA Cup Final (Graeme Sharp being clipped mid-air by Steve Nicol when preparing to dispatch a header into the net).

The famous free kick was actually awarded for Ipswich goalkeeper Paul Cooper handling the ball outside his area, an offence that Neville Southall would later be sent off three times for, starting at Chelsea the following season and then at Queens Park Rangers and Sheffield Wednesday just five weeks apart from each other in the inaugural 1992/93 Premier League campaign.

Cooper stayed on though, and Ken Rogers of the *Liverpool Echo* wrote, 'Sheedy bent the ball to the right of the keeper and into the net, only for the referee to disallow it with the defensive wall still not ten yards from the ball.

'Sheedy's response was to strike another viciously curling effort, this time into the other corner and Everton had made the perfect start with just five minutes on the watch.'

Recalling the incident to this author in the *Goodison Park: My Home* series, Sheedy said, 'Paul Cooper had edged over to his right-hand side, knowing I could put it in his top right-hand corner and he left a nice, little space, so I knew if I could get it up and over the wall with a bit of spin, away from the keeper, I've got a chance. As soon as I'd executed it, I knew it was in.'

A rare mistake from Southall gifted Ipswich a 15th-minute equaliser when Kevin Wilson's low, dipping drive from outside the area squirmed under his body, and with Dutchman Romeo Zondervan firing into the roof of the Everton net with a smart 31st-minute finish, the home side looked to be heading out of the competition until Mountfield's late leveller.

Also speaking on *Goodison Park: My Home*, Mountfield said, 'That's my most important goal because without that goal, we don't get the chance of the semi-final.

'Pat Van Den Hauwe is playing right-back at the time when he should have been left-back. He flicks the ball over his head, volleys it across and I get the touch on it.'

Everton lived to fight another day but unfortunately Harry Catterick did not as the Blues' legendary former manager collapsed and died aged 65 just after the final whistle, suffering a heart attack in the Goodison directors' box.

* * *

14 January 2007: Everton 1 Reading 1 (Sylvester Stallone adds a touch of Hollywood stardust to a dog of a game as 'Rocky' comes to Goodison)

Sylvester Stallone's rip-roaring trip to watch Everton brought a sprinkling of Hollywood stardust to Goodison Park with what proved to be a blockbuster appearance from the Tinseltown A-lister.

The fanbase can be notoriously fickle and they're certainly not easy prey for gimmicks – the Gwladys Street once booed when one of their number accepted his girlfriend's pitchside proposal of marriage – but there was genuine excitement in the air when the action movie acting star took to the turf.

To be fair to Stallone – who played the American goalkeeper Hatch in the cult 1981 football film *Escape to Victory* alongside the likes of Pelé and Bobby Moore – his Goodison cameo was also a performance he entered into with great gusto.

Invited by his Everton shareholder friend Robert Earl, who owned the Planet Hollywood restaurant chain, to come over and promote his latest production, *Rocky Balboa* – the sixth instalment of the boxing franchise series – Stallone strolled out to the centre circle enthusiastically waving a blue and white Everton scarf above his head while the strains of the iconic *Rocky* theme tune 'Gonna Fly Now' blared out over the stadium's public address system.

Taking his bow, while also wearing an Everton-branded jacket, Stallone lapped up the adulation of the crowd as chants of 'Rocky, Rocky' emanated from all four corners of Goodison.

But while 'Sly' was a smash hit with the Blues faithful, unfortunately the feature attraction proved to be a major flop.

Dominic King of the *Liverpool Echo* mused, '*The Rocky Horror Show* was avoided but on the day Sylvester Stallone came to town, Everton were once again left looking for *The Good Life*. Come on – did you expect anything else other than an introduction crammed full of cliches?

'While PR chiefs at Goodison Park can rightly reflect on a wonderful afternoon for the club, contrary to what one imbecilic radio commentator thinks [BBC Radio 5 Live's Alan Green apologised for describing Stallone's visit as a pathetic stunt and suggesting he left five minutes from full time to see whether his limousine was on bricks], manager David Moyes will be scratching his head for the next few days, wondering how his side can rediscover the Eye of the Tiger. Sorry. That's the last one.

'Stallone's visit to Liverpool was always going to be the main talking point, no matter what football Everton and Reading produced, but it's a good job the positive image the Blues projected diverted attentions away from a disappointing performance.

'Failing to build on a bright start, fuelled by the energy of a crowd hyped up by Stallone's memorable jig on the pitch before kick-off, it was left to Andrew Johnson to spare the blushes with a late header.

'Make no mistake, however, Everton were out of sorts. It would be far too convenient to blame the razzmatazz of Stallone's visit as the reason for Everton's lethargy, especially during an uneventful first half.

'The presence of a Hollywood megastar might well have been the little something needed for Everton to raise themselves and put on a show for a worldwide audience.'

Reading went ahead on 28 minutes through a Joleon Lescott own goal. King said, 'Having conceded a silly free kick, Reading took advantage of Joseph Yobo and Joleon Lescott retreating into their six-yard area to pile pressure on Tim Howard.

'He may have made a terrific save from Stephen Hunt's header, but the comedy of errors was completed when the rebound careered into Lescott then bobbled over the line.'

It was the kind of sucker punch to leave a bad taste in the mouth akin to Stallone's eye-popping reaction when taking a sip from a Goodison cuppa.

Thankfully, Everton got back up off the canvas to at least live to fight another day and earn a share of the spoils nine minutes from the end as 'Johnson atoned for a couple of earlier misses to convert Yobo's cross and register his eighth goal in as many games against Reading.'

Despite Green's cynical misgivings about Stallone's motives, he spoke passionately of the warmth of the Merseyside public and compared Scousers to the citizens of Rocky's home city of Philadelphia because it was 'a blue-collar town and the people are all heart'.

Indeed, the native New Yorker would remain an Evertonian from afar and made a virtual Goodison return, wearing a Blues replica shirt, in 2015 for the shooting of a scene in the film *Creed*, featuring real-life Scouse boxer Tony Bellew, for which he reprised the role of Rocky Balboa.

* * *

19 May 1977: Everton 2 Sunderland 0 (Visitors go down after dodgy finish at Coventry)

A couple of decades later, Everton would be involved in a brace of last-day relegation deciders themselves – one against Coventry City – but on this night, shady goings on some 120 miles from Goodison Park at Highfield Road would condemn Sunderland's fate.

With Tottenham Hotspur and Stoke City both already relegated, there was a three-way battle to stay in the division between Sunderland, Coventry and Bristol City who each had one fixture left with the latter pair facing each other.

The trio were all on 34 points, but Sunderland's superior goal difference ensured they controlled their own destiny.

Not only would a victory at Everton be enough to save them, a draw would be enough if the game at Highfield Road also ended all square while even a defeat for the Mackems would do the job if either Coventry or Bristol City beat the other.

Despite being marooned in mid-table with new manager Gordon Lee having replaced Billy Bingham in February and having nothing but pride to play for on the Thursday night fixture, the Blues maintained their sporting integrity by giving their all.

As Charles Lambert wrote in the *Liverpool Echo*, 'Everton were worthy winners, possessing a little too much in all departments for the north-easterners,' but the same could not be said for Sunderland's fellow strugglers who were going head-to-head.

Everton took the lead on 11 minutes when 'Bob Latchford ran clear of Colin Waldron to steer home a beautiful header from a Mike Pejic free kick', while they sealed the win late on as 'there was no cover available to pick up Bruce Rioch when he ran through the middle in injury time to collect a pass from Neil Robinson and score with a shot that Barry Siddall touched but could not keep out'.

Lambert pointed out that although the Blues were victorious, their role was one of bystanders in the sensational events of the evening.

He said, 'Strangely, for a team playing in front of its own supporters, Everton did not have a very big part in the drama of the night's football activities.

'The real story lay in events taking place off stage, and anyone whose interest went no further than the two points Everton gained was missing as much of the action as those playgoers who complained of rowdy behaviour in the theatre the night President Lincoln was shot.'

Lambert added, 'The night had its moments of hideous irony. News from Highfield Road was as eagerly seized upon as the action from the Goodison Park pitch, and when the false scoreline of Coventry 3 Bristol 1 somehow got around the ground, the thousands of Sunderland supporters at the Stanley Park end went into raptures.

'Then when the final whistle went, came the loudspeaker announcement that the score was Coventry 2 Bristol 1. Renewed celebrations on the terraces, but those around the press box knew that the score was in fact 2-2.

'Youngsters with red and white scarves danced in jubilation on the pitch, believing all had ended well – until at last, the truth dawned, and the brown ale suddenly turned flat.'

It turned out that the game at Highfield Road – delayed due to crowd and traffic congestion – still had ten minutes to go when the final whistle blew at Goodison Park.

Coventry had been 2-0 up but Bristol City had fought back to make it 2-2, a scoreline that would keep them both up now Sunderland had lost.

The result of the game at Goodison was flashed on to the Highfield Road scoreboard by chairman Jimmy Hill. Once both sets of players became aware of this, they tamely played out the remainder of the game without any real intent to attack.

Former Bristol City player Clive Whitehead recalled, 'We let Coventry have the ball, we let them keep it in their own half, they just knocked it about.

'I can always remember someone shouting to [future Everton striker] Mick Ferguson who was playing up front for them, "Oi, stay in your own half! You're not allowed in here."'

Players from both sides embraced as they left the pitch at the end of the game at Highfield Road and shared survival.

A Football League inquiry was subsequently held and while Coventry were reprimanded, the decision served as a mere slap on the wrist and the result stood, leaving a distinctly bad taste in the mouths of Sunderland supporters.

* * *

4 January 2012: Everton 1 Bolton Wanderers 2 (Goalkeeper Tim Howard scores)

In 147 years of football, Tim Howard remains the only goalkeeper to score for Everton – and he didn't even celebrate.

Some 63 minutes into a game against the Premier League's bottom club at Goodison Park, the American hit a wind-assisted 101-yard clearance up the field that bounced once just outside the D in front of the visitors' penalty area before wickedly sailing up in the air again to go over his opposite number Adam Bodgán's head and into the Gwladys Street goal.

Greg O'Keeffe of the *Liverpool Echo* wrote, 'Howard's punt bounced then arced over Bogdán's head – a unique moment in Goodison's modern history that is destined to be watched for many years to come.

'Classy as ever, the USA international was muted in his celebration of his only career goal in the Premier League due to empathy for his opposite number.'

Team-mates such as John Heitinga, Sylvain Distin, Leighton Baines and Howard's USA international colleague Landon Donovan all rushed to embrace him, but the embarrassed custodian refused to offer any cheers of his own.

He said, 'It was cruel. You saw the back fours and the keepers not being able to believe balls all night, and at the back one wrong step and it can be a nightmare.

'For our goal I was disappointed from a goalkeepers' union standpoint. You never want to see that happen. It's not nice, it's embarrassing, so I felt for Adam, but you have to move on from it.'

At least Howard's low-key response also spared him any further blushes because he might have come to regret wildly celebrating his opener given that struggling Bolton fought back to win 2-1.

O'Keeffe said, 'Just three minutes more had elapsed when Louis Saha misplaced a pass and Owen Coyle's side produced a slick move involving Kevin Davies and Nigel Reo-Coker before David N'Gog got a yard ahead of Distin and curled a fine finish inside Howard's right post.

'It got worse. The wind was a factor as Howard punched a wafted free kick away, and Chris Eagles reacted fastest to slip a wonderful pass to Gary Cahill that left Everton's defenders flat-footed and allowed the Chelsea target to score [in the 78th minute] with a low drive across the keeper.'

Indeed, O'Keeffe's *Echo* colleague David Prentice summed up the glum evening for the Blues with some gallows humour by declaring, 'Well isn't that just typically Everton FC? A pair of out-and-out strikers, the USA national team's all-time top scorer wide on the right – and not a single defender on the seven-man subs' bench.

'Then a goalkeeper goes and scores. But even more typically Everton, just minutes after Tim Howard was being congratulated for a highly unusual opener, Everton's defensive resilience cracked, and Bolton snatched a more conventional equaliser.

'And just when they needed a Cahill on the scoresheet, it was Bolton's Gary who obliged. With Phil Jagielka limping off holding his knee and Jack Rodwell beating the turf in frustration after pulling his hamstring again – a thoroughly wretched night off the pitch was matched on it. After a couple of promising results and performances, Everton were awful.

'The freak effort from Howard was the only occasion Bogdán was stretched all night, while Howard was called on to pull off two outstanding stops.'

Although two outfield players had started in goal for Everton in the club's early years – Hope Robertson in a 4-3 win at Newton Heath on 19 October 1892 and Jack Crelley for the first 12 minutes of a goalless draw at home to Manchester City on Christmas Eve 1904 after Leigh Roose and understudy Billy Scott arrived late due to fog – Howard became the first keeper to score for the Blues.

Neville Southall once netted in a 6-5 penalty shoot-out defeat at home to Charlton Athletic after a 2-2 draw in the Full Members' Cup quarter-final on 3 March 1987 but goals in shoot-outs don't count in the record books.

Howard was not the first goalkeeper to score at Goodison in the Premier League though, as that honour went to Peter Schmeichel who volleyed in from close range in the 92nd minute of Aston Villa's 3-2 defeat to Everton on 20 October 2001.

The Dane's effort was the first of six instances of goalkeepers scoring in the Premier League to date.

In addition to Howard's goal, Paul Robinson of Tottenham Hotspur and Stoke City's future Everton man Asmir Begović both netted with long punts upfield while Blackburn Rovers' Brad Friedel scored with a close-range shot and Liverpool's Alisson with a header.

* * *

28 December 1895: Everton v Small Heath (Abandoned, first hooliganism at Goodison as angry mob throw stones and threaten to burn down the stands)

This game is unique among all those included in the book as it was not completed, but given that it prompted the first act of major crowd trouble at Goodison Park, it remains a cautionary tale worth telling. These days we often think of football hooliganism as being a more modern blight that peaked in the 1970s and 80s as young men in post-industrial urban areas undergoing economic hardship used causing trouble in and around matches as an outlet for their violent frustrations.

While it might be true that those dark decades in terms of the game's prosperity and social standing served as low points when it came to football-related violence, the scope for crowds turning ugly has unfortunately existed from the very start.

Even before Goodison existed, there were reported crowd disturbances in Everton's very first Football League fixture, at home to Accrington at Anfield on 8 September 1888.

Thomas Taw wrote in *Football's Twelve Apostles, The Making of the Football League*, 'Those waiting were at an "utmost pitch of excitement" on a beautiful day. Some didn't pay: one "hulking fellow tore down a portion of hoarding" and 50 followed him through "the breach".

'A little urchin trespassed upon the grass and got a "free kick" from an elderly steward. A lithe young fellow went for the official without ceremony, leaving him prostrate with blood streaming from his face.'

Fast forward another seven years and as Thomas Keates wrote in his *Jubilee History of The Everton Football Club in 1928*, 'December 1895 was a harassing month for the directors, as, in the addition to the turnstile frauds, they had a riot to contend with.'

Just weeks earlier, concerns that the Blues' estimated crowds seemed to be consistently higher than the official tallies registered at the turnstiles, a plain clothes police investigation took place on a matchday at Goodison and resulted in a dozen turnstile operators, the groundsman and the club mechanic all appearing in court.

Although Everton had tried to move on from that scandal, they found more trouble brewing when their home match with Small Heath was abandoned before half-time.

Three days of continual rain after Christmas had turned the pitch into a mud bath. Confusion reigned as despite the atrocious conditions, players and officials from both clubs tried to harangue the referee into restarting the game and although they eventually convinced him, it was too late as some of the players had bathed.

Keates explained that despite the attendance being only one-third of the average, 'The bulk of spectators remained on the ground until it was announced that the game was abandoned. The gates were then opened, and the majority passed out.

'Quite a crowd, however, remained, and recruited by an army of street loafers who had entered, a howling mob fronted the office demanding their money back. The secretary tried to appease the brawling but in vain, and retreated when a stone was hurled at him.

'Director George Mahon did manage to get a hearing, and pointing out that it was impossible to tell who had paid and who had not, a free ticket was offered to all the demonstrators for the replayed match.

'The howling intensified, with the clamour for money. Stones were thrown at Mr Mahon, one of them smashing the thick glass face of the clock over his head.'

He added, 'It soon became evident that a great many hooligans had entered the ground and infected the mob with their rowdyism.

'Showers of stones flew about, every pane of glass in the office windows was broken, and woodwork was smashed and used as weapons.

'A crowd made for the grandstand and players' dressing rooms, and a cry of "fire the stands" was heard. The few policemen who prevented the raiding of the office were hurt yet kept very cool.'

Indeed, the nasty incident was reported by the *Liverpool Daily Post*, which wrote, 'When it transpired that no money was to be returned, an angry section of the crowd assembled in front of the office, trying their utmost to break down the railings leading into the committee's sanctum.

'A number of police and stewards did their best to keep the crowd back, and to a great extent succeeded.'

For the record, Everton won the replayed game 3-0 on Monday 3 February 1896 in front of another rather paltry 8,000 crowd which was less than a third of their season's best figure.

* * *

27 January 1991: Woking 0 Everton 1 (Everton the 'away' team at Goodison)

Goodison Park was Everton's home for 133 years but for this FA Cup tie against Woking, the Blues were officially the away side and duly made heavy weather of disposing of their non-league opponents.

Woking had been the toast of the nation in the previous round when they fought back from being 1-0 down at half-time to pull off a huge upset by defeating second-tier West Bromwich Albion 4-2 at The Hawthorns with their striker Tim Buzaglo netting a hat-trick.

The giant-killing earned them a plum fourth round tie with Everton and despite being drawn at home, they switched the game from their Kingfield Stadium to Goodison to enjoy the financial benefits of a bumper crowd on Merseyside (34,724 turned up) as well as giving their part-time players the opportunity to take to the field on one of football's most famous grounds.

As they officially remained the 'visitors', Everton had to forgo their home dressing room for the afternoon and with Woking turning out in their usual red shirts, white shorts and red socks, Howard Kendall's side wore their blue change shorts instead of white.

Before the first world war, when the Football League consisted of only two divisions of mostly northern-based clubs, the Blues would regularly face non-league opponents in FA Cup ties.

Many such clubs would eventually become members of the Football League and indeed top-flight outfits themselves such as Southampton, Portsmouth, Tottenham Hotspur and West Ham United with Everton slipping up on a few occasions, perhaps most infamously to minnows Glossop in 1914.

In the post-second world war era there were no such upsets with Altrincham's 1-1 draw at Goodison in 1975 before losing an Old Trafford replay 2-0 the only occasion the Blues failed to win against non-league opponents; it was also the only time they conceded a goal.

Woking pushed them all the way though as Ken Gaunt explained in the *Liverpool Echo*, 'Woking walked away from Goodison Park with cheers for souvenirs … not to mention a few goodies as well.

'The Vauxhall League side, six divisions and a world apart from Everton and their kind, bowed out of the FA Cup with their pride intact and their bank balance boosted.

'Kevin Sheedy's goal after 57 minutes took the Blues to a 1-0 victory. But the narrow win did little to humour the fans or ease manager Howard Kendall's embarrassment.

'And Woking's skipper Adie Cowler took delight after the game in telling whoever would listen that "it was difficult to tell who was the non-league side".

'Cowler's comments may have been a bit over the top. But there was only one team knocking the ball about – and it wasn't Everton. Woking keeper Tim Read was rarely tested or put under any pressure. In contrast, Neville Southall was kept on his toes.

'Read was back at the bank today, showing off his Goodison gift. The 19-year-old rookie swapped jerseys with his boyhood hero opposite number after the game. "That made my day," he said. His attitude summed up Woking's spirit. They didn't kick and didn't snarl. They just got on with what they do quite well and played the ball to feet.'

Everton had to wait almost an hour for their opening and for once the ready Scouse wit of the Gwladys Street was silenced by nerves.

Gaunt said, 'The home fans had to endure taunts of "Are you West Brom in disguise?" You could tell they were hurt for they didn't answer back.'

However, 'Just when it seemed Woking might hang on for a sensational result they finally cracked to a goal of the highest quality.

'Neil McDonald knocked the ball over, Graeme Sharp nodded it down and Sheedy applied the finishing touch. Young Woking keeper Read could only look on in admiration.'

The floodgates didn't open though, and in the end a single-goal margin had to suffice.

Gaunt added, 'If Blues fans were expecting a late flurry, they were sadly mistaken. Woking kept their heads, kept playing simple football, and made it difficult for Everton to dictate the pace.

'Woking deserved their marvellous ovation as the players and coaching staff went on a lap of honour while the Everton players as well as the referee and linesmen waited patiently to clap them off.

'Both sides had got what they wanted – Everton a place in the fifth round and Woking a lot of respect.

'And [after their trip to Goodison] Woking are not finished with Walton yet. Their next match is on Tuesday night in the Surrey Senior Cup against Walton and Hersham!'

* * *

15 November 1924: Everton 2 Arsenal 3 (Sam Chedgzoy corner confusion)

Sam Chedgzoy turned out 300 times for Everton and was part of the 1914/15 league championship-winning side but a century on from his playing career, he is arguably best-remembered for a single quirky moment in changing the laws of the game and even the facts behind that are shrouded by the myth surrounding the incident.

Football folklore claims that in a game for Everton at Tottenham Hotspur, Chedgzoy exploited a loophole in the rulebook to dribble the ball from a corner before scoring – rather than the conventional crossing or passing to a team-mate.

It's a great story, which has even been published in some previous books, but as the television programme *QI* has taught us on so many occasions when it comes to perceived general knowledge, it's not actually true.

Chedgzoy did attempt the feat, on more than one occasion in a single game – yet it was not against Spurs but rather their north London rivals Arsenal in a 3-2 home defeat for Everton at Goodison Park – and ultimately while his actions are credited with making football's governing bodies amend their laws, he did not score.

The outside-right was put up to his stunt by *Liverpool Echo* football writer Ernest Edwards.

A rewriting of football's laws rephrased the old Law 10 with the new Law 11 simply reading, 'A goal may be scored from a corner kick or from a free kick.'

This had left a grey area which enabled players to dribble the ball from the corner flag and Edwards wanted to highlight this by bringing the issue to a head.

Many years later, long-time Everton chairman and director Will Cuff recalled, '"Bee" [Edwards's pen name] offered a fee of £2 to Chedgzoy, with but one proviso, "Get that corner in the first 20 minutes if possible as I want to feed my newspaper clients around the country with the full story."'

As early as the first minute Chedgzoy was trying the trick, attempting to dribble the ball in from the Park End corner flag to score.

According to Cuff the stunned crowd, unaware of the arrangement, 'were getting waxier and yelled instructions as to what he should do with the ball'.

He added, 'It was the funniest interlude for years. Chedgzoy was hanging on to the ball to try and force a corner kick. The crowd shouted "centre, centre" but he wanted to hang on to force the ball on to a full-back's leg for a corner.'

In an act that would surely be frowned upon now, journalist Edwards was allowed into the Everton dressing room area at half-time by Cuff, to visit Chedgzoy and hand over the £2, and he remarked, 'Thanks for the fun.'

At the time, under the headline 'A sensation in football: Everton player takes the offensive in corner kick rule; pushing a vexed point to a conclusion', 'Bee' wrote in the *Echo*, 'Sam Chedgzoy of Everton broke the ice so far as pros were concerned when against Arsenal, he read the corner kick in the way the *Echo* has been reading it.'

He added, 'It may be recalled that the Liverpool Referees' Society unanimously voted against Bee's reading of the rule, but referee Griffiths waved Chedgzoy on without hesitation, and therefore was on the *Echo*'s side.'

When it comes to the telling of this particular tale, especially as reported by 'Bee' in the *Echo*, the goalscoring on the day seems almost inconsequential.

However, a topsy-turvy battle saw James Ramsay fire Arsenal ahead on 42 minutes with a shot that 'bumped against the crossbar and bumped off the boy's hand [goalkeeper Bob Jones who was actually 22] over the line'.

Everton drew level two minutes after the restart as 'Bee' declared, 'Bobby Irvine had the satisfaction of scoring one of the best goals ever seen on the ground,' but that's all he says about it despite earlier waxing lyrical, 'Two of the most remarkable incidents of the game were a throw-in by Arsenal's Billy Milne to his goalkeeper and a perfect Catherine wheel by Alec Troup round Jock Rutherford, who is twice his size.'

The Blues went ahead two minutes later when Frank Hargreaves 'nipped in' but Andrew Young 'hit a glorious drive' to restore parity on the hour mark before Ramsey 'scrambled the ball over the line' following a more orthodox corner to net the winner nine minutes from the end.

Following Chedgzoy's actions, the law was duly amended making it clear that the player taking the corner could only strike the ball once before another player must make contact.

* * *

23 December 1975: Everton 1 Manchester United 1 (Match held up for 14 minutes due to floodlight failure on 69 minutes)
At a time of year when most people's homes are lit up with Christmas decorations, the lights went out at Goodison Park and Everton blamed the subsequent delay to restore power on their failure to win.

When untangling and dusting off the Gordian Knot of wires that have lain dormant in our lofts since the previous January, many of us have suffered a blow out from a dodgy bulb at some point across the festive season but this wasn't supposed to happen to a leading First Division football club like the Blues.

As Rob Sawyer explained in his online article, 'The Age of Illumination – The Story of Goodison Park under Floodlights', 'A back-up diesel generator was installed to supply emergency power to essential lighting within the ground,' and, 'The Merseyside & North Wales Electricity Board gave assurances that the floodlights' supply could be switched to an alternative source within five minutes should a failure occur.'

However, despite the UK having seemingly seen the back of their electricity supply issues with the abolition of the three-day week, which lasted from 1 January to 6 March 1974, just two days before Christmas the following year, Everton's game with Manchester United was plunged into darkness in front of a 41,732 crowd.

Manchester United went into the match in second place but knew they would leapfrog Liverpool to go top of the tree on Christmas Day if they avoided defeat.

For their part, Everton sat ninth, but a victory would see them climb to within just three points of the summit.

With winger Gary Jones also having to miss the game with a neck injury, the Blues also drafted in homegrown prospect Ronny Goodlass – in more recent years a regular summariser on Radio Merseyside commentaries of Everton matches – for his first team debut at the relatively advanced age of 22.

The *Liverpool Echo* went with the headline 'Light relief for United! – Blackout dulls the Everton charge' and explained that after weathering an early storm from United, the hosts started to find their feet but were left to rue a gilt-edged chance that was squandered.

Alex Goodman of the *Echo* wrote, 'With Roger Kenyon in dominating form, Everton gradually settled down and they might have taken a 21st-minute lead when Alex Stepney fumbled the ball after a shot from the lively David Smallman, but Bob Latchford failed to connect with the rebound just a few yards out.

'It proved to be an expensive miss as United took the lead five minutes later with a stunning goal from Lou Macari. He had his back to goal 15 yards out but still managed to beat Dai Davies with a brilliant overhead kick.'

Latchford would redeem himself though, and Goodman added, 'The goal stung Everton into life and with Mike Bernard and Terry Darracott taking a grip on Steve Coppell and Gordon Hill, Bryan Hamilton and Martin Dobson busy in the midfield, they hit back five minutes before the break.

'When Bernard was fouled, he floated the ball into the penalty area from the free kick, Dobson and Hamilton helped it on with headers and Latchford volleyed it into the roof of the net from six yards.'

However, with the Blues pushing for a winner in the second half, the action came to an abrupt halt.

Goodman said, 'Everton manager Billy Bingham is left to reflect on what might have been if a fuse had not blown after 65 minutes of the game. It blacked out the floodlights and caused a 14-minute hold-up.'

A frustrated Bingham remarked, 'United did well in the first 20 minutes but we began to play much better after our goal. But then the game was a non-event when the players came back after the lights failure.'

The Blues boss's fellow Belfast boy, Bryan Hamilton, described as their star man on the night, concurred, 'We were doing well until the lights went out. The break did more harm than good.'

Everton officials must have been thankful for small mercies given that the fixture – in front of a crowd second only in size that season to the one that watched the visit of Liverpool for the Merseyside derby – was not abandoned completely, but the Reds might also have grumbled about their neighbours' loss of momentum caused by the power cut.

As Goodman observed, 'Liverpool are off the top of the First Division today, because the lights went out on Everton!'

* * *

8 August 2012: Everton 4 AEK Athens 1 (Failing to find the net in 328 competitive games for the Blues, Tony Hibbert scores in his testimonial)

'Hibbo scores – we riot!'

That was the mantra among Evertonians. They said it to each other, they had it printed on T-shirts and banners, and when he finally did, they were good to their word, albeit in an understandably jubilant rather than angry way.

Homegrown hero Tony Hibbert was one of their own: a lifelong Blue, living the dream and playing for his home city club. He was also a throwback to the days when full-backs defended first and foremost and weren't overly concerned with what they did in the final third of the pitch.

England 1966 World Cup winner Ray Wilson never scored for Everton in 154 appearances but as a full-back he was considered the doyen in his field and was once picked in an all-time World XI on *Saint and Greavsie* alongside the likes of Alfredo Di Stéfano, Diego Maradona, Johan Cruyff, Pelé and Ferenc Puskás.

Delving even further into history, Warney Cresswell, generally considered the Blues' best player in his position before the second world war and dubbed the 'prince of full-backs', netted just once in 308 games for the club.

While Hibbert couldn't claim to have operated at quite the same kind of levels as those two, he was the last of his kind in many ways.

Football was changing, with the evolution of attacking full-backs one of the biggest developments in the early decades of the 21st century, and Hibbert's successor in the Everton side would be the marauding Irish international Séamus Coleman who has gone on to net 28 goals for the club, including seven in the 2013/14 season alone.

Hibbert's 328 games were the most appearances from an Everton outfield player without finding the net but curiously he'd played further forward as a junior and was still primarily a midfielder when part of the Blues' 1998 FA Youth Cup-winning squad.

After over a decade of loyal service, Hibbert, who usually shunned the limelight, rarely doing interviews and feeling more at home enjoying the solitude of angling – he'd go on to purchase a 33-acre French carp fishery on the outskirts of Reims – was awarded a Goodison Park testimonial. Would this be his chance to finally shine?

Before the match against AEK Athens, Hibbert dismissed suggestions he'd be resorting to a cheap way of finally breaking his duck.

He said, 'I don't know why everyone is saying I should take a penalty. It's an easy way of scoring, isn't it? If I'm going to do it, I want it to be a 30-yarder!'

When his big moment came along, he wasn't far off.

Hibbert's long-awaited blockbuster was so significant it even put his Goodison debutant team-mate Steven Naismith's hat-trick in the shade.

The Scot, signed on a free transfer after his contract at Rangers was deemed void due to the financial collapse that forced them to reform, netted just 30 seconds into his home debut, lobbing the goalkeeper, and despite Taxiarchis Fountas volleying the Greeks level soon after, two more Naismith goals before the break, a header and a close-range effort from a rebound, put the hosts 3-1 up.

Hibbert's moment of destiny arrived in the 53rd minute. Greg O'Keeffe of the *Liverpool Echo* wrote, 'In the end, nobody can say they weren't warned. Tony Hibbert scored for Everton and Goodison rioted.

'Never mind Jessica Ennis or Usain Bolt. Take no notice of people who boast of being there when Mo Farah won Olympic gold.

'The sporting highlight of the summer arrived last night – and 17,508 Evertonians witnessed Tony Hibbert score for the first time in 309 games spanning ten years of his loyal Toffees career.

'There was a rumble of expectation around when the right-back strolled purposefully across the field to take a 20-yard free kick.

'The man of the moment had already unleashed a fierce effort over the bar in the first half and maybe, just maybe, this would be that fabled time. Perhaps there were many who didn't expect what happened next too.

'But, sure enough, Steven Pienaar teed it up and the defender rifled the ball through the wall and past Dimitris Konstantopoulos in the Gwladys Street goal.

'It would have been churlish to save it, not that the AEK Athens goalkeeper had a chance. "Tony Hibbert will score when he wants" sang the jubilant supporters as almost 1,000 fans poured on to the pitch to enjoy their good-natured and long predicted riot.'

David Moyes quipped, 'It was a genuine goal. I've been putting the wrong guy on the free kicks for too long!'

15

Ground structure

WHEN EVERTON'S new home first opened its doors in 1892, the journal *Out of Doors* proclaimed, 'Behold Goodison Park! No single picture could take in the entire scene the ground presents, it is so magnificently large, for it rivals the greater American baseball pitches.'

Newcastle United's St James' Park, which also opened in its current guise in 1892, and Wolverhampton Wanderers' Molineux, which appeared three years earlier, were both relatively basic but professional football was still very much in its infancy at this time and everyone knows that if you stand still at the game's highest level then you inevitably go backwards.

There were only three proper stands at Goodison at first but having spared no expense to build it, Everton would continue to develop the ground over the coming decades to ensure it remained one of the leading venues in the country.

That was certainly the case for the best part of a century but by the time the Premier League came around, the 'Grand Old Lady', with her numerous restricted views and lack of modern amenities, was showing her age and as many rivals either relocated or undertook substantial redevelopments following the turn of the 21st century, she increasingly became a relic of a bygone age.

A significant part of Goodison's charm though is her tightly packed stands, a feature that helps generate what has often been described as an intimidating 'bear pit' atmosphere.

While the ground has long since not been economically viable to serve Everton's aspirations – by its latter years it has dropped into the bottom three of the Premier League when it came to generating matchday revenues – US architect Dan Meis, who designed the club's new stadium at Bramley-Moore Dock, has tried to replicate that intimacy as best he can in a modern setting.

This has been done with steep terracing in close proximity to the pitch to ensure that the 'Spirit of the Blues' travels with the team as they and their fans move two miles down the road from Walton to Vauxhall.

Everton, who have only once enjoyed average gates of over 50,000 across a season with a figure of 51,603 in the 1962/63 title-winning campaign, are now looking forward to the prospect of a brighter future with scope to play in front of the biggest regular crowds in the club's history by relocating to their new home on the Mersey waterfront.

* * *

Main Stand

Having been the first club in the country to boast double-decker stands on all four sides of the ground, Everton's progression to be the first with a triple-decker stand should have enforced their position at the top of the English game.

However, bigger is not always better and in many ways, the new Main Stand built on Goodison Road between 1969 and 1971 came to represent the Blues' status as football aristocrats who did not adapt sufficiently with the times.

In hosting a World Cup semi-final alongside Wembley in 1966, Goodison Park was already the de facto number one club ground in England before the 'Mersey Millionaires' backed by John

Moores's fortune and vision made the decision to replace their 1909 Archibald Leitch-designed Main Stand.

The former structure had often been referred to as the 'Mauretania Stand' in its early years after Ernest Edwards of the *Liverpool Echo* – who also dubbed Anfield's largest terrace the 'Spion Kop' – declared that it resembled the side of RMS *Mauretania*, then the world's largest ship, which operated from the Port of Liverpool.

But just as the 1970s would see the construction of Chicago's Sears Tower as the world's tallest building at 1450ft, more than twice the height of New York City's Metropolitan Life Tower (700ft) which held the title when it too was completed in 1909, football stands were also moving on up.

While Goodison's old main stand cost £28,000 and was considered immense, the new stand, which produced a £1m bill, was nearly twice the size, and until 1974 when Chelsea opened their mammoth East Stand, it was by far the largest stand in Britain, holding 10,045 seats on the upper two tiers and originally standing 4,900 on the lower terrace.

Also, because the new stand was so tall, Goodison's floodlight pylons were taken down to be replaced by lamps mounted on gantries along the roof. The structure also boasted the luxury of having escalators to take fans up to the Top Balcony.

Such opulent features could not mask the flaws in the design though as 1971 also marked a year of equilibrium at the top of English football.

With Arsenal winning the First Division, they, along with Everton, Liverpool and Manchester United all shared the title for the most championships won with each of the quartet on seven apiece.

From the top of Goodison's Main Stand, Blackpool Tower is visible on a clear day, but perhaps the Blues should have been looking inland to the east for inspiration?

Five years earlier, Manchester United had used cantilever technology to redesign their North Stand column-free, allowing every spectator a completely unobstructed view.

In contrast, over half a century later, Goodison patrons – including the author, who had to choose whether to watch the penalty taker or the goal during Everton's UEFA Cup shoot-out against Fiorentina in 2008 – have been constantly straining their necks either side of the ground's infamous and numerous pillars and wondering what is happening when the ball disappears behind one of them in some kind of momentary Bermuda Triangle.

* * *

Rest of the ground

Goodison Park has a unique feature among football grounds due to the presence of the St Luke the Evangelist Church, which has been visible on matchdays for well over a century in the corner between the Goodison Road Main Stand and Gwladys Street End.

Everton's ground predates the present St Luke's building, consecrated in 1901, but a sketch from *Outdoors* magazine in 1892 of a match against Edinburgh-based Heart of Midlothian shows its wooden predecessor on the same site.

For over two decades from the 1960s there were also two clocks at opposite ends of the ground (the Goodison Road/Gwladys Street and Bullens Road/Park End corners) – initially on floodlight pylons – which featured the slogan 'Buy at/Eat at Littlewoods Stores', the company of majority shareholder John Moores.

These were taken down in 1985 but the view of the church has been partially obscured for both matchday fans and television viewers alike since 2000 with the installation of a couple of jumbotron screens in the same two open corners of the ground where the clocks were.

The Gwladys Street Stand – officially renamed the Howard Kendall Gwladys Street End in July 2016 nine months after the death of Everton's most successful manager – is traditionally home to the club's most vociferous supporters.

Blues captains usually choose to attack the 'Street End' in the second half if they win the pre-match toss and the two-tier stand holds 10,611.

The end also gives its name to Gwladys Street's Hall of Fame, an exclusive club to honour former Everton players and staff conceived by Dr David France.

Built in 1938 with its completion ensuring that Goodison Park became the first football ground with double-decker stands in all four corners (the later Goodison Road Main Stand is triple-decker while the Park End is now a single tier), the Gwladys Street's lower tier was a terrace until 1991.

Just two years after it was built, the Gwladys Street Stand suffered bomb damage during the second world war in 1940. The bomb had landed directly in Gwladys Street and caused serious injury to nearby residents and the bomb splinter damage to the bricks remained visible on the exterior of the stand. The cost of repairs was £5,000 and was paid for by the War Damage Commission.

Everton's directors' minutes say of the incident, 'It was decided also that Mr A. Leitch [junior; the ground's original architect Archibald Leitch senior had died the previous year] be instructed to value the cost of complete renewal of damaged properties and that a claim should be forwarded to the War Damage Claims department within the prescribed 30 days.

'The damage referred to included the demolition of a wide section of the new stand outer wall in Gwladys Street; destruction of all glass in this stand; damage to every door; canteen, water and electricity pipe and all lead fittings and the perforated roof in hundreds of places.

'On Bullens Road side, a bomb dropped in the school yard had badly damaged the exterior wall of this stand and the roof was badly perforated here also.

'A third bomb outside the practice ground had demolished the surrounding hoarding and had badly damaged glass in the Goodison Avenue and Walton Lane property.'

The Bullens Road Stand is also an Archibald Leitch creation, featuring his distinctive criss-cross steel latticework balustrades – also visible at Ibrox in his native Glasgow – that once adorned so many famous football grounds throughout the United Kingdom.

Holding 10,546, the two-tiered stand used to have a terrace in the paddock at the front of the lower tier and was built in 1926 at a cost of £30,000.

Since the rebuilding of the Park End in 1994, a section of both the upper and lower tiers of the Bullens Road closest to Stanley Park has usually been reserved for away fans.

The Park End, like the Gwladys Street End, was renamed in July 2016 as the Sir Philip Carter Park End after the club's long-serving chairman and director who died in April 2015. It was the most modern stand at Goodison Park and the only one without any pillars obstructing the view of fans.

A single-tier structure holding 5,750, it opened on 17 September 1994 having cost £2.4m and was the location for Goodison's scoreboard.

The structure was being built at the time of Everton's first 'Great Escape' against Wimbledon on the final day of the 1993/94 season and because there was only a skeleton of the stand at the time, some fans without tickets were able to take in the action from treetop vantage points in Stanley Park.

16

The last game

18 May 2025: Everton 2 Southampton 0 (Blue boys' final fixture)

Blue was the colour, on the pitch, in the stands and even in the air as after 133 years at the first purpose-built football ground in England, the final men's first-team match marked the end of an era at Goodison Park on what was a truly momentous day of both celebration and sadness.

Emotional Evertonians had been gearing up to say goodbye to Goodison all season and until just five days ahead of the Blues signing off with a 2-0 win over Southampton, this was set to be the ground's final fixture full stop.

However, on the Tuesday before the game the club announced that their home since 1892 was to be spared the bulldozers and instead, from the start of the 2025/26 campaign, would become the new venue for Everton's women's team.

The 'Grand Old Lady' had been given a new lease of life, prompting many to declare on the eve of the Saints' visit that this was now a party and not a wake.

There were no Sunday morning lie-ins for this high-noon showdown and eager to get to the ground early to show their support and soak up the atmosphere, fans started to congregate in great numbers around the streets that surround Goodison shortly after 8am.

This created crowd scenes more reminiscent of ultras in places like Turkey, the Balkans or South America rather than merry old England, football's spiritual home, but then Scousers in general, and Evertonians in particular have always been a passionate exception to the rule in this country and this was to be a sporting spectacle like no other.

The club had encouraged its fans to line the pavements between Walton Lane and Goodison Road to greet the Everton players with a coach welcome around 10am but over half an hour before the vehicle was scheduled to drive past, the roads were packed with a royal blue sea of humanity and there was no alternative but to abandon the venture, change the route and sneak David Moyes's men in around the back.

Once the throngs had relocated to their seats inside the ground, Goodison bounced and crackled like never before with lusty renditions of anthems old and new, including 'Spirit of the Blues', the song that inspired the title of this book.

However, as Andy Hunter of *The Guardian* observed, 'The La's song "There She Goes" captured the mood perfectly, sparking a mass sing-along before the second world war siren kicked in and Everton's men emerged to the sound of the *Z-Cars* theme for one last time at Goodison Park.'

Southampton had beaten the Blues twice that season, prior to Moyes's arrival, but despite holding Manchester City to a goalless draw the previous weekend to ensure they avoided matching Derby County's all-time Premier League low points total of 11, the division's basement side were in many ways the perfect guests when it came to being powerless to spoil Everton's party.

Although this was just the Blues' fifth league success at Goodison of the campaign – the joint-lowest in their history, along with 1957/58 – it was a 17th Premier League home win over the Saints, more than they had achieved against any other club.

While the game itself was in many ways secondary to the occasion, it was also imperative that Everton proved victorious and it was Iliman Ndiaye who wrote himself into the history books with a brace of goals at the Park End to secure such a result, either side of Beto having another two disallowed for offside.

His first, just six minutes into the contest, settled the hosts' nerves, picking up a loose ball and driving forwards to the edge of the area before despatching a cool, left-footed finish.

The Senegal international, who was the Blues' most entertaining performer of the historic season, then sealed the contest in first-half stoppage time, dribbling around Southampton keeper Aaron Ramsdale and tapping the ball into an empty net.

A post-match ceremony combined music, a parade of former players and lap of appreciation from the current team with Moyes proclaiming, 'We might be a club coming back together,' when handed a microphone to address the crowd.

As Joe Thomas of the *Liverpool Echo* concluded, 'The future at Hill Dickinson Stadium [as Everton's future home immediately became after a naming rights deal announced less than 48 hours before this game] offers Everton a chance for a future that seemed impossible as the club lurched from catastrophe to disaster.

'It is only possible because of what has been achieved at Goodison – think those survival-clinching nail-biters against Crystal Palace then Bournemouth – and so many more. This is a club that saw better days, glorious days, long before then. The hope is such glories will return, albeit at a new home.

'Whatever happens on the banks of the Mersey, it was Andy Gray who summed up this day best.

'"We might be leaving Goodison," he said, "but Goodison will never leave us."'

Bibliography

Books:

Ball, D. and Buckland, G., *Everton: The Ultimate Book of Stats and Facts* (Liverpool: The Bluecoat Press, 2001)

Buckland, G., *Money Can't Buy Us Love: Everton in the 1960s* (Liverpool: deCoubertin Books, 2019)

Buckland, G., *Boys From The Blue Stuff: Everton's rise to 1980s glory* (Liverpool: deCoubertin Books, 2021)

Buckland, G., *The End: From glory to a whole new ball game, Everton 1985–1994* (London: Toffeeopolis, 2024)

Corbett, J., *Everton: The School of Science* (London: Macmillan, 2003)

Corbett, J., *The Everton Encyclopedia* (London: deCoubertin Books, 2012)

Corbett, J., *Faith of Our Families – Everton FC: An Oral History 1878–2018* (Liverpool: deCoubertin Books, 2017)

France, D., *Gwladys Street's Hall of Fame* (Witham: Skript Publishing, 1998)

France, D. and Prentice, D., *Gwladys Street's Blue Book: 100 seasons at the top* (Witham: Skript Publishing, 2002)

France, D. and Prentice, D., *Virgin Blues: 100 seasons at the top* (Witham: Skript Publishing, 2003)

France, D. and Prentice, D., *Dr Everton's Magnificent Obsession* (Liverpool: Trinity Mirror Sport Media, 2008)

Inglis, S., *Football Grounds of Britain* (London: HarperCollins 1997)

Inglis, S., *Engineering Archie: Archibald Leitch – football ground designer* (London: English Heritage, 2005)

Johnson, S., *Everton: The Official Complete Record* (Liverpool: deCoubertin Books, 2016)

Keates, T., *Jubilee History of the Everton Football Club 1878–1928* (Westcliff-on-Sea: Desert Island Books, 1998)

Kendall, H., *Love Affairs & Marriage: My Life In Football* (London: deCoubertin Books, 2013)

Ponting, I., *Everton: Player by Player* (Enfield: Hamlyn, 1998)

Prentice, D., *A Grand Old Team To Report: 45 years following Everton Football Club* (Liverpool: Reach Sport, 2020)

Reid, P., *Cheer Up Peter Reid: My Autobiography* (Liverpool: Trinity Mirror Sport Media, 2017)

Rogers, K., *Goodison Glory: The Official History* (Derby: Breedon Books, 1998)

Sheedy, K., *So Good I Did It Twice – Kevin Sheedy: My Life from Left Field* (Liverpool: Trinity Mirror Sport Media, 2014)

Southall, N., *The Binman Chronicles* (London: deCoubertin Books, 2012)

Taw, T., *Football's Twelve Apostles: The Making of the League 1886–1889* (Southend-on-Sea: Desert Island Books, 2006)

Websites:

bluecorrespondent.co.uk

bbc.co.uk

britishnewspaperarchive.co.uk

dailymail.co.uk

evertonfc.com

evertonheritagesociety.com

evertonresults.com

theguardian.com

liverpoolecho.co.uk

mirror.co.uk

toffeeweb.com

wikipedia.org

youtube.com

Newspapers and magazines:

Barnsley Chronicle
Cricket and Football Field
Daily Express
Daily Herald
Daily Mail
Gazzetta dello Sport
Liverpool Courier
Liverpool Courier and Commerical Advertiser
Liverpool Daily Post
Liverpool Daily Post and Mercury
Liverpool Echo
Liverpool Mercury
London Daily News
The Mirror
Sunday Mirror

Podcasts and YouTube channels:

Behind Closed Doors
Goodison Park: My Home
Royal Blue podcast